KEIGHLEY COLLEGE LIBRARY
~~TEL. 01535 618519~~

To renew by telephone please give the barcode number on your Library card and the barcode number on the item to be renewed

19. APR. 2004	28 JAN 2011	TEL. NO! **(01535) 685010**
-3. JUN. 2004		Please check the CD/ DVD at the back of the book
-1. NOV. 2004	14. MAR. 2011	0 3 JUN 2015
17. DEC. 2004 -4. JAN. 2005	0 3 MAY 2011	2 5 NOV 2015
-4. APR. 2005	1 8 MAY 2011	2 0 NOV 2018
29 JUL 2005	2 2 NOV 2012	
15. DEC. 2006	2 7 NOV 2012 2 3 JAN 2013	
25 JAN 2007		
-5. FEB 2007	2 6 MAR 2013	
11. OCT 2007	2 0 MAR 2014	
DEC. 2008	2 0 MAR 2017	

He ... *for AQA*

Withdrawn

Heinemann
PSYCHOLOGY AS
for AQA

David Moxon   Kevin Brewer   Peter Emmerson

Heinemann
Inspiring generations

Heinemann Educational Publishers
Halley Court, Jordan Hill, Oxford OX2 8EJ
Part of Harcourt Education

Heinemann is the registered trademark of
Harcourt Education Limited

© David Moxon, Peter Emmerson, Kevin Brewer, 2003

First published 2003

07 06 05 04 03 02
10 9 8 7 6 5 4 3 2 1

British Library Cataloguing in Publication Data is available
from the British Library on request.

ISBN 0 435 80673 4

Edited by Des Brady

Typeset and illustrated by Tek-Art, Croydon

Original illustrations © Harcourt Education Limited, 2002

Cover illustration by Matt Buckley

Printed in the UK by Bath Press Ltd

Picture research by Thelma Gilbert

Acknowledgements
David Moxon would like to thank his family for all their patience and support while he was
working on this book. The authors would like to thank Susan and Sarah for all their help.

The publishers would like to thank the British Psychological Society for permission to
reproduce copyright material on the CD-ROM, and Anthony Skipworth for permission to
reproduce sample revision sheets on the CD-ROM.

Every effort has been made to contact copyright holders of material reproduced in this book.
Any omissions will be rectified in subsequent printings if notice is given to the publishers.

The publishers would like to thank the following for permission to reproduce photographs:

Alamy pp.135, 226; Gavin Boden pp.79, 98, 100; Bridgeman Art Library/ Museum of Fine Arts,
Houston p.269; Bubbles p.66, 96; Camera Press p.189; Corbis pp.4, 6, 7, 46, 214; Empics
p. 106; Sally & Richard Greenhill pp.17, 61, 71, 92, 132, 168, 198, 212; Hulton Archive pp.2,
4, 6, 8, 42, 51, 107, 174, 239; Hulton Getty p.229; Alexandra Milgram pp. 218, 219, 223,
225; David Moxon pp.118, 171; OSF p.35; Panos Pictures pp.76, 162; Popperfoto pp. 128,
207, 210; Rex Features pp.53, 55, 135, 152, 160, 193; Roger Scruton p. 182; Shout Pictures
p.40; SPL pp.2, 3, 4, 5, 31, 38, 84, 120, 126, 172, 173; Stanford University p.216; Still Pictures
p.75; Topham Picturepoint pp.2, 14, 38, 86, 157, 176; Wellcome Trust pp.62, 111, 186.

Tel: 01865 888058 www.heinemann.co.uk

Contents

Contents

Contents

Contents

Contents

CHAPTER 1 | INTRODUCTION TO PSYCHOLOGY

THE BEGINNING – GODS, PHILOSOPHY AND POSITIVISM

THE BEGINNINGS OF SCIENCE

Science has a long history, with influential minds appearing as far back as we can remember. In ancient Greece Archimedes (287–212 BC) carried out what we call 'physics' experiments, on problems such as why bodies float. Ptolemy (AD 90–168) defined the foundations of modern astronomy by putting together a model of the stars. In the thirteenth century Roger Bacon (1214–1292) performed experiments on water clocks.

However, many thinkers, among them the nineteenth-century French sociologist Auguste Comte, argue that science proper began during the Renaissance, when people like Copernicus revolutionized astronomy by arguing that the Earth went round the Sun and not vice versa. Galileo carried out experiments on gravity and developed the microscope. Both attracted the wrath of the Pope, who was the sole authority on what was 'knowledge' at this time. Reformers such as Francis Bacon contributed to the development of science.

Later still, the first scientific institution was formed in seventeenth-century Britain; it was called the Royal Society and enjoyed the patronage of King Charles II. One of its members was Sir Isaac Newton, who developed the first general model of physics. Even the power of the Roman Catholic church could not stop the development of what Comte termed **positivism**.

Fig 1.1 *Archimedes*

CD-ROM

To learn more about the people mentioned in this chapter, see CD-ROM Introduction: Key people in the development of psychology.

Fig 1.2 *Ptolemy*

Fig 1.3 *Auguste Comte*

Fig 1.4 *Francis Bacon*

Fig 1.5 Aristotle

KEY DEFINITIONS

POSITIVISM
Science based upon observable phenomena.

THEOLOGY
For Comte, a belief in the supernatural.

METAPHYSICAL
Of knowledge beyond the physical world.

AUGUSTE COMTE AND POSITIVISM

Comte argued that there were three forms of knowledge:
- **Theological** – the belief in a supernatural world
- **Metaphysical** – a term originally developed by the Greek philosopher Aristotle, used for knowledge beyond the physical world; Comte argued it was a technique for finding truth using methods such as logic
- **Positivist** – knowledge which, unlike the other two, is reality-oriented: it makes the positive step of taking its reference point from the world outside, as well as from the mind.

All three types of knowledge involve the development of theories or models of the universe, but only positivism requires such models to be tested in relation to the facts. Positivism is the word used by Comte to describe what we normally call **science**.

SCIENCE EXPANDS AND GROWS

For Comte, science is a type of knowledge that developed out of supernatural and logical knowledge, so that now the three co-exist in the modern world. Even so, in the last four hundred years science has grown quickly, incorporating in its earliest days the natural sciences such as physics, chemistry and later biology, as well as social sciences such as economics, sociology and psychology.

Comte's point was that they all share the same heritage: they are all different scientific perspectives on separate types of subject matter; they are part of the family of sciences. It is arguable therefore that psychology could not have existed before its foundation in the nineteenth century. Not surprisingly it is still laden with elements of superstition and philosophy. Even so, the problem of the soul has been abandoned in favour of something measurable like personality: the science of psychology has been born.

Fig 1.6 Wilhelm Max Wundt

Fig 1.7 Charles Darwin

Fig 1.8 William James

Fig 1.9 Hermann Ebbinghaus

 KEY DEFINITIONS

ASSOCIATIONISM
An approach in psychology that focuses on learning.

STRUCTURALISM

Many have argued that psychology began in Leipzig in 1879 when Wundt set up the first psychology laboratory. He was influenced by chemistry and Dalton's theory of atomic structure (small parts making up a whole). His research attempted to put together a psychology of colour, using the idea of sensations and feelings as the elements which formed 'psychological compounds' called colours.

Introspection (or careful thinking) was the technique he used to investigate these relationships. This involved training people to think about their sensations and feelings about colour and reporting them in detail, so that a pattern of elements could be built up which would define each colour (for example, redness is often associated with warmth). The problem was that these elements were always to a large extent going to be personal. This method lacked the sort of detachment necessary to provide knowledge that could be checked by other psychologists: the method was too heavily affected by the values of the respondent.

FUNCTIONALISM

Another strand involved in the development of psychology was related to the work of Charles Darwin. The **evolutionary** model that Darwin developed is a biological theory based on the notion that all life forms are in competition for survival: those that can adapt are successful, those that cannot become extinct. James argued that human psychology had a function or purpose in this process, both in terms of our ability to think and our facility for emotion. Along with Lange he developed a theory of emotion whereby we feel the emotion of 'fear' because we run: the theory assumes that emotions result from physiological changes.

Both Wundt and James were interested in unconscious psychological processes that could be accessed through the method of introspection, rather than through experiment. Other more experimental strands of psychology grew to eclipse these earlier models, offering a more detached approach related to the search for hard empirical (or factual) evidence.

ASSOCIATIONISM

One such strand was **associationism**, based on the importance of learning in our psychological make-up. Ebbinghaus tried to investigate how we develop associations between previously isolated stimuli. He discovered the limits of what we call the short-term memory, and that the strength of association between two separate elements is based on repetition and meaning.

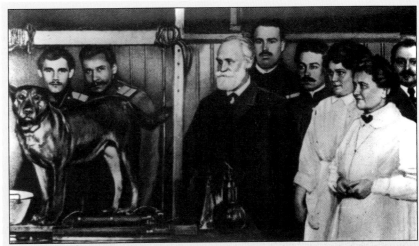

Fig 1.10 Ivan Petrovich Pavlov

In Russia, the physiologist Pavlov researched saliva production in dogs, and discovered that salivation could be stimulated with an empty food container (the dogs would learn to associate the container with food and thereby with salivation). The learning of an association between an involuntary action such as salivation and a neutral stimulus such as a bowl is called **classical conditioning**.

Pavlov extended his research to show that other stimuli, such as lights and sounds, could be associated with food to produce salivation. He developed the laws of conditioning, explaining how things could be unlearned or extended to other stimuli.

Edward Thorndike was interested in the relation between learning and voluntary behaviour. He developed an apparatus called the **puzzle box**, in which animal behaviour could be observed in the process of escaping from a box. He showed that a cat would accidentally use the catch to open the door of the box and then eat food positioned nearby. If the cat were constantly returned to the box it would find its way out again, but in an ever decreasing time.

From this research Thorndike formulated the **law of effect**, whereby animals, to improve their survival prospects, will show a preference for behaviour that is positively reinforced (encouraged), thereby eliminating behaviour that is not. The positive reinforcer is the food. The cat, through a slow process of trial and error, associates this reinforcer with the undoing of the catch on the door (this slow process involves eliminating other behaviour which is not linked with the reinforcer).

PSYCHOLOGY DEVELOPS FURTHER

Fig 1.11
John Broadus Watson

Fig 1.12
Burrhus Fredric Skinner

BEHAVIOURISM

Watson's influence

The work of Ebbinghaus, Pavlov and Edward Thorndike (see section 2) was undoubtedly influential on one of the major schools of psychology – **behaviourism**. Behaviourism is a very empirical model and is arguably a radical response to the lack of detachment of introspection (as used by Wundt; see section 2). One of the most influential people in this school was Watson. He wanted to wipe away old superstitious ideas that because animals do not have souls, we cannot experiment on them for human benefit. He took a **reductionist** approach by investigating the basic elements of psychology, but unlike Wundt, he wanted only hard measurable evidence.

Watson argued that the fundamentals of psychology were the reflexes. Cross your legs and tap the area of your knee just below the knee-cap: your leg will flex. The tap is the **stimulus**, the flexing of the leg the **response**. These were the basic behaviours. Watson argued that there were two types:
* Those that were instinctive, as researched by Pavlov
* Those that could be learned, as researched by Thorndike

According to Watson, psychology should be the research of these two types of behaviour.

However, such a theory oversimplifies the role of the brain: Watson argued that it was no more than a telephone exchange passing information around the body. But this psychological model offered the opportunity for experimentation and the possibility to support or refute its findings; that is, it had a proper scientific grounding.

The work of Skinner

Perhaps the most famous of all behaviourist psychologists was Skinner. In Skinner we can see elements of both Thorndike and Watson. Skinner developed a much more efficient version of the puzzle box so that he could repetitively monitor the relationship between stimulus–response units.

'Skinner boxes' were developed to research operant or voluntary learning. Into the box is placed a rat. The box has a bar that can be pressed by the rat, a food tray below and light above. It is otherwise bare. A hungry rat is placed in the box. From time to time it happens to press the bar. At first nothing happens when the bar is pressed; this is so the researcher can establish the base rate for bar pressing (that is, find out how often the rat tends to push the bar as a matter of course). Once the base rate has been measured, food is allowed into the tray each time the rat presses the bar – this is positive reinforcement (encouragement) for pressing the bar. Very quickly the rat learns the link between the two and bar pressing accelerates. If the food is then stopped, bar pressing declines and eventually returns to the base rate measure.

Skinner varied this by switching on the light while the reinforcer (food) was presented. He then managed to elicit bar pressing solely by switching on the light – this is secondary reinforcement.

These techniques were used to produce an array of evidence as to how **operant conditioning** works. They have much wider application than classical conditioning. For example, operant conditioning may explain much of human learning.

However, such an approach has difficulty in explaining how these small parts of behaviour form into patterns of complex behaviour or perceptions. If we ignore the brain as a processor of information (where information goes in and is changed by the brain to produce thinking and behaviour) we ignore some very significant psychological knowledge. Tolman, for example, suggested that changes take place in our brains as we learn about (or **internalize**) our world, and that such **cognitions** (thoughts) structure our perception and understanding.

THE GESTALT SCHOOL

Tolman was influenced by the Gestalt school, which began from the opposite end of the scale to behaviourism. This approach concerned the way the brain structures perception and experience holistically (as a whole): it assumed we never perceive anything in complete isolation. A Gestalt is a compound of related elements.

Fig 1.13 *The figure/ground rule in action: this picture changes depending on which areas you see as the figure itself and which as the background. It is either a vase or a pair of faces.*

Wertheimer argued that our brains organize our perceptions according to certain rules such as 'figure and ground' (see Fig 1.13).

Thus, when we perceive anything it is *in relation to something else*. Let's take as an example the 'rule of proximity'. Look at Fig 1.14. It is experienced as two groups of four rather than four groups of two.

Fig 1.14 *Two groups of four?*

The Gestalt psychologists argued that the brain is biologically structured to receive information from a world that is structured in the same manner. We see Fig 1.14 as two groups of four because that is how they occur in the brain. We perceive a world of patterns: therefore nothing is separate.

Another member of this school was Köhler. He carried out similar experiments to Edward Thorndike, except that he studied apes, not cats (see section 2). Köhler watched an ape in a cage try to grasp hold of a banana placed just beyond its reach outside the cage. Inside the cage was a stick placed in reasonable proximity to the banana. Eventually the ape seemed to make a leap of insight and see the connection between the stick and banana. It then proceeded to pick up the stick and use it to rake in the banana. Köhler argued that this was not the trial and error learning that Edward Thorndike had investigated. The ape had solved the problem by relating together, as a Gestalt, the banana and the stick.

Fig 1.15 *Max Wertheimer*

PSYCHOLOGY TAKES A NEW DIRECTION

 KEY DEFINITIONS

HYSTERIA
A psychogenic (originating in the mind) disorder in which the patient presents with a physical disorder – very common in Freud's time.

PRESENTS
Refers to when a patient consults a doctor.

PSYCHOANALYSIS

In the last quarter of the nineteenth century, Europe was plagued by an epidemic of **hysteria**. This presented as blindness, deafness, paralysis and convulsions, amongst a plethora of other mental and physical complaints. Sigmund Freud was aware that his medical training in neurology (study of the nervous system) was of little help in treating this condition.

Charcot had argued that the problem was psychological rather than physical, and had used hypnosis to treat the condition, with some success. Freud, with his colleague Breuer, began to explain this by arguing that hysteria was caused by the repression of traumatic experiences, which were released during hypnosis. This release provided catharsis, a sense of pleasure related to the reduction of tension, as a result of the recovery of the painful memories.

From such investigations Freud began to formulate his theory of the unconscious as a part of the mind about which we know little, but which has a powerful effect on conscious thinking and behaviour. Freud gives us a theory of the personality structured in terms of the id, ego and superego. In Freud's model:
• Human beings are motivated by innate unconscious drives, which are essentially self-centred.
• The drives build up tensions which need expression through behaviour.
• This in turn leads to tension reduction and the experience of pleasure, or catharsis.

Fig 1.16 Sigmund Freud

People are in a state of conflict, torn between their selfish drives and their need of others. This is rooted in the personality: in the battle between the id and the ego. The id (selfish drives) is innate. The ego is based in reality, and develops through stages in childhood as our experience of the world and its requirements increases. It is important that this process of development is smooth, leading to the growth of a strong ego that can control our id impulses (the superego develops the conscience); otherwise we will be outcast and potentially neurotic.

 KEY DEFINITIONS

NEUROSIS
A feeling of anxiety related to something that would not normally cause fear.

PSYCHOANALYSIS
A theory and a treatment based upon the teachings of Sigmund Freud.

Freud argued that bad experiences during ego development, where the battle between the id and the ego is not resolved successfully, lead to conditions such as anxiety, hysteria, phobias and so on. In this case we will need **psychoanalysis** to get at those repressed traumas and relieve the neurosis.

Freud and his associates had put together a theory that would dominate psychology until the 1950s, when serious doubts started to surface about the model. The major problem with the theory is that it seems untestable.

Many of Freud's concepts are not objective enough to be experimentally checked, and in recent years evidence of malpractice in his research have seen a decline in the popularity of psychoanalysis. However, there is no denying the importance of Freud's ideas for the development of psychology – if only because we can learn from our mistakes.

PSYCHOMETRICS

Another important strand of psychology emanating from the nineteenth century is **psychometrics**. Galton was interested in using statistics in order to correlate, or show the relationship between, intelligence and certain mental abilities. Spearman developed this further, suggesting that intelligence was comprised of a group of general abilities, linked with certain individual abilities. Binet developed an intelligence test to assess children with learning difficulties so that they could be allocated to schools with specialist help.

Since these early days psychometric testing has developed considerably and is now widely used by companies in staff recruitment. Hans Eysenck was involved in much of this work, developing inventories for the assessment of both intelligence and personality. Unlike Freud, Eysenck argued that human personality had two basic dimensions: extraversion/introversion and neuroticism. He put together this model on the basis of extensive testing using questionnaires.

The difficulty with this sort of approach is that it tends to over-simplify human psychology, and offers a rather rigid view by overstating the importance of genetics and understating the role of learning in our experience.

OVERALL CONCLUSIONS ON PSYCHOLOGY

From these beginnings, modern psychology has developed into a series of specialist areas reflected in the nature of your AS course. Thus, nowadays we focus on different areas including individual differences, developmental, cognitive, social and biological psychology, any of which may incorporate different aspects of the models described above. One thing is certain: psychology is extremely popular. This is partly because it is a child of our times: it gives us insight into our modern problems based on sound scientific principles. Because of this, it is a good grounding for much of what we do today, whether work or play.

You may be interested in pursuing psychology in further study, and perhaps even as a career. The CD-ROM provides information on careers within psychology and Web addresses which you may find useful as you progress through the book.

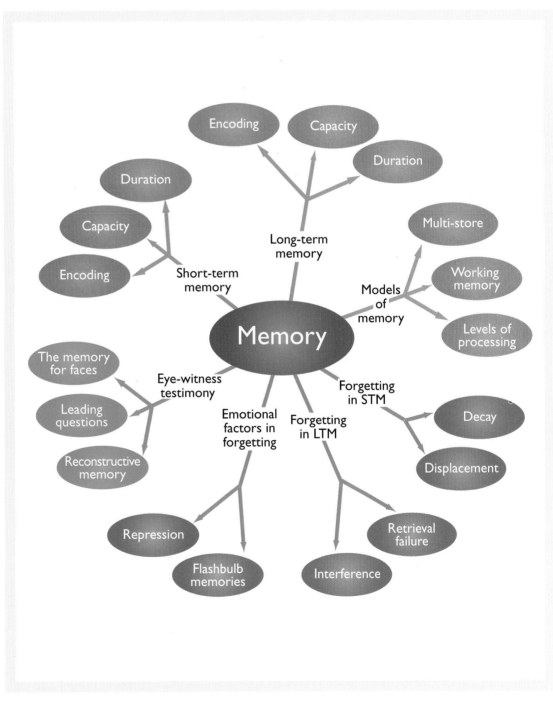

To prepare for the AQA exam you need to know the following things.

Short-term and long-term memory
- Encoding
- Capacity
- Duration

Models of memory
- Multi-store model
- Working memory model
- Levels of processing model

Forgetting

Explanations of forgetting in short-term memory
- Decay
- Displacement

Explanations of forgetting in long-term memory
- Retrieval failure
- Interference

Emotional factors in forgetting
- Flashbulb memories
- Repression

Eye-witness testimony
- Reconstructive memory (Bartlett)
- Leading questions (Loftus)
- Memory for faces

INTRODUCTION

Justin was never able to remember anything at school. Facts teachers taught him went in one ear and out the other. At the time he wasn't able to understand why and he always assumed he was a bit stupid. Three million pounds of personal fortune and two successful businesses later, he was able to understand why he'd found school so hard. He was brilliant at remembering things that interested him.

Fig 2.1   *Clive Wearing only has a short-term memory.*

CD-ROM

Memory: Clive Wearing

IMPORTANCE OF MEMORY

Memory is so important that everything we do and are is based upon it. It is taken for granted until, in rare cases, individuals lose their memory abilities. For example, after having a stroke, some people can no longer remember the names of everyday objects. They will be able to describe an object, but cannot recall its name. This is known as **agnosia**.

Other rare cases include that of Clive Wearing, who has only had a short-term memory since he contracted a brain disease. For him, life is like waking up every couple of minutes. He keeps a notebook by his bed in hospital, and writes things like: 'At last, I am awake' every few minutes. Yet he remembers much, including his musical skills, from before the illness.

Just as disturbing is Alzheimer's disease, in which the memory slowly deteriorates with the onset of the illness. In time the individual's personality and self are lost.

PROCESSES OF MEMORY

Memory is made up of three parts or processes.

Encoding

This is the placing of information into the memory store. It is not generally an automatic process: you must pay attention in order for the information to be encoded. However, it is different in the case of traumatic experiences: these become encoded in the memory and cannot be forgotten, despite the desire to forget them. This is what happens in post-traumatic stress disorder (classically suffered by some soldiers who have seen combat).

Storage

The information must be kept in memory until it is needed at a later date. Information is stored in different ways, and possibly in different parts of the brain, depending on what type of information it is. The memory for skills such as riding a bike (**procedural memory**), for example, is stored differently to the memory for facts (**semantic memory**) or personal autobiographical memories (**episodic memory**).

In some cases, it is possible to remember how the information was acquired (**explicit memory**). In other cases, you have no conscious recollection of how you know something: you just know it (**implicit memory**). This type of memory usually applies to skills: for example, you may not remember learning to tie your shoelace, but you are able to do it just the same.

Retrieval

The ability to recall information when needed is obviously very important. In quiz programmes, the winners are people with a good memory for the answers. In fact, it is their ability to retrieve the relevant information that matters most. The same mechanism is paramount in exams – recall at the appropriate time. That is not to say that encoding and storage are not important – you cannot retrieve memories that are not present.

DIFFERENT WORDS FOR THE THREE STAGES

As you may have noticed different terms are often used for the three stages of memory. These are listed in the table:

Names for process	Description of process
encoding/registration/reception/acquisition	putting information into memory
storage/retention	keeping information in memory for later use
retrieval/recall	bringing information out from memory when needed

CONCLUSIONS

Memory involves three processes: encoding (putting the information into memory), storage (retaining the information in memory), and retrieval (recalling it when required).

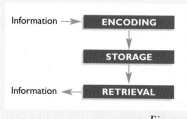

Fig 2.2

WHAT FACTORS AFFECT MEMORY PROCESSES?

As you read this section, remember the basic processes of memory as outlined in Fig 2.2.

Encoding

Factors that affect the process of encoding (inputting information into memory) are as follows:

- **Attention** – attention must be paid generally. Attention paid to specific aspects of stimuli improves encoding (if you look at a group of people, your recall is likely to be better if you notice and focus on individual faces).
- **Arousal** – memory ability is reduced by high levels of arousal. For example, when someone is in a state of panic their perception is very focused but their encoding abilities are reduced.
- **Expectations** – information is encoded much quicker if it fits expectations, and sometimes ignored if it does not (if you expected doctors to be male, you might remember a particular female doctor less). On the other hand, the unexpected is sometimes remembered better than the expected. (Imagine if after a year of wearing a grey suit to school, your maths teacher turned up one day in green cycling shorts!)

Storage

The following factors affect storage of information in the memory:

- **Stereotypes/assumptions** – information is stored in categories based on stereotypes and assumptions, and information that does not fit may be forgotten (as with expectations affecting encoding above). That is why people tend to remember more examples to back up their stereotypes than examples that contradict them.
- **'Efforts after meaning'** – this phrase was coined by Bartlett (1932) (see section 16), and is related to how memories are actively filed away in categories that make sense. In other words, we do not simply remember what we see. We also remember the assumptions we made at the time of encoding.

Retrieval

There are a number of types of retrieval. They are as follows:

- **Free recall** – remembering information without any external cues (reminders).
- **Cued recall** – normally the use of external cues to help focus the search in memory for the required information. (A 'cue' may be anything that acts as a reminder.) For example, traditional storytellers use cues in the environment around them to help in their long stories. Memory improvement techniques focus on teaching the use of cues to increase recall.

Fig 2.3 In redintegration a cue, in this case a picture, opens a chain of memories.

- **Recognition** – remembering something when it is seen; for example, seeing the answer to a question and remembering that it is correct. However, there can also be false recognition.
- **Recollection** – retrieval of information by establishing a particular context in the mind. For example, you might remember past classmates at school by first visualizing the classroom then 'looking around' in your memory.
- **Zeigarnik effect** – remembering something you thought you had forgotten when you are not thinking about it. The brain searches for memories even when not consciously thinking about them.
- **Relearning** – when something is revisited it can be very clear in the memory, even when you think it is forgotten completely. A good revision technique is to review learnt material on a regular basis.
- **Redintegration** – this is where a cue, such as hearing a particular song, opens a chain of memories.
- **Reconstructive memory/confabulation** – 'recall' of events that did not occur. This means that your mind fabricates imaginary experiences.

The above definitions mention 'cues' a lot. It is important to remember that cues can be both external (such as a photograph) and internal; a mood can be a cue. For more information about the types of cue related to each of the types of retrieval, see Fig 2.4. Note that some types of retrieval can be associated with both internal and external cues.

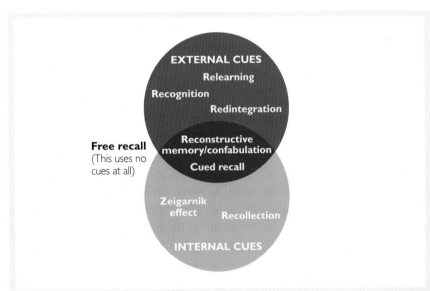

Fig 2.4 Different types of cue associated with different types of retrieval.

CONCLUSIONS

As you can see, memory is not a consistent straightforward process. Various factors affect the three stages we have been discussing (encoding, storage and retrieval), and the final recall stage can take various forms. Keeping the various stages clear in your head will help you remember the information you need.

SECTION 4 | THE TWO-PROCESS MODEL OF MEMORY

DIFFERENT STORES

Atkinson and Shiffrin (1971) proposed the two-process model to explain memory. They described memory as having two separate stores: **short-term store or memory** (STS/STM) and **long-term store or memory** (LTS/LTM). There are also **sensory memories** related to each sense (such as sight, hearing and so on). This is therefore a **multi-store model**. It is also a structured model; that is, memory stores have defined characteristics, such as capacity (see below), that do not change. Different types of memory are stored in different parts of the brain.

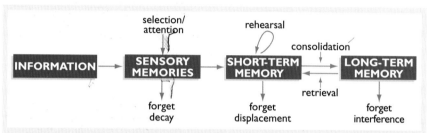

Fig 2.5 The two-process model. The 'two processes' are rehearsal and consolidation. For mechanisms of forgetting, see sections 10, 11 and 12.

The model is outlined in Fig 2.5. It is often referred to as an information-processing model. Let us now discuss some of the important terms in more detail.

MEMORY PROCESSES IN THE TWO-PROCESS MODEL

- **Rehearsal** – repeated re-entering of the information into the system: for example, repeating a phone number out loud to remember it for a short period of time before dialling.
- **Repetition** – repeating of information leads to its transference from the short-term store to the long-term store, and storage of memories there.
- **Consolidation** – the process by which memories become embedded in long-term memory. There needs to be a period of time for the memories to be filed away, or else they will be forgotten. Concussion from banging of the head, as in sports, can inhibit the process of consolidation.

SENSORY MEMORY

This occurs within each sense (for example, hearing) and is a literal impression of the stimulus for a very short time of about 1–2 seconds. It allows the opportunity to further process the information if it is important, or ignore it if it is not.

Sperling (1963) showed participants three rows of four letters for 1/20 of a second (50 milliseconds). Immediately afterwards they could recall four letters correctly, but with only a 1 second delay, recall dropped by half. Recall availability in sensory memory is momentary and easily lost.

CHARACTERISTICS OF THE DIFFERENT MEMORY STORES

	Short-term memory	Long-term memory
Duration of storage	30 seconds	No apparent limit
Capacity	Limited to about 7 bits of info (± 2)	No apparent limit
How memories stored (method of coding)	Auditory (sound)	Semantic (meaning), visual, auditory
How info enters system	Attention	Repetition
How info is maintained in system	Rehearsal	Repetition

WHY IS IT CALLED AN INFORMATION-PROCESSING MODEL?

The two-process model shares many features of general information-processing models. These features are described below, with examples from the two-process model.

- *Information flows through the system.*
  In the case of memory, information always flows from sensory memory to short-term memory to long-term memory.
- *System is divided into separate stages (sub-systems).*
  There are three separate memory stores.
- *Information enters the system at the same point every time, and follows a set sequence.*
  In our model, information always enters through sensory memory.
- *Each sub-system has limited capacity and duration.*
  The short-term store is limited to 30 seconds and seven bits of info.
- *At each stage information is coded or recoded for that sub-system.*
  The short-term memory uses auditory information; the long-term memory uses semantic, visual and auditory information.

CONCLUSION

As we have seen, in this model memory has separate stores for short-term storing of information, and for long-term retention of memories. Information is transferred from the short-term store to the long-term store by repetition.

INTRODUCTION

What was the number of that video shop? James ran a few combinations through his mind but none of them seemed right. He'd have to use the phone book. He ran upstairs and found it stuffed into a drawer. Eventually he found the number. He closed the book and ran back downstairs, chanting the number over and over in his mind: '0208 234 6587, 0208 234 6587, 020….'

Suddenly there was a tremendous crash from the back bedroom. James stopped halfway down the stairs, turned and ran back up again. His cat passed him at great speed going in the opposite direction. A shelf had collapsed, breaking a number of ornaments, and breaking James's concentration – the telephone number was gone.

WHAT ARE THE FUNCTIONS OF SHORT-TERM MEMORY?

Short-term memory is a limited part of memory, like a desk-top in an office. It is for holding information that is needed at the time, and as a passing-through station for information moving to and from long-term memory.

- To keep information available because it is currently needed. An example is a phone number found in the phone directory just before dialling.
- To pass information to long-term memory for storage to use later.
- To retrieve information that is needed now from long-term memory.

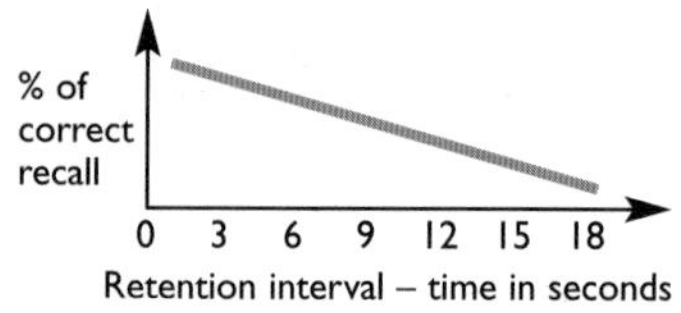

DURATION

Information can be held in short-term memory for only about 30 seconds, unless it is re-entered through rehearsal. Ideally information will be transferred into long-term memory, through consolidation, if it is required for later.

Rehearsal tends to be acoustic (that is, repeating the information out loud) and is easily interfered with. This is shown with the Brown–Peterson technique (Brown 1958, Peterson and Peterson 1959). Participants are asked to remember sets of three letters for a few seconds. In the intervening time, they are asked to count backwards (an interference task). Accurate recall declines over time, and only 30% is recalled after 9 seconds and 10% after 18 seconds (see Fig 2.6).

CAPACITY

The capacity of the short-term store is limited and relatively small. George Miller (1956) coined the phrase 'magical number seven plus or minus two'. For him, the capacity is five to nine bits of information, with

Fig 2.6 Brown–Peterson results

CD-ROM

Memory: the Brown–Peterson technique.

KEY DEFINITIONS

BROWN–PETERSON TECHNIQUE
A technique for testing the effect of length of retention interval on recall in short-term memory. Participants remember three letters for 3–18 seconds. There is a distractor task in the intervening time, for example counting backwards.

an average of seven (7 ± 2). However, subsequent research has shown that this figure varies.

Firstly, the figure depends on what type of information is being recalled. Solso (1979) summarizes the average information recalled in short-term memory according to information type as follows:

Numbers	7.7
Colours	7.1
Letters	6.3
Words	5.5
Geometrical shapes	5.3
Random forms	3.8
Nonsense syllables e.g. XBK	3.4

It has also been discovered that the short-term memory has seven **'pigeonholes'**; more than one piece of information can be put into each pigeonhole. The use of **chunking** allows information to be combined, and increases the capacity of the short-term store. For example, an undergraduate student called 'SF' (quoted in Jones and Davies 1989) was able to increase the short-term memory capacity from 7 digits to 28 by combining the random numbers into athletics times, ages and dates (which were meaningful to SF), and thus put more information into each pigeonhole in short-term memory. Eventually, after 20 months of training, SF was able to recall up to 80 digits immediately after hearing them.

Let's look at an example of chunking in action. Here someone is attempting to recall 12 digits, both without chunking and with chunking:

Without chunking:

STM pigeonhole	1	2	3	4	5	6	7					
Digit	2	0	0	1	1	0	6	6	1	9	9	9

Only 7 digits are recalled.

With chunking: digits combined (here into years):

STM pigeonhole	1	2	3	4	5	6	7
Digits	2001	1066	1999				

All 12 digits are recalled.

CONCLUSION

Short-term memory is limited in capacity to around seven bits of information, and limited in duration to 30 seconds. It is a limited part of memory for storing information needed at the time; for example during a conversation, to store a question someone has asked you and also store what will be your reply (which might involve information retrieved from long-term memory) (see Fig 2.7).

Fig 2.7

SECTION 6 | LONG-TERM MEMORY

INTRODUCTION

David sat with his grandma and grandad in their back room. He loved to hear stories of when his grandparents were younger. His grandad was telling him about the time he had just left Kings Cross station driving a passenger train when a bomb exploded nearby. Considering it was during the Second World War he had been very lucky. David was always surprised what an amazing memory his grandad had at 82 years old.

KEY DEFINITIONS

VERY LONG-TERM MEMORY
The capacity to remember events for a very long time, sometimes decades.

HOW LONG DOES LONG-TERM MEMORY LAST?

The long-term memory is like a filing cabinet in an office, where information is stored, in an organized fashion, for use at a later date. It is not filed away like a video recording of the events, but is organized by categories, themes, and semantic links.

It appears that there is no limit to the length of retention of long-term memory. People in old age can remember events in their childhood across more than 60 years. This length of retention is sometimes called **very long-term memory** (VLTM) or 'permastore' (a relatively permanent memory) (Bahrick et al 1975).

It is often difficult to test memory over a very long period of time. However, Bahrick et al (1975) were able to test long-term recall using school records. Seven groups of participants, who had left school between 3 months and 47 years ago, were asked to recall certain things about their classmates. The level of recall was high, even after such a long period as 47 years.

The table below is a sample of the results of Bahrick et al for some of the groups, showing approximate mean different levels of recall for different types of information.

Time since leaving school	9 months	25 years	47 years
Name recognition: recognizing names from list	90%	75%	75%
Name matching: matching picture and name together	95%	not tested	60%
Picture recognition: recognizing classmates from selection of pictures	95%	95%	70%
Free recall of names	70%	50%	40%

(After Bahrick et al 1975)

HOW IS LONG-TERM MEMORY ORGANIZED?

Long-term memory uses a system of organization that makes retrieval relatively easy. Information is linked together: this is what happens during consolidation (the process during which memories become embedded in long-term memory). There is also evidence that during sleep new memories are filed away in the correct categories.

If people are given 20 words randomly to remember, for example, they will recall them in categories linked together (Bousfield 1953). Also, organizing material you have to learn makes use of this principle, and increases recall (Bower et al 1969).

Memories are organized by general links (for example 'canary' links to 'bird'), as well as personal links (for example, 'canaries' might link to the nickname of Norwich City football team), and the strength of the link depends on how often the memory is recalled. This is known as the **spreading activation model** (Collins and Loftus 1975).

KEY DEFINITIONS

SPREADING ACTIVATION MODEL
A model of how memory is organized based on links that are personally important.

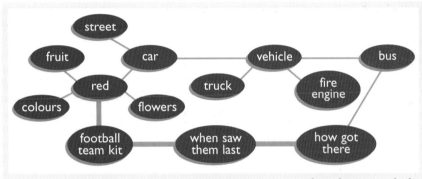

Fig 2.8 Examples of memory links

CONCLUSIONS

In long-term memory, there appears to be no limit on the amount of information that can be stored (capacity) nor on how long (duration) it can be stored for. People in old age may remember events more than 60 years in the past.

Memories are organized and linked together. They can be organized by categories, themes and semantic links. This is a good principle to remember when you are learning material, for example for an exam.

THE WORKING MEMORY SYSTEM

IS THE SHORT-TERM MEMORY MORE COMPLEX?

Baddeley and Hitch (1974) proposed the working memory system as an extension of the short-term memory in the two-process model of memory (see section 4). The working memory system sees the short-term memory as active, and not just a passing-through point for information going in and out of long-term memory. Furthermore, Baddeley and Hitch argue that the short-term memory is sub-divided into four parts: **central executive**, **articulatory loop**, **primary acoustic store** and **visuo-spatial scratch pad**. See below for more discussion of these terms.

With the working memory system, short-term memory varies depending on the type of information (for example visual or acoustic) and the task that memory is required for. This model allows that, rather than having a single capacity, individuals have the capacity to perform two tasks at the same time (such as driving a car and talking). To some degree, the working memory system is a combination of the sensory memory and short-term memory from the two-process model (see section 4). It is believed that each part of the system is situated in a different part of the brain.

COMPONENTS OF THE WORKING MEMORY SYSTEM

See Fig 2.9 for a diagram of the working memory system.

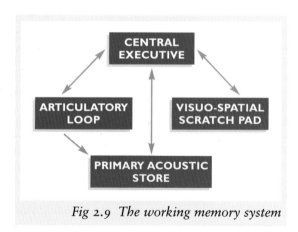

Fig 2.9 The working memory system

KEY DEFINITIONS

CENTRAL EXECUTIVE
(In the working memory model)
The controlling element of the system.

Central executive

In the working memory system, this is the controlling element, and is linked to the other three parts of the model. It does not store any information itself; instead it has a limited amount of attention that can be allocated to the other components. It is not restricted to a particular mode.

KEY DEFINITIONS

ARTICULATORY LOOP
A component of the working memory system. It stores information in acoustic form for a short time.

KEY DEFINITIONS

PRIMARY ACOUSTIC STORE
In Baddeley and Hitch's system, this holds and receives auditory information.

VISUO-SPATIAL SCRATCH PAD
This part of the working memory system stores and deals with visual and spatial information.

Articulatory loop

This is also known as the 'inner voice'. This component holds information of the acoustic type (in fact, words ready to speak), and includes the verbal rehearsal loop. This is a means of keeping information needed right now in the memory for a brief period by repeating it out loud (for example, muttering the phone number you've just been given while desperately searching for a pen!). Information can only be maintained in this way for a short period of time. Its capacity is limited by the time taken to speak the information held (usually two seconds), not the number of items.

Primary acoustic store

This is also known as the 'inner ear'. Not surprisingly, this also stores information of the acoustic type; it receives auditory information, which can be held for a short period. For example, this might include what was last said by the teacher as you are writing down notes.

Visuo-spatial scratch pad

Also called the 'inner eye', this component stores and deals with visual and spatial information; for example, driving along a familiar road and thinking about the next bend.

See Fig 2.10 for an example of the working memory system in action.

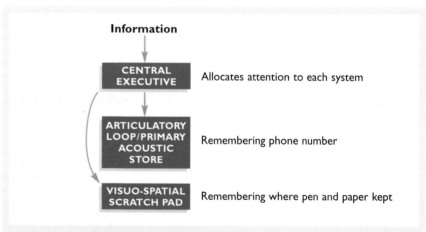

Fig 2.10 The working memory system: remembering a phone number heard on the radio while finding a pen and paper to write it down

CONCLUSIONS

The working memory system sees the short-term memory as being divided into four parts: the central executive, the articulatory loop, the visuo-spatial scratch pad and the primary acoustic store. A simple way to see this model is as a multi-store model of short-term memory. (Remember how we used the term 'multi-store' in section 4.)

DEPTH OR LEVEL OF PROCESSING

HOW DO WE UNDERSTAND THINGS?

This approach is different to the two-process model (see section 4) and the working memory system (see section 7) because it is an explanation of memory processes rather than a memory model. In this approach, memory is seen as a by-product of the processing of information, that is, how information is perceived and understood by the senses. The durability of the information (what we call memory) relates to the depth of functioning involved in that process of perception and understanding.

The concept of depth or level of processing was proposed by Craik and Lockhart (1972): 'Trace persistence is a function of depth of analysis, with deeper levels of analysis associated with more elaborated, longer lasting, and stronger traces'. 'Trace persistence' here means the individual memory.

Incoming information is subjected to a series of analyses: which level of analysis depends on the nature of the stimulus and the time available for processing. There are three levels of processing: **orthographic**, **phonological** and **semantic**. In Fig 2.11 these are graded from a 'shallow' to a 'deep' level of processing.

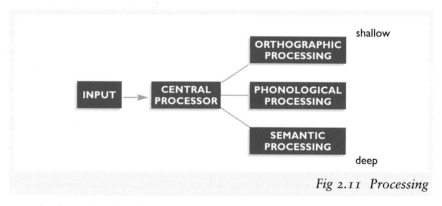

Fig 2.11 Processing

Let's look at these levels in more detail.

Orthographic

This level concentrates on the structure of the stimulus. It is seen as relatively shallow processing. An example might be the shape of a word shown to you; for instance, is it written in capital letters?

It is **unlikely** that the memory would be recalled.

Phonological

This level of processing concentrates on the phonetic aspects of the stimulus. In the example of a word being shown to you, phonological processing might concentrate on the sound of the word.

It is **possible** that the memory would be recalled.

KEY DEFINITIONS

ORTHOGRAPHIC PROCESSING
Concentrates on the structure of the stimulus.

PHONOLOGICAL PROCESSING
Concentrates on the phonetic aspects of the stimulus.

Semantic

This level of processing concentrates on the meaning of the stimulus. If you were shown a word, semantic processing might deal with the meaning of the word, and links to other words/meanings.

It is **likely** that the memory would be recalled.

RESEARCH EVIDENCE

Craik and Tulving (1975). Depth of processing and retention of words in episodic memory. *Journal of Experimental Psychology.*

Aims

To see whether depth of processing influences recall of information.

Procedure

Participants were asked questions about a list of words, and then given an unexpected memory test for the words. This was an **incidental** learning task; this means the participants were not expecting a memory test (this is important).

The words were divided into four groups, and each was investigated with one of the following types of question:

a   Is the word written in capital letters? (Orthographic processing)
b   Does the word rhyme with another word? (Phonological processing)
c   Is the word one of a particular category? (Semantic processing)
d   Would the word fit a particular sentence? (Semantic processing)

It was expected that the participants would recall more words from categories **c** and **d** because these required deeper processing of the information.

Findings

The average percentages recalled of words based on questions asked were **a** 15%, **b** 35%, **c** and **d** 70%.

Conclusions

Deeper processing leads to better recall.

SUMMARY

In this model, memory is simply a by-product of the processing of information. The deeper the information is processed, the more likely it is to be remembered.

SECTION 9 | FORGETTING

INTRODUCTION

Andrew began to panic – she was getting closer. This could wreck his chances of securing the deal. She was beginning to smile... almost in talking range. Her hand was beginning to rise ready for the customary shake. What was her name? What was it? He'd only been working with her for the last – six years!

'Hello Andrew, nice to see you again.'

'Hi – hi there – how are you... Lisa?'

Phew! Remembered in time.

'Sorry. I'm Lucy.' She smiled embarrassedly.

She wasn't half as embarrassed as Andrew.

WHAT IS FORGETTING?

'Forgetting' means being unable to retrieve information from memory when it is required. It occurs for a number of reasons.

Short-term memory

Forgetting in short-term memory can be due either to decay or to displacement.

Long-term memory

Forgetting in long-term memory can be due to:

*   **Lack of availability** – information is no longer in the long-term memory; for example, because of brain damage
*   **Lack of accessibility** – information is still in the long-term memory but cannot be retrieved, because of interference or retrieval failure (see sections 11 and 12)

Types of forgetting

Different types of forgetting are:

*   **Complete**
*   **Partial or distorted recall**
*   **Inaccurate recall (confabulation)** – this is recall of events that did not take place

THE WORK OF HERMANN EBBINGHAUS

Hermann Ebbinghaus (1885) studied his memory over many years using nonsense trigrams (a trigram is a group of three letters, for example XBV). He produced the **forgetting curve**, which shows that most forgetting occurs in the first hour after learning (see Fig 2.12).

For example, one hour after learning some trigrams, Ebbinghaus could recall only 44% of the information correctly, and one week later only 21% of the information. Thus about 56% of material was forgotten in the first hour after learning, but only another 23% was lost in the first week.

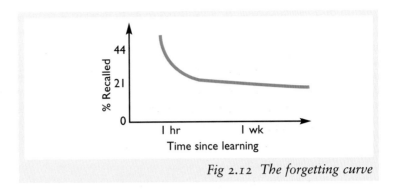

Fig 2.12 *The forgetting curve*

The forgetting curve has been also been found to apply for meaningful information.

Ebbinghaus also showed that forgetting can be overcome by **overlearning**. This involved him continuing to study the list of nonsense trigrams even after the whole list could be recalled without error.

CONCLUSIONS

Forgetting occurs for different reasons, depending on whether we are considering short-term memory or long-term memory. In long-term memory, forgetting may be due to lack of availability or lack of accessibility.

Forgetting can be complete or partial. Another issue is that of confabulation – the mind making up memories of events that did not in fact occur.

The next four sections will look at the areas we have touched upon here in more detail.

HOT EXAM HINT

Apply what you have learnt about memory to your revision. Do not test your recall immediately after reading the information, but wait at least two hours.

SECTION 10 | FORGETTING: SHORT-TERM MEMORY

INTRODUCTION

'You can't expect me to remember that,' said Katy. 'There's far too many numbers in that barcode.'

'Well, just try,' said the supervisor.

What a terrible first day as a 'checkout chick', thought Katy. Barcodes with 14 numbers – how could anyone remember that many digits?

HOW ARE THINGS FORGOTTEN IN SHORT-TERM MEMORY?

Forgetting in short-term memory occurs for two main reasons:

- **Decay** – the information can only be stored for a certain amount of time.
- **Displacement** – only a certain amount of information can be stored, and it is removed (displaced) if more information arrives.

The best way to remember things for longer is to transfer them to long-term memory.

Let's look at the two processes of forgetting in short-term memory in more detail.

KEY DEFINITIONS

MEMORY TRACE
Physiological change in brain made by new memory.

DECAY

When a new memory is formed in short-term memory it leads to a physiological change in the brain. This is known as a **trace**. This trace may be a change in neurons (specialized cells that transmit nerve impulses) and their connections in the brain; it may be down to biochemical changes; or both. Psychologists are still researching this.

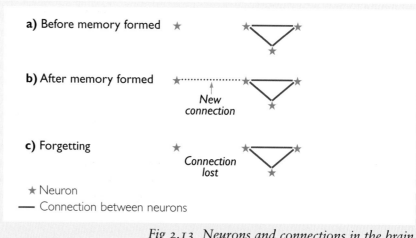

a) Before memory formed

b) After memory formed
New connection

c) Forgetting
Connection lost

★ Neuron
— Connection between neurons

Fig 2.13 Neurons and connections in the brain

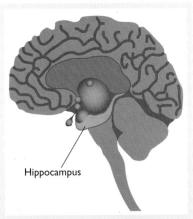

Fig 2.14 *The hippocampus*

Fig 2.15 *Aplysia*

Decay in this memory trace occurs quickly: the physiological changes in the brain are lost, and so the information is forgotten. Short-term memory tends to have a duration of about 30 seconds (see section 5). The memory trace can be reactivated by rehearsal or consolidation (section 4).

Research has shown that traces can be made permanent. Eric Kandel found that structural changes occurred in the neurons in the hippocampus (part of the brain) of sea slugs (aplysia) when there was repeated stimulation of the animal (quoted in Eysenck and Keane 1999). We believe similar processes occur in the human brain. This is a permanent memory trace, as found in the long-term memory.

DISPLACEMENT

Short-term memory is believed to be able to hold about seven **slots** of information (see section 5). Any more information leads to the displacement of the original information, which is therefore lost (forgotten).

Look at the following example. Here a person is asked to try to remember a list of ten words read out to them: dog, cat, head, chair, table, bed, cloth, fire, brown, horse. Observe how their short-term memory arranges the information, and what happens when all the slots are full.

Slot	1	2	3	4	5	6	7	
	dog →							
	cat	dog						
	head	cat	dog					
	chair	head	cat	dog				
	table	chair	head	cat	dog			
	bed	table	chair	head	cat	dog		
	cloth	bed	table	chair	head	cat	dog	
	fire	cloth	bed	table	chair	head	cat	*'dog' is forgotten by displacement*
	brown	fire	cloth	bed	table	chair	head	*'cat' is forgotten*
	horse	brown	fire	cloth	bed	table	chair	*'head' is forgotten*

CONCLUSIONS

Forgetting in short-term memory is linked to the limitations of that store of memory. It is limited in the amount of time it can store information (information is lost by decay), and also by its capacity (information is lost by displacement).

SECTION 11 | FORGETTING: LONG-TERM MEMORY AND INTERFERENCE

INTRODUCTION

'You're so lucky,' said Clare. 'All those trips to America. Did you visit a place called Manuuchos when you were in New York?'

'Where's that?' said Bill.

'You don't know where Manuuchos is? It's a really big bar in Central Manhattan.'

'Yeah – is it a big glass place?' said Bill. 'I think I know it – to be honest I've probably been in there loads of times. I just never really noticed.'

WHY DOES FORGETTING OCCUR IN LONG-TERM MEMORY?

Forgetting may occur in long-term memory because the memories cannot be retrieved. Memories that are too similar become fused and it is difficult to recall a particular one. For example, memories for regular events, such as eating breakfast, are so similar that it is very hard to remember a particular occasion unless it was distinct for some reason (that is, something different happened – such as finding a twenty pound note in your cereal). In the case of similar events like these, people tend to recall a general idea (or **schema**) of what usually happens during that event, rather than each actual event itself.

KEY DEFINITIONS

INTERFERENCE
When the similarity of memories makes it difficult to locate a particular memory.

Interference occurs when the similarity of memories makes it difficult to locate a particular memory. There are two types of interference, which have been tested experimentally: **retroactive inhibition** or interference (RI) and **proactive inhibition** or interference (PI).

Experiments in this area use two lists of words that contain similar words. For example:

List A	List B
hit	hot
dog	dig
older	elder
bet	bit
pen	pin

Participants are asked to learn the two lists of words, one after the other, and then recall just one of the lists. They tend to confuse the lists. This is an example of forgetting due to interference. The more similar the items, the greater the interference. One memory inhibits recall of another.

Let us look at the difference between retroactive interference and proactive interference.

WHAT IS RETROACTIVE INTERFERENCE?

This is where information learnt afterwards interferes with recall of the desired learnt information. This effect **increases** with the time between learning and recall.

- **List A** is learnt first.
- **List B** is then learnt.
- **List A** is then recalled.
- **List B** interferes with the recall of **list A**.

PROACTIVE INTERFERENCE

This is where information learnt beforehand interferes with recall of the desired information. Note that this effect, unlike that of retroactive interference, **decreases** with time between learning and recall (be careful not to get them confused).

- **List A** is learnt first.
- **List B** is then learnt.
- **List B** is then recalled.
- **List A** interferes with the recall of **list B**.

McGeoch and McDonald (1931) found that the recall of a list of words can be interfered with in different ways by having different additional items to remember. Their experiment required the participants to learn a list of ten words, then learn another list of various things (like nonsense groups of letters), before attempting to recall the original list.

Average no. words recalled from original list	Second list
4.5	Control group; no second list
3.68	Numbers
2.58	Nonsense groups of letters (e.g. 'XBVK')
2.17	Unrelated words
1.83	Words of opposite meaning
1.25	Words of similar meaning

(After McGeoch and McDonald 1931)

This shows that interference not only occurs with words that look or sound the same (as in the 'hit'/'hot', 'dog'/'dig' example above), but also with words that have similar or opposite **meaning**.

CONCLUSIONS

Competing memories (that is, memories that are similar) make it difficult to locate particular items in recall. This is known as interference. Interference can be retroactive or proactive, and in words can be related both to superficial similarities and to semantic links (semantic refers to 'meaning').

HOT EXAM HINT

Apply what you have learnt about memory to your revision. Do not study two similar topics together as this will cause interference.

FORGETTING: LONG-TERM MEMORY AND RETRIEVAL FAILURE

INTRODUCTION

Rashmi was on that boring old motorway heading back to university. It was starting to get dusk and he was thinking about all the things he would have to do when he got back. He had the radio on, as background music, something to accompany his thoughts. Suddenly 'The Boys of Summer' by Don Henley started up. He turned it up and was completely transported back in time. He was with Michelle again, it was a hot summer, and one of the best holidays he'd had. For about two minutes he relived the past – and almost missed his junction.

KEY DEFINITIONS

CUES
Prompts that aid recall; can include words, smells and music.

THE LINK BETWEEN CUES AND RETRIEVAL

Cues are things that aid recall, and retrieval may fail because of lack of cues. There are two types of cue: external and internal. Let us consider in turn these two types of cue, and how they can affect recall (or failure to recall).

EXTERNAL CUES

Within external cues, there are different groups. We shall look at these in turn.

Physical context

Physical context can play a part; for instance the place where learning took place can increase recall. As information is encoded, so are aspects of the physical environment. Returning to the same environment will produce cues that aid recall. This is often used with eye-witnesses to crimes or accidents: they are taken back to the site of the event to aid their recall. However, if the event was emotionally very painful for the witness, then this approach actually reduces recall. Evidence for the role of physical context is provided by the work of Godden and Baddeley (1975) (see opposite).

Verbal context

Words can also act as cues. The name of a place you have been on holiday might aid recall of things that happened there.

Other cues

Other cues can include appearance, smells or a piece of music. People can associate a particular song or melody with a particular period in their lives.

INTERNAL CUES

The mood or mental state of a person during learning can act as cues for recall. For example, if you learn something while drunk it may be harder to recall it while sober – and vice versa:

Learning state	Retrieval state	Level of recall
Sober	Sober	Good
Drunk	Drunk	Good
Sober	Drunk	Poor
Drunk	Sober	Poor

This has also been found with people who suffer from mania (characterized as the opposite of depression – but not a pleasant experience!), who can only remember certain things when in the manic state and not when calm. There is evidence that this link between mood and memory applies with all moods generally (see section 13).

RESEARCH EVIDENCE

Godden and Baddeley (1975). Context-dependent memory in two natural environments. *British Journal of Psychology.*

Aims

This study set out to test learning and recall in two different environmental situations.

Procedure

The participants were deep-sea divers, and the experiment compared memory both on land and underwater in diving equipment. The experiment took place by the side of a swimming pool (land) and under ten feet of water in the pool. There were four sets of experiments (including two controls), each using the task of learning a list of forty words and attempting to recall them.

Group	Learning	Recall
Control 1	Land	Land
Control 2	Underwater	Underwater
Experimental 1	Land	Underwater
Experimental 2	Underwater	Land

Fig 2.16 Deep-sea divers were used in Godden and Baddeley's research.

Findings

The mean percentage recalled for each of the four experiments was calculated:

Control 1	35%
Control 2	28%
Experimental 1	23%
Experimental 2	20%

Conclusions

Recall was better when it took place in the same environment as learning, because physical cues aid retrieval. Changing environments leads to a lack of cues and retrieval failure.

SUMMARY

Retrieval depends upon cues to help find the memory, and forgetting can occur through lack of cues. As we have seen, cues such as words, smells, music, physical environments and even moods can have an effect on memory.

FORGETTING AND EMOTIONS

INTRODUCTION

Alex wanted to tell his new girlfriend about his unhappy childhood, but found it very difficult to remember specific things. He told her about how he generally remembered his dad hitting and pushing his mum and her crying, but he couldn't recall any specific incidents. He remembered that they got divorced when he was seven, but he couldn't remember specifically being told. It seemed that memories of his unhappy childhood lacked detail – they had somehow become diluted.

KEY DEFINITIONS

REPRESSION
Term used by Sigmund Freud to describe a process he proposed by which unpleasant memories are forced into the unconscious mind, and are consequently forgotten by the conscious mind.

UNCONSCIOUS MIND
The part of the mind not open to direct scrutiny.

HOW IS RECALL AFFECTED BY EMOTIONS?

Recall and forgetting are influenced by the emotional content of the memory. According to Sigmund Freud, unpleasant memories will be forgotten through **repression**. This is the process by which painful and threatening memories are pushed into the unconscious mind, and cannot be remembered by the conscious mind. However, these memories can still exert an influence on the individual.

Not everyone is convinced by this idea. Alan Baddeley (1990) says: 'There is no doubt that powerful negative emotions can induce amnesia, although the extent to which the patient is totally unable to access stressful memories … is very hard to ascertain'. In fact, many people recall unpleasant memories that they would rather forget (as in post-traumatic stress disorder, often suffered by those who have experienced some powerful emotional trauma, such as war).

FOR CONSIDERATION

Have you ever noticed how when you are sad you tend to remember only negative memories? This is one of the reasons why depressed people find it hard to see things positively.

MOOD AND FORGETTING

The current mood of the individual can influence the type of memories recalled. Rinck et al (1992) asked participants to learn words of different types ('strongly toned' words, that is, with pleasant or unpleasant associations – such as 'hate' or 'love'). Later, when the participants were in different moods, they were unexpectedly given a memory test. The type of words recalled was linked to the mood of the participant at recall. This is known as the **mood congruent effect**. It only applies for words with strong associations, not those with weak ones.

- When participants were 'happy' at the time of the memory test, they recalled approximately 50% of the words with pleasant associations, and approximately 30% of the words with unpleasant associations.
- On the other hand, when participants were 'sad' at the time of the memory test, they recalled only around 30% of the words with pleasant associations, and approximately 40% of the words with unpleasant associations.

SUMMARIZING THE RELATIONSHIP BETWEEN EMOTIONS AND MEMORY

This information draws on Gilligan and Bower (1984).

- Recall is best when a person's mood matches their mood at the time of learning (**mood-state-dependent recall**):

Mood at learning	Mood at recall	Level of recall
Sad	Sad	Good
Sad	Happy	Poor

- Free recall of information is linked to mood (**thought congruity**).
- Increases in mood intensity lead to increased access to memories of an associated type (**mood intensity**). Thus the happier the person becomes, the more pleasant memories can be retrieved. This has important implications because depressed and unhappy individuals tend only to retrieve negative memories.
- Material with emotional associations is learnt best when the individual is in a similar mood to the material (**mood congruity**).

Type of material	Mood at learning	Level of recall
Sad	Sad	Good
Sad	Happy	Poor

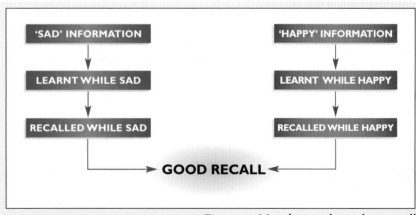

Fig 2.17 Mood-state-dependent recall

CONCLUSIONS

Forgetting can be influenced by the emotional content of the memory. Freud suggested that unpleasant memories are more likely to be forgotten. Later research has investigated the effects of congruence of emotion of the memory and mood at the time of recall.

FLASHBULB MEMORIES

INTRODUCTION

What were you doing when you heard about the twin towers disaster in New York? I was sitting at my desk working, and a colleague came in and almost in passing said, 'Isn't it terrible news in America?'

'What do you mean?' I replied.

'Haven't you heard? Two planes have crashed in New York.'

I was totally shocked and went straight on the Internet to read all about it. I have a very clear recall regarding the event. For some reason I can remember it word for word.

KEY DEFINITIONS

FLASHBULB MEMORIES
Vivid memories for a particular event (public or personal) outside the context of other memories of that time.

WHAT ARE FLASHBULB MEMORIES?

Flashbulb memories (FBMs) are vivid and detailed memories that are recalled out of context of the rest of a person's life. They can be of major public events, like the death of a president or a rock star, or of major personal events, like one's wedding day. That they are recalled 'out of context' means that surrounding memories of other aspects of a person's life (which are usually required for recollection) will be forgotten long before the FBM.

FBMS OF PUBLIC EVENTS

There are probably a number of important public events that you remember, without necessarily recalling much about what was happening in other areas of your life at the time. Some public events in the USA that have been studied for FBMs are:

- The assassination attempt on President Ronald Reagan (30 March 1981)
- The *Challenger* space shuttle disaster (28 January 1986)

Fig 2.18 Striking public events such as the loss of the Challenger space shuttle and the resignation of Margaret Thatcher can lead to flashbulb memories (FBMs).

Correspondingly important events in the UK that have been studied in connection with FBMs include:

- The Hillsborough stadium disaster (15th April 1989)
- The resignation of Margaret Thatcher as Prime Minister (22 November 1990)

Brown and Kulik (1977) investigated the nature of FBMs in US students. The students were asked to recall recent key events in US history, such as the assassination of President Kennedy. They found that the students were likely to remember six kinds of information about the time they learnt about the news (known as the **reception event**):

- Where they were when they were told the news (place)
- Details of what they were doing at the time they were told (event)
- Who the person was who gave them the news (informant)
- Their feelings on hearing the news
- The feelings of others
- What happened afterwards (aftermath)

On this evidence, it seems it really is true when people say everyone remembers where they were when Kennedy died!

Because individuals cannot remember other aspects of their lives at the time (that is, context which is usually needed for recollection), Brown and Kulik believe that FBMs are a different type of memory to normal. Their level of accuracy is believed to be greater, and they have more **longevity** than other memories (they are retained over a longer period). The surprisingness (or suddenness) and the emotional impact are important factors. It is felt that the emotions print the event into the memory. This is why this is sometimes called the **Now Print Theory**.

Another point to remember, however, is that FBMs for important public or private events are commonly rehearsed (people tend to go over and over them), and this may explain their vividness in recall.

FBMS OF PERSONAL EVENTS

FBMs are also found for personal events. Some common personal events which cause FBMs for US students are:

- Accidents
- Witnessing accidents
- First date
- First kiss
- Graduation/prom night

CONCLUSIONS

FBMs are vivid emotional memories for important events (public or personal), where the individual is able to remember where they were when told about a public event, or where they experienced a personal event. The individual is unable to remember what was happening in their lives at that time apart from that event.

KEY DEFINITIONS

THE NOW PRINT THEORY
The theory that the emotional impact of a surprising or sudden event prints that event into the memory.

SECTION 15 | EYE-WITNESS TESTIMONY: INTRODUCTION

INTRODUCTION

The police officer began writing in a notebook. He was resting on the bonnet of the Volvo V70. 'Okay sir, what speed would you estimated the Honda was going when it hit the wall?'
'It's hard to remember,' said Bob. 'I wasn't really paying that much attention – I just heard a very loud bang.'

Fig 2.19 Recall of an accident by eyewitnesses can be influenced by various factors after the event.

KEY DEFINITIONS

EYE-WITNESS TESTIMONY
The memory of witnesses who were present at accidents or crimes.

WHAT IS EYE-WITNESS TESTIMONY?

When individuals witness crimes or accidents, their recall is important, for example to provide a description of events for a court. This is eye-witness testimony. But the memory of such events is not an infallible video tape: it can be changed and influenced.

WHAT FACTORS CAN INFLUENCE EYE-WITNESS TESTIMONY?

Eye-witness memory may be influenced by the following factors:
- Information added at retrieval to make sense
- Information added after the event but recalled as part of the event
- Assumptions recalled as facts
- Wording of question at retrieval (can influence memory)

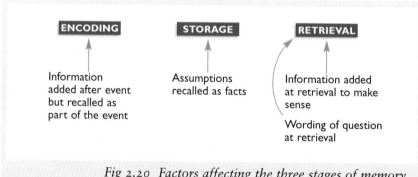

Fig 2.20 Factors affecting the three stages of memory

These will be discussed in greater detail in sections 16–20. For now we shall look at some concrete examples of these and other factors that can affect the accuracy of a witness's statements.

The witness
- Physical condition – for example, was the witness drunk?
- Stress of the event – can distort perception

The environment

- Viewing conditions – for example, was it night or day?
- Exposure duration – that is, the length of the event
- Significance of the event at the time – for example, you might see a getaway car drive past and only learn of the crime much later
- Time lapsed between event and recall

The suspect

- Disguise
- Changed appearance
- The **weapon effect** – if a criminal uses a weapon, witnesses tend to focus on it, to the exclusion of other information about the situation ('All I could see was the gun barrel pointing toward me')

The police

- How the witness was interviewed (nature of the police questioning) – for example, a leading question might affect the nature of the witness's recollections
- Methods used – for example, an identity parade

MORE ABOUT WITNESS ACCURACY

Eysenck (1984) believes that the recollection of an event is 'fragile and susceptible to moderation'. Buckhout (1974) showed that accuracy of recall is poor. He staged a 'crime' in front of 141 students in a lecture theatre: a male intruder ran into the lecture theatre, grabbed a bag, and ran out. The main findings from questioning the students later were as follows:

- Students would overestimate the length of the incident (by 2.5 times) (for example the incident lasted 10 seconds, but was recalled as 25 seconds).
- Descriptions of the intruder were on average only 25% accurate.
- 40% of the students identified the correct suspect from six photographs. More importantly, 60% got it wrong.
- Furthermore, 25% of the students identified an innocent bystander at the front of the lecture theatre as the suspect from the six photographs.

In addition, the confidence of the witness is not an indicator of accuracy ('That's him, officer, I'm absolutely positive'). Witnesses can be very confident of accuracy even when wrong.

CONCLUSIONS

The memory of eye-witnesses is not an infallible video tape of the event, but is a reconstruction which can be inaccurate. Confidence of accuracy is not related to actual accuracy of recall. The next few sections will go on to consider factors affecting eye-witness testimony in greater detail.

EYE-WITNESS TESTIMONY: BARTLETT 1

INTRODUCTION

If you remember from the previous section, Bob was having trouble recalling the events surrounding an accident. Let's continue with the story…

'So just give me some idea of the speed,' said the police officer. 'It doesn't have to be exact.' Bob was thinking. His recall of events was poor; however, he remembered the loud bang. It seemed logical that the faster the car was going the louder the bang would be. That must mean the car was travelling fast. He looked across at the vehicle. The front was totally crushed.

'I reckon it must have been doing 50 miles per hour.'

'50 mph. Thanks a lot sir.'

Bob realized he hadn't used his memory to work this out. He'd used his logic. Oh dear!

Fig 2.21 Frederick Bartlett

KEY DEFINITIONS

EFFORTS AFTER MEANING
Reconstruction of memories to make sense of them, rather than just remembering what actually happened.

BARTLETT AND EFFORTS AFTER MEANING

When we recall events, we add information at retrieval in order to make sense of our recollections. Frederick Bartlett (1932) was the first to emphasize the interpretation process in recall. To go back to the video tape analogy from section 15: when a memory is recalled, it is not simply a question of finding the correct point on the video tape; the memory must be reconstructed at the time of recall. This means that the memory can be distorted from the original information. Bartlett called this process **efforts after meaning** – making sense of the past memory.

This process can be tested by asking participants to remember information that does not make sense to them. When they recall the information, it will be distorted to fit with what makes sense to them. To demonstrate this, Bartlett used a Native American folk story called 'The War of the Ghosts'. Read the story. In the next section we shall see how Bartlett used the story.

THE WAR OF THE GHOSTS

One night two young men from Egulac went down to the river to hunt seals, and while they were there it became foggy and calm. Then they heard war-cries, and they thought. 'Maybe this is a war party'. They escaped to the shore, and hid behind a log. Now canoes came up, and they heard the noise of paddles, and saw one canoe coming up to them. There were five men in the canoe, and they said: 'What do you think? We wish to take you along. We are going up the river to make war on the people'.

One of the young men said: 'I have no arrows'. 'Arrows are in the canoe', they said.

Fig 2.22 'The War of the Ghosts'

'I will not go along. I might be killed. My relatives do not know where I have gone. But you', he said, turning to the other, 'may go with them'. So one of the young men went, but the other returned home. And the warriors went on up the river to a town on the other side of Kalama.

The people came down to the water, and they began to fight, and many were killed. But presently the young man heard one of the warriors say: 'Quick, let us go home: that Indian has been hit'. Now he thought: 'Oh, they are ghosts'. He did not feel sick, but they said he had been shot.

So the canoes went back to Egulac, and the young man went ashore to his house, and made a fire. And he told everybody and said: 'Behold I accompanied the ghosts, and we went to fight. Many of our fellows were killed, and many of those who attacked us were killed. They said I was hit, and I did not feel sick'.

He told it all, and then he became quiet. When the sun rose he fell down. Something black came out of his mouth. His face became contorted. The people jumped up and cried. He was dead.

(Bartlett 1932)

To find out how Bartlett used this story to demonstrate efforts after meaning, turn to the next section.

EYE-WITNESS TESTIMONY: BARTLETT 2

BARTLETT'S EXPERIMENT

Bartlett (1932) conducted a study using the story 'The War of the Ghosts' (see section 16). The story was given to US participants to remember. They were then tested for recall in two ways:

- **Repeated reproduction** – recall of the story at different times after reading, such as 1 hour after reading and 1 day after reading
- **Serial reproduction** – the first person recalls the story; a second person recalls the first person's version, and so on. You may recognize this as very similar to the party game 'Chinese Whispers'.

What Bartlett found

In both cases (repeated reproduction and serial reproduction), recall by the participants showed evidence of changes: they tried to make sense of the story, rather than simply remembering it. The pattern of changes in the recall of the story was as follows:

- **Rationalization** – new information was included to make the story logical to the listener.
- The order of the events was transformed.
- Individuals omitted information that they felt was not relevant or they did not understand.
- The story was shortened.
- The story became more conventional according to US culture and story-telling – more like the type of story participants were used to hearing.
- Individuals changed the emphasis of importance, for example to focus on one part.
- **Drifting** – the more often the story was told with serial reproduction, the more the meaning changed.

KEY DEFINITIONS

RATIONALIZATION
A process of recalling memories in such a way as to make them appear logical – even if events are twisted in the process.

This showed that recall is an attempt to make sense of the information or the event, and not an exact memory. Now we shall look at an example of an individual's recall of the story. Compare it with the original (section 16).

EXAMPLE OF RECALL OF 'THE WAR OF THE GHOSTS'

Two youths were standing by a river about to start seal-catching, when a boat appeared with five men in it. They were all armed for war.

The youths were at first frightened, but they were asked by the men to come and help fight some enemies on the other bank. One youth said he could not come as his relations would be anxious about him; the other said he would go, and entered the boat.

In the evening he returned to his hut, and told his friends that he had been in a battle. A great many had been slain, and he had been wounded by an arrow; he felt no pain, he said. They told him that he must have been fighting in a battle of ghosts. Then he remembered that it had been queer and he became very excited.

In the morning, however, he became ill, and his friends gathered round; he fell down and his face became very pale. Then he writhed and shrieked and his friends were filled with terror. At last he became calm. Something hard and black came out of his mouth, and he lay contorted and dead.

(Bartlett 1932)

Analysis

- Rationalization – the participant's narrative is more coherent than the original in terms of time (for example, 'in the evening', 'in the morning').
- The order of events is changed – the 'ghosts' realization comes later in the participant's version.
- Omissions – the participant leaves out names of places, and dialogue.
- Shortened – the participant's version is around 180 words; the original was around 330 words.
- More conventional to US storytelling – last paragraph, for example, is less disjointed and more flowing.

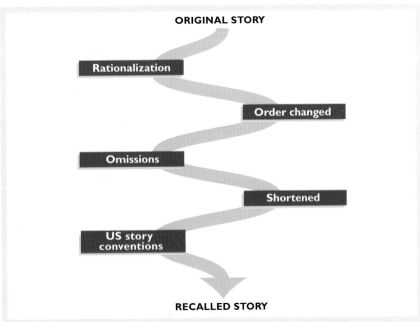

Fig 2.23 Various factors may influence recall.

CONCLUSIONS

Bartlett showed that people recalled 'The War of the Ghosts' in an adapted form to make sense to the listener. This demonstrates the rationalization and restructuring involved in efforts after meaning (reconstructing memories to make sense, rather than just recalling things as they were).

EYE-WITNESS TESTIMONY: LOFTUS 1

Fig 2.24 Elizabeth Loftus

HOW ADDITIONAL INFORMATION CAN ALTER MEMORY OF AN EVENT

Research has shown that information can be added to a particular memory after the event itself, and later recalled as part of the event itself. This is clearly another important factor to consider when evaluating eye-witness testimony. Elizabeth Loftus showed this phenomenon in her 1975 experiment.

RESEARCH EVIDENCE

Loftus (1975). Leading questions and eye-witness report. *Cognitive Psychology*.

Aims

This study set out to investigate whether misleading information after an event can be recalled as part of the event.

Procedure

A total of 150 students were shown a three minute film of a car driving in the countryside, followed by an accident. Afterwards the students were questioned about the film. Half were asked misleading questions, for example, 'How fast was the car travelling when it passed the barn?' (there was no barn in the film). One week later, all the students were questioned again about the film.

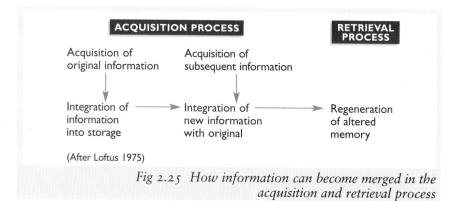

Fig 2.25 *How information can become merged in the acquisition and retrieval process*

Findings

The group who had been asked the misleading questions were more likely to recall a barn in the film (17.3% probability, compared with 2.7% for the group who had not been asked the misleading question).

Conclusions

Misleading information after an event can be recalled later as part of the original event.

CD-ROM

Memory: Loftus' research

SOURCE ERROR
Confusion of two events (sources) as if they were one memory.

A REAL-LIFE CASE STUDY

Information after the event can lead to **source errors** – the person confuses the origin of two different memories as if they were one event. Aronson et al (1999) report the case of Private Todd Bunting.

On 19 April 1995 the federal buildings in Oklahoma City were bombed, killing 168 people. Initial reports suggested that there were two suspects, working together. This belief was based on the eye-witness testimony of people like Tom Kessinger (a truck rental office mechanic), who said he had seen Timothy McVeigh (later convicted of the bombing) with another man, renting a truck the day before the bombing. Kessinger gave a brief description and police continued to hunt for the second suspect.

Later investigation found that Kessinger was describing Private Todd Bunting from Fort Riley, Kansas. However, Private Bunting turned out to have nothing to do with the bombing.

The explanation was that Bunting had indeed rented a truck the day before the bombing, but on a separate occasion to McVeigh. Kessinger had confused these observations, and when recalling could not distinguish that the memories had different sources.

CONCLUSIONS

Information added after an event can be recalled as part of the original event. This is shown by the experimental study done by Elizabeth Loftus, and the case reported by Aronson et al shows clearly how it can affect real-life eye-witness testimony.

In the next section we shall look at more of Loftus's work on recall.

EYE-WITNESS TESTIMONY: LOFTUS 2

HOW CAN WORDING OF QUESTIONS AT RETRIEVAL INFLUENCE MEMORY?

At the retrieval stage, the wording of questions about an event can influence the actual recall. Loftus and Palmer (1974) showed participants a film of a car accident. Later the participants were asked questions about the events, but different words were used in the questions. This was found to influence the participants' estimate of the car's speed. One version of a question was 'How fast was the car going when it smashed?' Other versions of the question replaced the word 'smashed' with 'collided', 'hit' and 'contacted'. This affected the average speed recalled as follows:

- 'smashed': 40.8 mph
- 'collided': 39.3 mph
- 'hit': 34.0 mph
- 'contacted': 31.8 mph

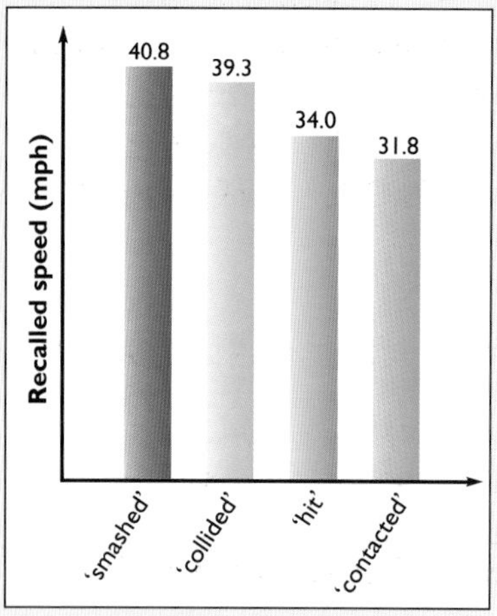

Also, participants will recall a non-existent broken headlight in a crash if the question implies its existence – for example, asking 'Did you see the broken headlight' rather than 'Did you see a broken headlight?' (Loftus 1996).

Fig 2.26 The effect of question wording on memory

RESEARCH EVIDENCE

Loftus (1975). Leading questions and eye-witness report. *Cognitive Psychology.*

Aims

This study aimed to investigate how information after the event can influence recall of the actual event.

Procedure

A total of 150 students watched a one minute film about a car going through a 'stop' sign, turning right and crashing. Afterwards, all participants were asked ten questions about the film, with one question being altered.

- For half the students (group 1), the question was 'How fast was the car travelling through the "stop" sign?'
- For the other half (group 2), the question was 'How fast was the car travelling when it turned right?'

One week later the participants underwent a memory test about the film. The key question was: 'Was there a "stop" sign in the film?'

Findings

53% of group 1 students recalled seeing a 'stop' sign, compared with 35% of group 2.

Misleading questions immediately after the event can influence later recall of the event.

It has also been found that delaying the misleading information to one week later has an even stronger effect on memory.

WHY DOES THIS HAPPEN?

The reason that the wording of a question can influence memory is that at the time of recall, memories of the event are reconstructed. It is important to emphasize again that memory is not like a complete video tape that can be rewound and studied at will. When information is recalled it is reconstructed from representations in memory. Leading or misleading questions by lawyers in court or the police during interview affect the reconstruction of the memory.

DO MISLEADING QUESTIONS ALWAYS INFLUENCE MEMORY?

The answer is no. There are certain situations where memory is unaffected:
- If participants believe the questioner already knows what actually happened
- If questioning follows the original order of events
- If misleading information is blatantly misleading
- If warnings are given beforehand about misleading information
- If participants are given time to study questions (including the misleading ones) carefully

FOR CONSIDERATION

It is ethical to ask participants misleading questions to deliberately confuse their memory?

ASSUMPTIONS RECALLED AS FACTS

In one of her many experiments, Elizabeth Loftus (1979) showed how previous associations can become worked into the memory for an event.

In a short film, person A is seen talking with person B. Later in the film person A is seen committing a burglary with an unseen accomplice. In recall about the film, participants tended to remember person B as the accomplice because of the previous association.

CONCLUSIONS

The way in which a question is asked can influence the recall of an event. Misleading questions (or leading ones) can affect a person's memory: obviously this might be crucial in a court case.

SECTION 20 | EYE-WITNESS TESTIMONY: CONCLUSIONS

JUST HOW UNRELIABLE IS EYE-WITNESS TESTIMONY?

It could be concluded from the studies in sections 18 and 19 that eye-witness testimony is far from perfect and needs to be used with caution. Buckhout (1974) emphasizes that 'Perception and memory are decision-making processes affected by the totality of a person's abilities, background, attitudes, motives and beliefs, by environment and by the way his recollection is eventually tested'.

Varying influence of misleading information

However, not all memories are distorted. Loftus (1979) showed viewers a film about a red purse being stolen from a handbag. After the film, viewers were asked whether they saw the 'brown' purse being stolen. At a memory test one week later, only 2% of them recalled a brown purse in the film.

This indicates that the memory for major facts is not easily misled.

There are key aspects to the influence of misleading information after the event. It tends to only influence memory if:
- It is about minor details of the event.
- It is given after a delay.
- The witness is not aware that false information may be being given.

DO LAB RESULTS REFLECT REAL LIFE?

Almost all of the research is lab-based experimental work, usually with students watching a short film followed by questions. Certainly the work of Elizabeth Loftus (sections 18 and 19) follows this pattern. This type of research tends to paint a very negative picture of eye-witness accuracy. But can we extrapolate these results to real-life witnesses?

Evidence challenging lab results

There are a limited number of real life studies to challenge the conclusions of the lab experiments, and these suggest that eye-witness memory is more accurate than first thought.

In particular, in a Canadian study by Yuille and Cutshall (1986), the researchers made use of a local shooting and robbery in Vancouver, and found that the accuracy of recall did not decline even after five months. The shooting took place outside a gun shop in view of several witnesses, and involved the thief firing two shots and the shop-owner firing six.

KEY DEFINITIONS

ECOLOGICAL VALIDITY
The applicability of laboratory studies and results to real life.

FOR CONSIDERATION

Lab-based studies allow experimenters a greater degree of control, but have low ecological validity.

Fig 2.27 Results from laboratory studies cast eye-witness testimony in a rather negative light. However, it seems that where real-life events are concerned, eye-witness memory is in fact good.

Thirteen of the twenty-one witnesses were traced five months after the event by the researchers. The level of accuracy of recall was 'truly impressive' when compared with the original police reports.

Misleading questions from the researchers had no effect on accuracy of recall. Any errors in information were due to the position of the witness at the time of the incident rather than recall of false information (confabulations). Those witnesses deeply affected by the event were the most accurate. So when an event is meaningful to the witness, rather than an experimental video, then eye-witness memory is good.

CONCLUSIONS

Most experiments on eye-witness testimony find it to be quite unreliable and easily distorted. However, not all such memories are distorted, and real-life studies show that eye-witness memory can be very accurate.

INTRODUCTION

Ivan is a freelance make-up artist who often does work for the police. He is commissioned to make up the participants of a line-up to resemble the suspect. For example, if the suspect has a mole on their cheek, or a beard, Ivan is instructed to create these features in the other participants. By having everyone in the line-up looking similar, it increases the validity of the choice if a witness is able to identify the suspect.

KEY DEFINITIONS

FACE RECOGNITION UNITS
Part of the memory that contain information about features of known faces.

CD-ROM

To learn more about face recognition, see CD-ROM Memory: Photofit faces.

WHAT IS FACE RECOGNITION?

Face recognition is a specific example of recognition memory. It involves not only recognition of the features of the face, but also the link to other knowledge about that face – the person's name (if known), semantic information about the person (if known; for instance their address) and where you have seen or met them before. Thus the process of face recognition has two main stages:

- The face is compared with a set of stored descriptions called **face recognition units** (**FRUs**), and this produces a feeling of familiarity or not.
- The memory store is activated to recall facts about the person, including retrieval of their name (if it is known).

The concept revolves around how face information is stored. There are a number of possibilities:

- A separate image stored for each face seen. This would take up a large amount of memory space.
- An average face (prototype), and details of how each face differs from this. This makes the distinctiveness of the face important.
- Focussing on individual parts of the face. For example, the shape of the head would be most important, followed by eyes and mouth in full-face pictures, and the nose for profiles.

It has been noted that recognition for upside-down versions of famous faces is poor (Valentine 1988). This would challenge the last explanation.

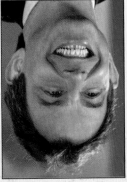

Fig 2.28 Can you recognize these famous faces upside-down?

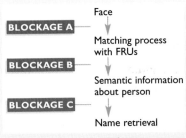

Fig 2.29 Model of recognition of familiar faces

RECOGNIZING FAMILIAR FACES

Recognition of familiar faces is a process that occurs step by step in a particular order – feeling of familiarity, recall of information about the person and, finally, name retrieval. See Fig 2.29.

Young, Hay and Ellis (1985) asked students to keep diaries of familiar face recognition errors, and this produced over 1000 incidents. The researchers analysed the errors for different types:

- Errors because of blockage at point A – failure to recognize a familiar face because, for example, appearance has changed
- Errors because of blockage at point B – feeling of familiarity about face, but no information recalled about the person or their name
- Errors because of blockage at point C – feeling of familiarity and some information recalled about the person, but no recall of their name

However there were no errors involving a feeling of familiarity and name retrieval without any other information recalled about the person, nor involving name retrieval without a feeling of familiarity about the face.

CONCLUSIONS

Face recognition is a specific version of the recognition process in memory. It requires the recognition of the features of the face, and then links to the name (when known) and/or where the person was seen last. The next section will discuss face recognition some more, and examine how it links to eye-witness testimony.

FACE RECOGNITION AND EYE-WITNESS MEMORY

Many factors can affect the face recognition process; this clearly has implications for eye-witness testimony.

Recognition of faces is poor if the face changes between the encoding (for instance, when a witness last saw a suspect) and the presentation of possibilities for recognition (for example an identity parade). The change could be a change in glasses, hairstyle, beard or even expression.

Patterson and Baddeley (1977, quoted in Brewer 2000) compared the accuracy of recall of a face that had changed in some way between the first and second times the participants saw it. They found that, for example, a change of wig reduces the accuracy of recall to 50%, while a change of wig and beard leads to only 30% accurate recall. These figures compare with 70% accuracy when the face does not change.

The accuracy of face recall is also influenced by the length of time since the face was seen; the seriousness of the crime; the number of previous encounters with the suspect; and characteristics of the witness, such as attention to detail.

Shapiro and Penrod (1986) reviewed 128 studies of facial recognition and concluded that:

Fig 2.30 Would you recognize these as the same person?

- Recognition of one's own race is better than recognition for other races.
- More time and attention spent looking at the face leads to greater accuracy.
- Accuracy is reduced by distractions.
- The upper part of the face is more important for recognition.
- Training does not improve recognition.
- The length of time since first seeing the face is important.
- Other factors that are influential include presenting many pictures of faces at the same time; this can reduce accuracy.

FACE RECOGNITION AND METHODS USED BY THE POLICE

Identity parades

A common practice used by the police is to place a suspect in an identity parade with five or six other people. The witness then has to pick out the suspect. If the witness has to face the line of people directly before pointing out the suspect, it can make them nervous and thereby reduce recall. Use of a one-way mirror increases the accuracy of recall in identity parades.

Fig 2.31 An identity parade

The problem generally with identity parades is that the police tend to choose people who look roughly similar. This is a legal requirement to avoid suggestion, but it tends to make accurate recall more difficult.

Mugshots

Another method used by the police is to get the witness to look through books of mugshots (photographs of known criminals) to find the suspect.

Wells (1993) set up an experiment where participants saw a calculator taken from a room where they were waiting. Afterwards there was 58% correct identification of the suspect from a choice of six photographs. But Buckhout (1974) showed that participants trying to identify the 'criminal' from a mock-up crime would simply pick out the most unusual photograph from a group of photographs, even though 75% of participants had not seen the person before.

The most confusing method for recall is to show mugshots and then have an identity parade. This leads to confusion between recognition and episodic memory. In other words, the witness may recognize a face in the identity parade, but not know whether it comes from the original event or from the mugshots. This is a source error (see section 18).

Photo-fit systems

Traditionally, a photo-fit could mean a police artist creating an impression of the suspect from the witness's recollections, or the use of a series of cards with parts of the face being combined to give the photo-fit. This latter practice is very restrictive, and assumes that individual features can be discriminated and combined to make the face.

Recent research suggests that in fact the whole face is recalled by witnesses. Because of this, computer-based photo-fits, such as 'E-Fit' or 'CompuFit', are based around the whole face.

CONCLUSION

Face recognition in eye-witness situations can be poor because of a change in appearance of the face through, for example, disguise. Many other factors can influence the accuracy of recall. There are a number of methods used to enlist witness recall in crime detection, and also to aid the recall itself.

FOR CONSIDERATION

Research finds that recognition of voices is poorer than recognition of faces, except for people who are famous for their voices; for example, a sports commentator.

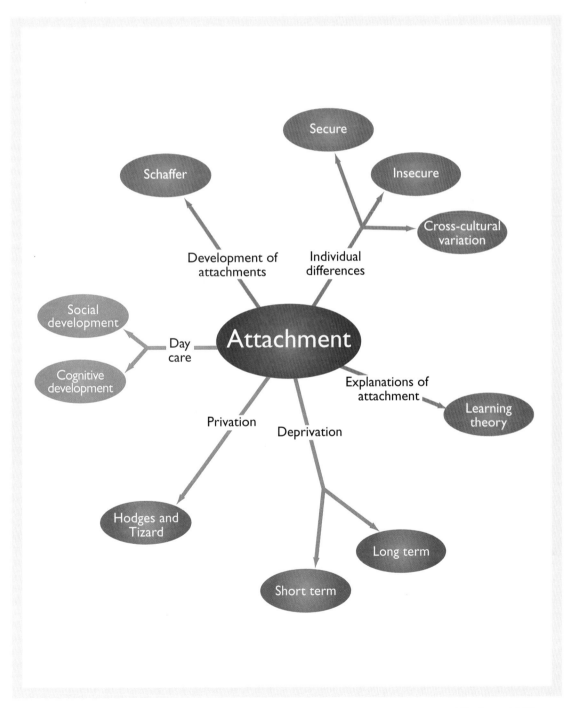

To prepare for the AQA exam you need to know the following things.

Attachments in development
- Schaffer – the development of attachments
- Ainsworth – secure and insecure attachments

Cross-cultural variations

Explanations of attachment
- Learning theory
- Bowlby

Deprivation and privation
- Short-term and long-term effects
- Bowlby
- Hodges and Tizard

The effects of day care on social and cognitive development

INTRODUCTION

Even though Malcolm was now in his mid-thirties, he still felt better when his mum was around. She always knew what to do, just like she did when he was little. His knew his mum would have an answer to his problems with Victoria – good old mum, what would he do without her?

KEY DEFINITIONS

AFFECTIONAL BOND
A 'relatively long-enduring tie in which the partner is important as a unique individual and is interchangeable with none other' (Ainsworth 1989).

ATTACHMENT
This is a type of affectional bond and is 'a special sense of security and comfort in the presence of the other' (Bee 1997). Alternatively: 'The forming of a close, emotional tie between mother and baby' (Sylva and Lunt 1982).

ATTACHMENT BEHAVIOURS
While affectional bonds and attachment are internal states and cannot be directly observed, attachment behaviours are observable, for example crying, clinging behaviour.

CD-ROM

To learn more about stranger fear, see CD-ROM Attachment: Advice for medical professionals.

KEY DEFINITIONS

PRIMARY ATTACHMENT OBJECT
The person, usually an adult, to whom the child forms their first and most important attachment.

SEPARATION ANXIETY
The level of distress shown by the child when separated from adults to whom they are attached.

DEFINING ATTACHMENT

Attachment relates to the formation of a bond between an adult (usually a parent, traditionally the mother) and a baby. It is a two-way relationship, and is usually seen as aimed at a specific person only. However, recent research has shown that there can be multiple attachments.

WHAT ARE THE SIGNS OF ATTACHMENT?

Traditionally there are a number of clear indicators shown by the baby of an attachment being formed:

- The infant seeks to be near the other person (**primary attachment object**), including watching them or trying to get their attention.
- The infant shows distress on separation from that person. This is known as **separation anxiety**.
- The distress of separation anxiety ends on reunion with the primary attachment object.
- Fear of strangers and handling by unfamiliar people. The level of this fear varies from child to child. At the extreme, the child will show all the signs of real fear. The peak is often at nine months old (Emde et al 1976). Also, how the stranger approaches is important. If the stranger approaches slowly, or if the stranger is still while the infant can move around, less stranger fear is produced, and in fact a positive reaction sometimes occurs (Bretherton and Ainsworth 1974).

WHAT IS THE PURPOSE OF ATTACHMENT?

One purpose of the early attachment is to provide the infant with a model for adult relationships and attachments. Bowlby (1969) sees the attachment as an 'internal working model' for future relationships. If the model is one of reliability and security, this will lead to healthy adult development.

In addition, at a more practical level attachment makes sure the baby is fed and cared for while still unable to be independent.

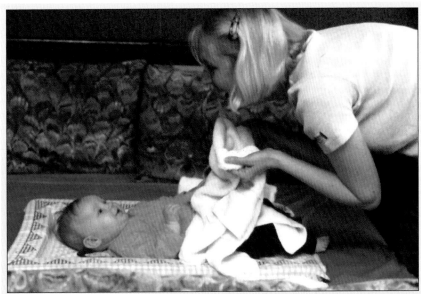

Fig 3.1 Attachment is important for the child's development.

Also, attachment gives the baby the security that allows them to explore their environment. Attachment is important because the bond enables the child to feel secure in strange environments and so move away from the mother. Ultimately attachment develops to help detachment.

Rheingold (1969) placed 24 ten-month-olds in one room, either alone or with their mothers. The infants could see into another room where there were toys. Only when the mother was present would the infants explore the other room (though continually returning to check the mother was still there). When alone, the infants were too afraid to move.

CONCLUSIONS

HOT EXAM HINT

You may be asked about the definitions of attachment behaviour. Memorize the examples given in this section.

Attachment has clear signs. These signs include the child wanting to be near the attachment object (for instance the parent), and showing distress when they go away (separation anxiety). Then the child will be consoled on reunion with that person. Fear of strangers is another important sign.

DEVELOPMENT OF ATTACHMENTS

STAGES OF ATTACHMENT

As a baby grows, it is possible to trace different phases in the development of his or her attachment to others. Schaffer (1977) sees attachment as developing gradually in a number of stages in the first year of life:

- **0–1.5 months:** asocial phase
- **1.5–6 months:** indiscriminate attachment phase
- **7–12 months:** specific attachment phase
- **12 months plus:** multiple attachment phase

These different stages are studied below.

Asocial phase (0–6 weeks)

In the first 6 weeks or so, the child responds to social and non-social stimuli in the same way (for example, the mother's voice seems to elicit no different response to a random noise).

Indiscriminate attachment phase (1.5–6 months)

In this phase, infants are attracted to humans rather than inanimate objects. The increasing complexity of the stimulus is important (blank face, then face and eyes, then face, eyes and mouth, and so on). There is no preference by the infant for who provides their care. 'These attachment behaviours are simply emitted rather than being directed towards any specific person' (Ainsworth 1989).

Specific attachment phase (7–12 months)

At this stage in its life, based on the development of the memory, the infant shows a clear preference for one person, the primary attachment object (see section 2). The infant is capable of forming an emotional bond with this one person, whose company and attention is actively sought. A key sign of the child developing an attachment is separation anxiety (see section 2).

Tennes and Lampl (1966) observed 27 infants at monthly intervals between the ages of 3 and 23 months old. The average age of onset of separation anxiety was 8 months old, but individual differences ranged from 4 to 18 months old. Kagan et al (1978) noted that infants attending day care tended not to cry on separation from the mother (a sign of separation anxiety) before 7 months old. The level of crying peaked at 13 months old and declined thereafter.

Generally, separation anxiety appears in the third quarter of the first year of life, which coincides with the development of recall memory at around 9 months old, and of object permanence. If children show separation

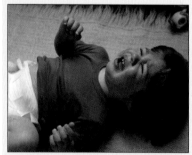

Fig 3.2 Separation anxiety is a sign of the specific attachment phase.

KEY DEFINITIONS

OBJECT PERMANENCE
The knowledge that an object exists even though it is no longer physically present.

anxiety at an earlier age, it may be due to changes in routine and environment, rather than a sign of attachment.

However, there is disagreement over the peaking of separation anxiety: some believe it peaks at 1 year old, others believe that it remains constant until the child is 2–3 years old.

Multiple attachment phase (12 months plus)

Schaffer added an extra stage. His research showed that infants could have equal attachments with more than one adult. However, these attachments are in a hierarchy: mothers are most preferred in times of distress, and fathers for playing (Schaffer 1996).

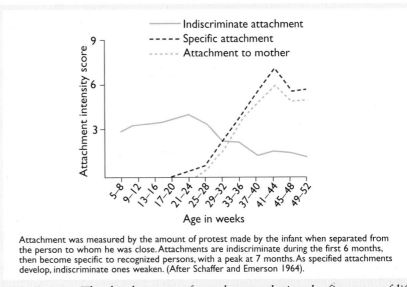

Attachment was measured by the amount of protest made by the infant when separated from the person to whom he was close. Attachments are indiscriminate during the first 6 months, then become specific to recognized persons, with a peak at 7 months. As specified attachments develop, indiscriminate ones weaken. (After Schaffer and Emerson 1964).

Fig 3.3   The development of attachments during the first year of life

FURTHER STAGES

Other researchers (for example Marvin 1977) have added extra stages in the development of attachments:

- Relationship develops as two-way (2–3 years old) – before this time the adult is purely a resource to the child
- Lessening of the proximity to the adult, and the development of attachment based on affection, trust and approval (5 years plus)

SUMMARY

The stages of development of attachments have been confirmed by naturalistic observation studies: for example children's behaviour studied in London parks (Anderson 1972).

HOT EXAM HINT

You may be asked about the stages in the development of attachment. Memorize the stages given in this spread.

These stages have been classified as: no attachment; indiscriminate attachment phase; specific attachment phase (7–12 months old); and multiple attachment phase. The specific attachment phase is the first stage of attachment behaviour. In the next spread we shall move on to look at multiple attachments.

INTRODUCTION

Naomi was very close to her grandma and grandad. She had spent so much time with them when she was young, they had become her surrogate parents. When they weren't around she missed them very much, always asking when grandma and grandad were coming around. Her behaviour often confused teachers at school, with one of them even believing that her grandad was her dad – how embarrassing!

HOW MANY ATTACHMENTS CAN A CHILD FORM?

 FOR CONSIDERATION

In some cultures it is customary for older daughters to care for their younger siblings. In this way they themselves might become the primary attachment object.

The traditional view is that infants will form one special attachment, usually to the mother. From this viewpoint, if the child did form other attachments, it would be at the expense of this main attachment. However, the work of Schaffer and Emerson (1964) showed that infants could become attached to a number of adults equally, and without any detrimental effects on the attachment with the main caregiver.

RESEARCH EVIDENCE

Schaffer and Emerson (1964). The development of social attachments in infancy. *Monographs of Society for Research into Child Development.*

Aims

This study aimed to observe the development of attachments in real-life situations over the first 18 months of a child's life.

 KEY DEFINITIONS

SEPARATION UPSET
The sign of attachment used by Schaffer and Emerson. Their criteria for separation upset included:
• Protest made when the baby was left alone in a room
• Protest made when the baby was left with other people than the mother
• Protest made after being put down from the mother's knee
• Protest made when left outside the house in a pram

Procedure

This was a longitudinal observational study of 60 Glasgow infants ('longitudinal' simply means it took place over a period of time). The infants were observed in their homes at 4-weekly intervals by the researchers in the first year of life, with a final visit at 18 months old. The main criterion for attachment was **separation upset**. The mothers were also asked to report aspects of their relationship with the infant: for example, their feeding practices, and occasions when the child showed separation upset.

Findings

Many of the infants had multiple attachments: in fact, a majority of the children by the age of 18 months. These included fathers, brothers, sisters, grandparents and close neighbours.

Although there is usually one strong attachment, other attachments were of varying intensity. At 18 months old, only half of the infants were principally attached to their mothers.

Age	Children showing more than one attachment	Children showing five or more attachments
7 months	29%	10%
10 months	59%	
18 months	87%*	33%

(* 75% showed attachment to fathers)

Another important finding was that attachment does not necessarily relate to the amount of time spent with the child, or to who does the caretaking functions. It is the quality and intensity of the interaction with the infant that matters (see section 11).

Schaffer and Emerson observed individual differences between the babies in their attachment behaviours – for example, some liked to be cuddled, others not. The latter group sometimes actively resisted cuddling, and this seems to be linked to the child's temperament (see section 8).

Conclusions

'... there is ... nothing to suggest that mothering cannot be shared by several people ... being attached to several people does not necessarily imply a shallower feeling towards each one, for an infant's capacity for attachment is not like a cake that has to be shared out. Love, even in babies, has no limits' (Schaffer and Emerson 1964, quoted in Sylva and Lunt 1982).

GRANDPARENTS

Research has shown the importance of one of the multiple attachments in particular: that to the child's grandparents. For example, it is quite common for grandmothers to share caregiving (particularly when the child's parent is a single mother, who may need more time to devote to earning money to support the child, and so on). The role of the maternal grandmother is important in Afro-American families. Biological grandparents also play an important part among Native Americans; however, if there are none, then an unrelated older person can be involved. Cox's study in Polish families (2000) showed how grandparents share their knowledge and experience.

CONCLUSIONS

Schaffer and Emerson (1964) showed in their study that the majority of children can have multiple attachments of equal intensity (for example to mother, father and grandparents) without detrimental effects on any of the attachments. This challenges the traditional view that multiple attachments dilute the attachment to the main caregiver.

FOR CONSIDERATION

Only in recent history in the West have children tended to be brought up solely by one or two parents. Throughout history, and indeed throughout the world, it has been and is more common to be brought up by an extended family.

INTRODUCTION

'I don't know how you dare take Stewart to the nursery,' said Cathy. 'He always makes such a fuss when you leave him – aren't you ashamed?'

'Not really,' said Karen.

'My Oscar just runs off – doesn't even look back. It's so nice to have an independent child.'

'Aren't you the lucky one,' said Karen sarcastically.

Fig 3.4 The strange situation

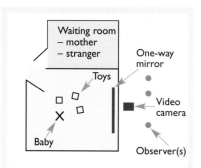

Fig 3.5 The assessment set-up. Note the mother and the stranger are out of sight of the baby, in a waiting room; they can, however, hear the baby so the mother can return if he or she is very upset.

WHAT IS THE STRANGE SITUATION?

The **strange situation** is a traditional method for assessing the level of attachment between the infant and the mother. It was developed by Mary Ainsworth. It involves a series of episodes where the child is left alone and adults come in and out of the observation room, and lasts 22 minutes in total. The key elements are a period of separation between the child and the mother, a reunion, and the appearance of a stranger.

The experiment is set up as in Fig 3.5.

The details of the eight 'episodes' in the assessment are as follows (after Ainsworth et al 1978):

1 The mother and the child enter the strange room (30 seconds).
2 The mother remains passive as the child plays (3 minutes).
3 A stranger enters (3 minutes).
4 The mother leaves and the stranger responds to the child (3 minutes, or less if the child is very distressed).
5 The mother returns; the stranger leaves; the mother leaves again (3 minutes).
6 The child is alone (3 minutes; again, less if the child is very distressed).
7 The stranger returns (3 minutes; less if the child is very distressed).
8 The mother returns and the stranger leaves (3 minutes).

The original study concentrated on attachment to the mother, but the same principles can apply to any adult to whom the child is attached. The baby is usually 1 year old. Their reactions are observed (and can be videotaped).

In order to assess the infant's level of attachment to the mother, ratings of the following are made on a seven point scale: proximity and contact seeking towards mother; contact maintenance with mother; resistance on reunion with mother; and distance interaction between infant and mother; and a rating of the separation distress shown by the infant.

DETAILS OF PATTERNS OF ATTACHMENT SCORING

These examples are described according to Ainsworth et al (1978). Note they depend on how the child responds to the mother leaving and returning, and how the child responds to strangers. For example, for a secure attachment, the observer would consider the behaviours listed (for example, 'Caregiver is a secure base for exploration') and assess them by the numbered criteria.

Secure attachment

Caregiver is secure base for exploration:
1. Child will readily separate from mother to explore toys
2. Sharing of play with mother
3. Contact with stranger in caregiver's presence
4. Readily comforted by mother when distressed

Actively seeks contact or interaction upon reunion:
1. If in distress: immediately seeks contact, which terminates distress
2. If not in distress: greets caregiver and is happy to see them

Anxious–resistant attachment

Poverty of exploration:
1. Difficulty separating from mother to explore; needs contact
2. Wary of new situations and people

Difficulty settling upon reunion:
1. Mixes contact seeking with resistance to contact
2. Continues to cry even when in contact with mother
3. Alternatively, shows passivity throughout

Anxious–avoidant attachment

Independent exploration:
1. Readily separates from mother to explore
2. Little sharing of toys with mother
3. Contact with stranger when caregiver absent

Active avoidance upon reunion:
1. Turning away, moving away, looking away
2. No avoidance of stranger

CONCLUSION

This section details the experimental set-up of the strange situation as used by Ainsworth et al. In the next section (6) we shall look at results from the assessment and what we can conclude from them.

RESULTS OF THE STRANGE SITUATION ASSESSMENT

Section 6 looked at the experimental set-up of the **strange situation** assessment used by Ainsworth et al (1978). In their original studies they used 56 middle-class children from Baltimore. According to the children's reactions to the situation, three types of attachment were described: types A, B and C. These were primarily classified in terms of each child's responses to the mother leaving and returning, and their response to the stranger.

The main points are as summarized below:

Type of attachment	A	B	C
Name	Anxious–avoidant	Securely attached	Anxious–resistant
Response to mother leaving	Little distress	Distress	Angrier than A or B, or passive
Response to mother returning	Avoid closeness; ignore or casually greet her	Seek contact; calmed by her presence	Seek contact but resist; e.g. want to be picked up, but then struggle to get down
Response to stranger	No distress; treat as mother	Distress when alone; OK when mother present	Actively resist contact
Note	Generally no attachment formed to mother	Classic example of attachment	Child wants mother, but cannot trust her: ambivalent

Besides these, other behaviours were also noted and classified into the three types A, B and C. These other behaviours are detailed below:

Type of attachment	A	B	C
Seeking proximity to mother	Low	High	High
Maintaining contact with mother	Low	High	High
Crying on separation	No	Yes	High or low (extremes)
Crying on reunion	No	No	High or low (extremes)
Other		Playful; less inhibited; sociable; explores	Visually checks mother all the time; clinging

Evaluation

Here is a summary of the main points to consider when evaluating the strange situation:

What is being measured? Is the child's behaviour due to attachment type, or could the factor of temperament play a part?

Problems with classification. Questions have been raised over the classification of the different insecurely attached types, and over categorizing children who respond differently in different episodes of the situation.

Are attachment types permanent? Could a child's attachment type change over time? Also, could it be indirectly affected by the assessment itself?

Stranger's behaviour. The behaviour of the stranger is very artificial in this set-up.

Different attachment types for different attachment objects? Might a child display a different attachment type with a different caregiver, for instance the other parent?

Older children. The strange situation can only be used with young children.

CD-ROM

Attachment: Evaluation of the strange situation

KEY DEFINITIONS

TYPE D ATTACHMENT
Disorganized/disoriented (insecure) attachment.

TYPE D ATTACHMENTS

There are some behaviours that do not fit into the three types. More recently, Main and Solomon (1990) have suggested a fourth type of attachment (D): **insecure attachment: disorganized/disoriented.** Here the child shows confusion, apprehension and contradictory behaviour patterns simultaneously (for example, moving towards the mother but avoiding eye contact). Types A and C attachments are seen as 'organized insecurity', while type D is seen as 'disorganized and incoherent behaviour'.

After the introduction of the type D attachment, past assessments of infants were reviewed and re-classified; for example, past misclassification as 'secure' (Type B) among high-risk children (maltreated). However, category D is not accepted by all researchers (Thompson 1998).

CONCLUSIONS

Mary Ainsworth found three types of attachment behaviour shown by children in the **strange situation:**
- Type A: insecure attachment: anxious–avoidant
- Type B: secure attachment
- Type C: insecure attachment: anxious–resistant

Subsequent research has noted a fourth type of attachment behaviour (type D) in the strange situation assessment. This is called 'insecure attachment: disorganized/disoriented'.

HOT EXAM HINT

You may be asked about the different types of attachment found in the strange situation assessment. They vary in how the child responds to the mother (parent) leaving and returning, and to strangers.

ATTACHMENT TYPES AND FUTURE DEVELOPMENT

DO ATTACHMENT TYPES PERSIST DURING CHILDHOOD?

Before you read this section, look back at the three attachment types A, B and C described in sections 5 and 6. We are going to consider whether these classifications still hold true as the person develops into childhood and then adulthood.

There is evidence that the type of attachment noted in the strange situation assessment (sections 5 and 6) at 1 year old will show itself in the child's behaviour even at 10 years old. For example, type A (anxious–avoidant) attached children are seen to be hostile with peers at 2 years old and have poor self awareness at 10 years old (Holmes 1993). More of Holmes's findings are detailed below:

- **Type B:** at 2 years old this type of child will call for their mother when needed. At 6 years old they can cope with the idea of separation.
- **Type A:** at 2 years old these children are hostile and distant towards their peers. At 6 years old they are over controlled ('keeping it in').
- **Type C:** at 2 years old these children have low-level dependency. At 6 years old they are under controlled ('impulsive').

CHILDHOOD DIFFERENCES

Waters et al (1979) found that children rated as securely attached (type B) at 15 months old were 'social leaders' at 3½ years old. Their nursery school teachers described them as forceful, self-directed and eager to learn. On the other hand, those children with insecure attachments were rated as socially withdrawn, less curious and less forceful in pursuing goals. However, these effects were not due only to the type of attachment, but also to the temperament of the child.

Similarly, securely attached children have been rated at school age as more confident in class, less dependent on teachers and having greater social skills (Erickson et al 1985).

Securely attached children are different to insecurely attached children in the following ways:

- They are more sociable with peers, and with strange adults.
- They have higher self esteem.
- They are more flexible and resourceful.
- They have lower dependency.
- They tend to have fewer tantrums and less aggressive behaviour.
- They tend to be more compliant and less rebellious.
- They have more empathy (that is, they are more able to imagine the feelings of others).
- They have fewer behaviour problems.

 **FOR CONSIDERATION**

The characteristics of children who learn well include: self-directed and eager to learn, flexible and resourceful, and independent.

- They have better problem-solving skills.
- They indulge in more complex symbolic play (the symbolic play of insecurely attached children is simpler). (Symbolic play involves using an object to represent something else.)

Fig 3.6 Is happiness an indicator of secure attachment?

ADULT DIFFERENCES

Response to stress

Some researchers have argued that the attachment type has effects even into adulthood. Mikulincer et al (1993) looked at the response of Israeli adults to Scud missile attacks by Iraq on Israel during the Gulf War. The reactions were different, and depended on the type of attachment styles shown by the participants as children:

- Type A: repressed or distanced emotions
- Type B: coped with help of emotional support
- Type C: very emotional response

Adult relationships

Hazan and Shaver (1990) argue that many aspects of adult behaviour can be understood based on the attachment type as a child. The areas include love relationships, work behaviour and religious behaviour.

McCarthy (1999) found that type B attached women had more success in romantic relationships and friendships than types A and C women (aged 25–44 years old). Type A people had particular problems with romantic relationships, and type C with friendships.

CONCLUSIONS

The type of attachment shown at 1 year old is linked to future behaviour in childhood and adult life. In middle childhood, securely attached children are more sociable with their peers and have better social skills. In adult life, they have more successful romantic relationships. Children with insecure attachments show the opposite behaviours.

FOR CONSIDERATION

Cross-cultural research is a good way to compare behaviour across different societies.

INDIVIDUAL DIFFERENCES IN ATTACHMENT

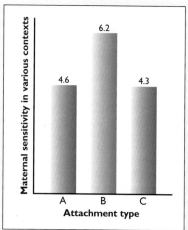

Fig 3.7 Relationship of maternal sensitivity with child's attachment type.

THE ROLE OF THE PARENT

There is a tendency to focus upon the infant's attachment, and to ignore the role of the parenting style in the development of attachment. Mary Ainsworth, from her work with the strange situation assessment (see sections 5 and 6), and observation of children in their own homes (for example Tracy and Ainsworth 1981), has noted four aspects of parenting style:

- Parents of securely attached children tend to be more sensitive to the child's views than parents of insecurely attached children.
- Parents of securely attached children are more accepting of the changes the baby has caused in their life.
- They are also more likely to co-operate with their child's play (whereas parents of insecurely attached children are more likely to interfere with it).
- Parents of securely attached children are more accessible to the child's desires (rather than ignoring those desires).

The relationship between parenting styles and type of attachment can also vary with the temperament of the child. A type A attachment can result from either a rejecting/ignoring parenting style, or a child with low sociability/emotional reactivity, or both these factors. Similarly, a type C attachment can result from either an ignoring/insensitive parenting style, or a highly irritable child, or both.

However, care must be taken not to blame the parent(s) of insecurely attached children for being insensitive. 'This is most unhelpful for parents already struggling with a difficult baby' (Jarvis 2001).

SENSITIVITY OF THE MOTHER

Ainsworth and Bell (1970) describe the 'insensitive mother' as one who 'gears her interventions and initiations of interactions almost exclusively in terms of her own wishes, moods and activities. She tends either to distort the implications of her baby's communications, interpreting them in the light of her own wishes or defences, or not to respond to them at all' (quoted in Sylva and Lunt 1982).

Obviously these traits can affect the development of the child. Evidence for this has been given by Thompson (1998), who collected data from six studies and used it to compare maternal sensitivity in various contexts in the three different attachment types of children (as defined in section 6). Note that a higher score implies a more sensitive mother:

Attachment type	A	B	C
Sensitivity in various contexts	4.6	6.2	4.3
Sensitivity during feeding	5.2	6.1	5.5
Sensitivity during play	5.2	5.8	4.9

However, the responsiveness of the mother can be trained. In Holland, Van den Boom (1994) gave 50 lower-class mothers with highly irritable babies three sessions of responsiveness training soon after birth. The children were then assessed using the strange situation at 1 year old. 62% of the children were classed as securely attached, compared with 22% in the matched control group (whose mothers had received no responsiveness training). Juffer et al (1997) used similar training techniques with parents in Holland who had adopted children from Sri Lanka and Korea.

COMBINING THE FACTORS

The type and the strength of the child's attachment is influenced by a number of factors:

- Intensity of interaction between the child and the primary attachment object (for instance, the mother) (rather than the amount of time spent together)
- Sensitivity of the adult: Clarke-Stewart (1973) categorizes maternal behaviour as 'positive emotional expression' (for example, touching child, smiling); 'contingent responsiveness' (proportion of cries responded to); and 'social stimulation' (non-caregiving interaction with infant, like playing)
- Consistency and predictability of the adult's behaviour
- Response of parent to child's personality (for example, if a child does not settle the parent may become irritated)

Thus a secure attachment is a combination of the child's temperament, the adult's personality and the situation.

Attachment is not an automatic process, and there is evidence that lack of bonding can lead to problems. For children, it will influence their later development, while a lack of bonding by the parent(s) can be linked to abuse of the child.

CONCLUSIONS

Mary Ainsworth noted four aspects of parenting behaviour that influence the attachment behaviour:

- Whether the parent is sensitive to the child's view or not
- Whether the parent is accepting or rejecting of the changes in their life caused by the baby
- Whether the parent is co-operative or interfering with the child's play
- Whether the parent is accessible to the child's desires, or ignores them

The attachment depends on the interaction between the child's temperament and the parents. Children with an 'easy' temperament are often associated with type B attachment; a 'difficult' temperament is often associated with type C; a 'slow to warm' temperament is often associated with type A.

CROSS-CULTURAL DIFFERENCES IN ATTACHMENT

INTRODUCTION

One of the most amazing things about my visit to East Africa were the trips I took to the outlying villages. Women would walk miles for water and to trade food and other goods. Children would walk miles to school everyday. But one of the most bizarre sights I recall was mothers carrying their children wrapped tightly to their backs. It would have been fine if we were talking about babies, but some of these kids were four or five. I remember thinking: can't they walk?

KEY DEFINITIONS

ETHNOCENTRISM
Tendency to judge all other cultures and societies from one's own standpoint (and assume the superiority of that standpoint). For example, assuming behaviour shown in the West to be universal.

WHY STUDY CROSS-CULTURAL DIFFERENCES?

Most studies in psychology come from the West, and from the USA in particular. It is important to study cultures and societies from around the rest of the world to see how people behave. Simply to assume that behaviour in the West is 'normal' is to be ethnocentric.

Advantages and benefits

Through cross-cultural research we can:
- Discover whether certain behaviour is universal (not affected by culture)
- Gain insight into other cultures

Disadvantages and difficulties

- It is expensive and time-consuming to travel to other countries.
- Findings may rely on the observer's interpretation of what they see; also there may be communication problems.
- Groups may not be comparable (it can be difficult to extrapolate findings between different sets of people).

CRYING ON SEPARATION

As we have seen, the child's response to separation from the parent is an important psychological indicator. However, research from around the world has shown that there are cultural differences in the age of crying on separation.

For example, in kibbutz children in Israel (who are cared for in communal nurseries), around a quarter cry on separation from the attached adult at 5 months old. This peaks at 15 months old and then declines.

In contrast, among the Kalahari bush people, few children cry at 5 months old, but all do at 15 months old, and it continues even at 25 months old (Cox 2000). Western studies find crying on separation begins at 7 months old and peaks at 13 months old (section 3).

ATTACHMENT STAGES

Cross-cultural research has found similar ages for Schaffer's stages in the development of attachment (see section 3); for example, among Kalahari bush people in southern Africa (Kagan 1984). Ainsworth (1967) noted the specific form of attachment at a slightly younger age (5–6 months old) among the Ganda people in Uganda, where the infants are permanently carried by their mothers at all times.

Fig 3.8 Kalahari bush people

Another interesting cultural difference was found among the Efe people of Central Africa (Tronick, Morelli and Ivey 1992). In these societies, there are extended families, and the children are cared for by all adults and older children – whoever is available at the time. Though this communal caring system continues, after 6 months old the infants show a preference for the mother to be with and to care for them.

CONCLUSIONS

Many studies of different cultures around the world find slight differences in behaviour. For example, attachment may form at a younger age in children permanently carried by their mothers, who are used to skin-to-skin contact, when compared with Western children.

Cross-cultural research is valuable in that it allows us to investigate whether certain behaviours are universal or cultural in origin.

HOT EXAM HINT

When you are evaluating a piece of research, the location of the study can be considered. For example, the findings of studies in the USA may not be applicable to other parts of the world.

CROSS-CULTURAL STUDIES OF THE STRANGE SITUATION

CROSS-CULTURAL DIFFERENCES

The original study and classification of attachment behaviour was based on American infants, and it was assumed that attachment 'type B' (secure attachment) was normal. (Look back at sections 5 and 6 for a reminder about attachment types and the strange situation assessment). However, cross-cultural studies with the strange situation have found differences in the distribution of attachment types. The table below shows approximate type classification results by country:

Country	A (%)	B (%)	C (%)	No. of studies
USA	21	67	12	18 (incl. Ainsworth et al 1978)
Sweden	22	74	4	1
Israel	7	64	29	2
West Germany	35	57	8	3
Great Britain	22	75	3	1
Netherlands	26	67	7	4
Japan	5	68	27	2
China	25	50	25	1
Overall average	21	65	14	32 studies in 8 countries

(After van Ijzendoorn and Kroonenberg 1988; averages calculated by Cowie 1995)

FOR CONSIDERATION

Would attachment types in Germany be the same after reunification?

These results show a marked variation in proportions of classified types.

- The country with the lowest proportion of type A children seems to be Japan, and the country with the highest, West Germany (as was when the figures were compiled).
- China has the lowest proportion of type Bs.
- Great Britain appears to have the highest proportion of type Bs and the lowest proportion of type Cs; Israel seems to have the highest proportion of type Cs.

Takahashi (1990) urges care when comparing results in the strange situation between cultures. For example, Japanese infants are never left alone at 12 months old, and this could explain the difference in results compared with US children. In addition, the terms used in the assessment, such as 'secure', may have different meanings. Grossman et al (1985) claim the findings in West Germany show that infants are trained to be more independent at an earlier age. Thus the measures within the strange situation are of limited use when moving between cultures.

Fig 3.9 China has the lowest proportion of type B attachment types of the eight countries studied.

Subgroup differences

It is worth pointing out that there are further differences when specific groups are studied in different countries. The table below shows approximate type classification results in some of these groups:

Country	Group studied	A (%)	B (%)	C (%)
Sweden	With fathers (not mothers)	25	71	4
Israel	With kibbutz metapelet (nanny)	15	52	33
*Chile	Extreme underweight	23	50	23
*Germany	With fathers	54	41	2
*Holland	With fathers	31	64	1
USA	Chinese–Americans	25	50	25
USA	Poor Hispanic people	30	50	20

* The remainder were unclassifiable in these groups.

(After Thompson 1998)

FOR CONSIDERATION

Researchers from the West need to be careful when interpreting behaviour around the world. It is all too easy to assume that behaviour in the West is the norm.

CROSS-CULTURAL DIFFERENCES IN INTERPRETATION OF BEHAVIOUR

There are also cultural differences in the perception of the child's behaviour. Harwood and Miller (1991) watched mothers' reactions to the strange situation with all attachment types from various countries.

Anglo-American mothers saw autonomous behaviour of the children more favourably (for example, not crying on separation was seen as a sign of independence), while Puerto Rican mothers favoured signs of obedience (for example, the child not crying because he or she was told not to by the mother).

CONCLUSIONS

In her Western study, Mary Ainsworth found that about two-thirds of children showed a secure attachment (type B) in the strange situation, about 20% type A and approximately 10% type C (see sections 5 and 6). The percentages of children showing these types of attachments vary around the world.

For example, nearly 30% of children in Japan show type C attachment behaviour, and one-third of West German children show type A.

THEORETICAL EXPLANATIONS OF ATTACHMENT BEHAVIOUR

THEORETICAL EXPLANATIONS OF ATTACHMENT

Theoretical explanations for the infant's attachment to the primary attachment object (for example a parent) have two main thrusts: the explanation is either that the child relies on that person for its survival (for example, food), or that the caregiver fulfils certain other needs (such as stimulation).

Early theories: survival factors

Early theories of attachment concentrated on the infant's survival needs being satisfied as the basis of the attachment. Sigmund Freud (1926), for example, talked of a primary drive for food that the mother satisfies, and so the infant acquires a secondary drive for the mother. Eventually the mother becomes desired in her own right (that is, an attachment is formed). The same explanation can be given using the concept of classical conditioning. The baby's hunger is reduced by the mother, and through association, the baby acquires a drive for the mother herself.

Ethologists see attachment in humans as similar to 'imprinting' in non-human animals (a young animal's development of recognition and trust fopr its own species). Imprinting is 'biologically programmed' in animals. John Bowlby was influenced by these ethological ideas. He noted that when a child is being cared for, the child's behaviour, such as smiling, instinctively rewards the caring behaviour and encourages it to continue. The smile in this situation is a 'social releaser' which triggers the parent's instinct to care for their offspring.

Recent theories: non-survival factors

Other theories focus upon non-survival factors (such as comfort and stimulation). They claim that the fulfilment of these other needs is the basis of the infant's attachment. For example, Harlow and Zimmerman's work with monkeys (1959) shows that comfort and security are important (see section 14).

Schaffer and Emerson (1964), studying Scottish infants, found that attachment was based on responsiveness to the infant's behaviour, and that the total amount of stimulation provided was important (for example talking, touching and playing). This is known as the **sensitivity responsiveness theory**. In their research, it was found that for 39% of the infants the primary attachment object was not the main caregiver (usually the mother) but the father. Though the infant would only see the father briefly each day, the intensity of the interaction was the basis of the attachment.

KEY DEFINITIONS

CLASSICAL CONDITIONING
Learning behaviour through association.

KEY DEFINITIONS

ETHOLOGY
The study of instincts to explain animal and human behaviour.

It is not necessarily the quantity of the time spent together but the quality of it that matters. Schaffer and Emerson also found that the infants could be attached to both parents (and other adults, such as grandparents), but in different ways.

FOR CONSIDERATION

THEORETICAL EXPLANATIONS OF SEPARATION ANXIETY

There are a number of different explanations.

The **ethological viewpoint** sees it as an innate reaction evolved to protect the young from harm by keeping the caregiver nearby. However, children show separation anxiety even in familiar situations, and towards adults who are not their caregivers.

The **'conditioned anxiety hypothesis'** suggests infants learn to fear separation because in the past it has been associated with bad experiences, e.g. hunger (compare classical conditioning). However, Ainsworth (1967) found infants in Uganda showed strong separation anxiety despite being only rarely separated. In addition, the level of protest by infants varies with the situation (e.g. lab vs. home).

The **cognitive viewpoint** suggests children learn 'familiar faces in familiar places': they protest only when they cannot understand where the primary attachment object has gone or when they will return.

Fig 3.10 *Having their mothers nearby can give children greater confidence.*

DOES THE STRENGTH OF THE SEPARATION ANXIETY REFLECT CLOSE ATTACHMENT?

Though separation anxiety is used as an index of the child's attachment having formed (see section 3), it is not necessarily a reflection of the closeness of the attachment.

The amount of distress shown varies with the individual child and their level of fearfulness and irritability. Greater habitual contact with parents does not equal greater separation anxiety. Infants reared on a kibbutz in Israel with little parental contact have shown as much distress in a strange room as American children used to greater parental contact (Maccoby and Feldman 1972).

Distinction can be made between the 'strength' and the 'security' of the attachment. 'Strength' is the intensity with which attachment behaviours are displayed. 'Security' refers to how confident the child is that the primary attachment object will be there in time of need, or how confident the child is in using them as a safe base from which to explore a new environment.

The relationship between 'security' and 'strength' of the attachment can operate in two ways. Firstly, there can be greater 'strength' because of less 'security'. For example, anxiety due to past rejection can lead to greater attachment shown by the child (such as being 'clingy' after separation from the mother). On the other hand, greater 'strength' of attachment can also be down to greater 'security'. For example, securely attached children show strong emotions at reunion with the primary attachment object and in their following behaviour.

CONCLUSIONS

Traditional theories of attachment supposed that the child became attached to whoever cared for them in the basic sense (for instance, gave them food). But more recent ideas assume that attachment is based upon more than on who feeds the child. For example, the responsiveness of the adult to the child's non-biological needs, and the quality of this interaction, are important factors.

INTRODUCTION

'I can't believe those children,' said Jenny. 'They're always out on the streets late at night, getting up to no good. Do you know what I saw them doing yesterday?'

'What?' said Roy.

'Dragging people's wheelie bins away and then emptying all the rubbish out.'

'Didn't you say something?'

'What, and get abused – no thanks.'

'I blame the parents. They're never around. When was the last time you saw any one of those kids with their parents? They don't give a monkey's.'

Fig 3.11 John Bowlby

KEY DEFINITIONS

MATERNAL DEPRIVATION HYPOTHESIS
The breaking of the special bond between an infant and its mother (or mother-substitute), or lack of opportunity to form such a bond (for example if living in a children's home), will have detrimental effects in the child's later life. The major problems will be juvenile delinquency and affectionless psychopathy (antisocial behaviour coupled with an inability to form emotional relationships).

JOHN BOWLBY – PSYCHOANALYST

John Bowlby spent over 40 years of his life studying children; particularly the effects of the early years upon later development. He was especially interested in children who were separated from their mothers when young, or deprived of such a relationship in the pre-school years (for example, children in residential nurseries).

John Bowlby was a psychoanalyst (someone who seeks to treat people by studying the interaction of their conscious and unconscious minds). He was influenced by the work of Sigmund Freud, who believed that what happened in a child's first five years of life determined their adult personality.

MAIN WORKS

Forty-Four Juvenile Thieves: case histories of delinquent teenagers in post-Second World War Britain (1946; originally appeared in 1944)

Maternal Care and Mental Health: World Health Organisation (WHO) report on children in institutions and hospitals (1951; became *Child Care and Growth of Love* in 1953; enlarged version in 1965): proposed maternal deprivation hypothesis

'Attachment and Loss' series: pulling together all his ideas
- Volume 1: *Attachment* (1969)
- Volume 2: *Separation, Anxiety and Anger* (1973)
- Volume 3: *Loss, Sadness and Depression* (1980)

BOWLBY'S IDEAS

Bowlby's work on the mother-child relationship has a number of strands:
- **Attachment theory or the internal working model.** The internal working model is a kind of 'cognitive map' of the self, others and relationships that individuals have. It is formed in infancy through the attachment experience with the primary caregiver. For example, 'an

anxiously attached child may have a model of others in which they are potentially dangerous and therefore must be approached with caution, while their self-representation may be of someone who is demanding and ready and unworthy to be offered security' (Holmes 1993). This theory includes the concept of **monotropy**.

- **Maternal deprivation hypothesis** (see section 13).

FAMOUS QUOTATIONS

Importance of mother–child relationship

'Mother love in infancy is as important for mental health as are vitamins and proteins for physical health' (1951)

'What is believed to be essential for mental health is that an infant and young child should experience a warm, intimate and continuous relationship with his mother (or permanent mother-substitute – one person who steadily "mothers" him) in which both find satisfaction and enjoyment' (1951)

Consequences of lack of mother–child attachment for the child's later development

'Prolonged separation of a child from its mother (or mother substitute) during the first five years of his life stands foremost among the causes of delinquent character development and persistent misbehaviour' (1946)

'... prolonged deprivation of the young child of maternal care may have grave and far-reaching effects in his character and so on the whole of his future life. It is a proposition exactly similar in form to those regarding the evil after-effects of German measles before birth or deprivation of vitamin D in infancy' (1953; quoted in Holmes 1993)

DID BOWLBY CHANGE HIS IDEAS?

Many of Bowlby's ideas were challenged and criticized over the forty years since he wrote them. There is a dispute by writers over whether Bowlby accepted the criticisms and changed his ideas, or remained unchanged.

Jarvis (1998) believes that by 1969, Bowlby had dropped the concept of monotropy, and came to accept that some infants can hold multiple attachments with adults, that is, attachments in addition to that to the mother or even instead of it. However, Gross (1998) argues that the term 'monotropy' was reiterated by Bowlby in 1988.

CONCLUSIONS

John Bowlby's work has been very influential in the area of child development. In this section we have looked at the key ideas of monotropy and the maternal deprivation hypothesis. In the next few sections we shall look more closely at Bowlby's ideas, and also at the opposition to them.

MATERNAL DEPRIVATION HYPOTHESIS

FOR CONSIDERATION

Some writers argue that Bowlby's ideas produced guilt among mothers who did not stay at home with their young children. 'Mother working full-time' is in Bowlby's list of circumstances likely to damage children. Women who had worked in factories during the war thus left those jobs for returning soldiers, and went back to the home. The traditional social order was re-established. It is not clear whether Bowlby intended this, or that his ideas were used to promote 'traditional social values'. Whatever, many working mothers still feel guilt when they place their young children in day nurseries; is it detrimental to the children? (See sections 20, 21 and 22.)

CD-ROM

Attachment: Konrad Lorenz

KEY DEFINITIONS

PSYCHOSOMATIC
Both physical and psychological in origin.

AFFECTIONLESS PSYCHOPATHY
An inability to feel affection for or care about other people.

CD-ROM

To learn more about the perceived irreversibility of the effects of early separation, see CD-ROM Attachment: John Bowlby.

BACKGROUND

John Bowlby first proposed the maternal deprivation hypothesis in 1951. He believed that children separated from or deprived of mother love and attention would have problems as adults.

These ideas were proposed in a particular historical context: society after the Second World War. There were concerns about the breakdown of society, with a perceived increase in juvenile delinquents (for example 'teddy boys'). Many people linked these concerns with the separation of children from their families in the evacuations during the war. Children living in cities, towns and areas of high risk for German bombing had been sent to live in the country with relatives – or complete strangers – for up to two or three years. This was maternal deprivation.

MAIN POINTS OF THE MATERNAL DEPRIVATION HYPOTHESIS

Critical period

Attachment should be formed between the child and the mother in the first year of life, preferably. Bowlby (1951) believed that 'even good mothering is almost useless if delayed until after the age of $2\frac{1}{2}$ years'. According to him children cannot form attachments after this **critical period**. The idea of the critical period comes from work with geese and ducks by Konrad Lorenz.

Monotropy

This theory assumes the dominance of a single attachment to the mother (or mother-substitute). The father, for example, was viewed as of little importance here: 'A biological necessity but a social accident' according to one supporter of Bowlby.

Effects of maternal deprivation

- **Short term:** protest, despair and detachment
- **Long term in childhood:** separation anxiety (fear of separation happening again is manifest in psychosomatic reactions like asthma); increased aggressive behaviour; greater demanding of mother; clinging behaviour; school phobia/refusal; enuresis (continued bed-wetting); physical growth problems
- **Long term in adolescence and adulthood:** delinquency; affectionless psychopathy; intellectual retardation

Irreversibility

Bowlby believed that the effects of early separation cannot be reversed.

THE FORTY-FOUR THIEVES STUDY

According to Bowlby, the most important long-term effects of maternal separation or deprivation were juvenile delinquency and affectionless psychopathy. The basis of this argument is his 1944 study.

RESEARCH EVIDENCE

Bowlby (1944). Forty-four juvenile thieves: their characters and home life. *International Journal of Psychoanalysis.*

Aims

This study aimed to see whether juvenile delinquents had any history of early maternal separation.

Procedure

Bowlby looked at case studies of 44 'juvenile thieves' (teenagers convicted of theft) and 44 'disturbed adolescents' (teenagers with mental health problems) to see how many had experienced early maternal separation – in particular, a period of 6 months or more of separation in the first 5 years of their lives. Bowlby used detailed interviews with the participants, and the collection of personal records about them. This is the case study method. Bowlby was also interested in diagnosing affectionless psychopathy.

Findings

Of the 'juvenile thieves' group, 40% reported prolonged separation compared with 5% of the 'disturbed adolescents' group. Of those in the 'juvenile thieves' group classed as 'affectionless psychopaths', 12 of 14 had had prolonged separation, compared with just 5 out of the remaining 30. None of the 'disturbed adolescents' group was classed as an 'affectionless psychopath'.

Conclusions

Bowlby concluded that maternal separation led to delinquency and affectionless psychopathy.

Criticisms

- The study was retrospective – the participants were asked to recall any separation at a young age, at least 10 years prior to the study.
- There were no experimental controls – Bowlby knew which group was which (therefore there was possible bias); no random sampling of participants; no random distribution between both groups.
- The conclusion by Bowlby ignored those in the 'juvenile thieves' group who were showing delinquent behaviour and had not been separated from their mothers (some 60%). It might seem more logical to conclude that *lack* of maternal separation leads to delinquency.

HOT EXAM HINT

You may be asked about Bowlby's maternal deprivation hypothesis. It will help if you present the ideas in an organized way, as in this section.

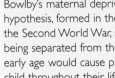

FOR CONSIDERATION

Bowlby's maternal deprivation hypothesis, formed in the context of the Second World War, suggested that being separated from the mother at an early age would cause problems for a child throughout their life. He believed that this effect could not be reversed. The hypothesis depends on a number of important ideas including monotropy and the critical period. The next section looks at evidence to support Bowlby.

EVIDENCE SUPPORTING BOWLBY

SUPPORTING STUDIES

Though Bowlby's own research is limited, he was influenced over the years by a number of other studies, both with humans and non-human animals. The main influences are:

- Lorenz (1935): imprinting among greylag geese (see section 13)
- Harlow and Zimmerman (1959): rhesus monkeys raised in isolation
- Robertson's work with hospitalized children (see section 15)
- Spitz (1945): mothers and babies in prison
- Goldfarb (1943): children in residential nurseries

We shall now look at some of these in more detail.

HARLOW AND ZIMMERMAN (1959)

Harlow and Zimmerman (1959). Affectional responses in infant monkeys. *Science*.

Aims

This study aimed to investigate the effect of maternal deprivation on rhesus monkeys raised in isolated cages. It also set out to investigate whether the monkeys would form an attachment to a 'surrogate mother' who fed them.

Procedure

Fig 3.12 This monkey was raised alone in an isolated cage, with a wire-mesh towelling 'mother'.

Eight infant monkeys were reared from an early age in separate cages. In each cage were two models of 'mothers' made of wire mesh; one of these was covered with towelling that the monkeys could cling to, and felt similar to monkey hair. The monkeys were kept in isolation until they reached adulthood, and then placed with other monkeys.

Findings

Two main areas of findings came from this research:

- The monkeys preferred the towelling-covered model, even when bottle feeding was done by the other model. When scared by a wind-up teddy bear model in the cage, the monkeys clung to the towelling-covered model, showing evidence of an attachment.
- In the long term, these monkeys showed problems as adults: they were timid, had difficulty mating, and were inadequate parents themselves.

Conclusions

- Attachments can be based on more than just who feeds the infant (see section 11). Here, for instance, it could be based on touch.

- Rearing monkeys in isolation causes long-term problems in social and emotional development.

Criticisms
- How far can we apply the findings from rhesus monkeys to humans?
- The problems in adulthood were later found to be due to social deprivation, not specifically maternal deprivation. Monkeys reared in separate cages but allowed twenty minutes per day to play with other monkeys did not show such emotional and social problems.
- There are also concerns about the ethics of animal experiments.

CD-ROM

Attachment: Harlow's research

FOR CONSIDERATION

EVALUATION OF SPITZ (1945)
- The study only looked at poor-quality institutions.
- The study failed to consider causes other than maternal deprivation for the babies' behaviour.

FOR CONSIDERATION

EVALUATION OF GOLDFARB (1943)
The children fostered immediately were not randomly chosen (as the fostering process would tend to favour the more outgoing ones). It could be that these children were more intelligent to start off with than the children left in the institution.

SPITZ (1945)

This was an observational study of 123 babies whose mothers were in prison. They lived together for the first few months (the babies were often born in prison), and then the children would be separated from their mothers for at least 3 months when 1 year old. These babies showed 'hospitalism': depression manifest in loss of appetite and failure to gain weight.

GOLDFARB (1943)

This was a study of two groups of fifteen children matched for mother's education and occupational status. One group lived in a children's home from 6 months to $3\frac{1}{2}$ years old, and was then fostered. The other group were directly fostered after leaving their biological families at a similar age: in other words, they spent no time in a children's home. At $3\frac{1}{2}$ years old, those in the former group showed lower intelligence, poorer abstract thinking, less social maturity and sociability and less rule-following than the other group. Similar differences were found at 10 and 14 years old. The IQ difference between the groups was as high as 20 points.

CONCLUSIONS

These studies influenced Bowlby's theories on maternal deprivation. We shall look more at the proposed effects of maternal deprivation in the coming sections.

EFFECTS OF MATERNAL DEPRIVATION: SHORT TERM

INTRODUCTION

Alison is worried. She has spoken to her GP about Bethany's behaviour at nursery, and the doctor is puzzled. In the early days Bethany had always made such a fuss when Alison left her, crying and even clinging to her legs. Now the teachers are saying that Bethany isolates herself from the other children and just sits in the corner, often rocking to and fro. Most worryingly of all, Bethany has started to get aggressive with her mum. Every time she is picked up from nursery, she kicks and hits Alison, and more recently has started biting.

Maternal deprivation will affect children both in the short term and in the longer term as adolescents and as adults. The long-term effects are discussed in sections 16 and 17. The main short-term effect is a loss of attachment by the child.

THE ROBERTSON FILM

In 1952, James Robertson produced a short film about the experiences of children under 5 years old separated from their mothers while in hospital. Many of the children were kept in isolation because of their illnesses.

The children were seen to show three stages of distress at the separation:
• Initial protest
• Despair
• Denial or detachment and loss of interest in parents

Initial protest

The children would cry and call for their parents immediately after separation, and reject nursing staff's attempts to console them.

Fig 3.13 Robertson studied children who had stayed alone in hospital.

Despair

Then came misery, apathy and bored indifference. The child had stopped crying and protesting. They isolated themselves from their peers, sat listlessly staring into space and ate little.

Denial or detachment and loss of interest in parents

The child appeared to recover from the despair, but the protests reappeared on reunion with the parents. The child clung to the parent(s) (called 'mummyishness'), but, at the same time, rejected and was angry at them. The attachment bond had been broken and needed to be re-established, if possible. There are long-term effects of even short separations (for example 10 days) like these.

KEY DEFINITIONS

MUMMYISHNESS
The tendancy of a child to physically cling to its parents.

Bowlby and Robertson (1952) confirmed these stages with a wider study of 49 children aged between 1 and 4 years.

ARE SHORT-TERM EFFECTS OF SEPARATION THE SAME FOR ALL CHILDREN?

Subsequent research since the Robertson film has shown that there are a number of factors that determine how the child will be affected in the short term by the separation.

These factors, and their key aspects, are listed below:

- **Age of child:** 6–7 months to 3 years old (with peak at 12–18 months) is the worst time for separation.
- **Gender:** it has been found that boys are generally more disturbed and vulnerable than girls.
- **Temperament:** more active babies are less affected.
- **Existing relationship with mother:** if there is a more stable attachment, the child is better able to cope.
- **Experience of previous separations:** separation is easier to cope with if it has happened before.
- **Familiarity of environment:** an unfamiliar environment is more stressful to a child separated from his or her mother.
- **Level of stimulation in environment:** boredom and understimulation are more stressful.
- **Duration of separation:** a separation of less than 3 weeks is less distressing.
- **Type of separation:** happy separations allow better coping with bad ones in future.
- **Quality of substitute care:** for example, in the Robertson and Robertson fostering experiment (see below).

Child	Age (y)	Fostered for (days)
Kate	2.5	27
Thomas	2.4	10
Lucy	1.9	19
Jane	1.5	10

Fig 3.14 Lengths of fostering

THE ROBERTSON AND ROBERTSON FOSTERING EXPERIMENT

Robertson and Robertson (1971) fostered for short periods a number of young children who had been left in institutions. The fostering of the children prevented 'bond disruption' with the parents and this reduced the degree of disturbance for them.

Even fostering for only a few days can be important. Fig 3.14 shows lengths of fostering for children in the Robertson and Robertson experiment.

CONCLUSIONS

Studies have suggested there are three stages in the short-term effects of maternal deprivation. Children separated from their parent(s) go through protest, then despair, then denial or detachment. Sections 16 and 17 will look at the long-term effects of maternal deprivation.

LONG-TERM EFFECTS OF MATERNAL DEPRIVATION: BOWLBY'S SIDE

BOWLBY'S HYPOTHESIS IN ACTION

A key part of Bowlby's maternal deprivation hypothesis was the inevitable long-term effects for the child of separation from the mother in the early years. Bowlby and his supporters produced a long list of ills that were supposed to be the consequences of the maternal deprivation. Furthermore, the consequences were seen as irreversible even if the child formed attachments in later childhood or adult life; it was the first 2–3 years that mattered most (the **critical period**).

LONG-TERM EFFECTS OF MATERNAL DEPRIVATION

Delinquency

According to Bowlby, the problems of maternal deprivation could lead to criminal behaviour in adolescence. Evidence includes Bowlby's own study (1946) (see section 13) and Douglas (1975).

Using a longitudinal study (a study over a period of time), Douglas followed until adolescence a sample of children born in one week in 1946. The aim was to see the effects of early hospitalization (and therefore separation from parents) upon later life. In adolescence, those children who had had repeated or prolonged hospitalization in the early years showed 'troublesome behaviour', delinquency, poorer reading scores and unstable job histories (that is, changing jobs regularly and being unemployed for long periods).

Affectionless psychopathy

This is the inability to form relationships or feel emotions for other people. Again evidence is provided by Bowlby (1946) (see section 13).

Depression

Evidence that deprivation causes depression is given by Spitz (1945) (see section 14).

Intellectual retardation

Evidence for deprivation causing intellectual retardation is given by Goldfarb (1943) (see section 14).

Growth retardation

According to Bowlby and his supporters, children deprived of their mothers were found to be undersized for their age and did not develop physically in the normal way (see Fig 3.15).

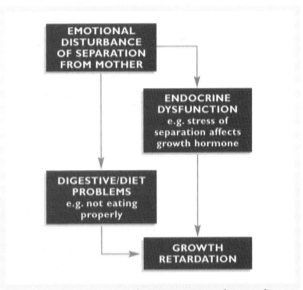

Fig 3.15 Factors contributing to growth retardation

The two factors mentioned in Fig 3.15 can cause growth retardation, but it is important to mention that this is not just because of maternal deprivation. Any long-term serious emotional stress in the child's life can have the same effects. The link to maternal deprivation is not taken seriously these days.

Enuresis

Babies separated from their parents for long periods show prolonged bed-wetting for several years after.

OTHER EFFECTS OF MATERNAL DEPRIVATION

Babies raised in children's homes or residential nurseries show a variety of adverse reactions (Bowlby 1951):
- Diminished interest, that is, lack of reaction to stimulation (appears at 2–3 months)
- Excessive preoccupation with strangers (3–4 months)
- Blandness of facial expressions (6–7 months)
- Ineptness in new social situations (10–11 months)
- Exaggerated resistance to new situations (11–12 months)
- Relative retardation in language behaviour (12–15 months)

HOT EXAM HINT

You may be asked about the effects of maternal deprivation. It is important to show that there are different effects, both long term and short term.

CONCLUSIONS

John Bowlby argued that the long-term effects of maternal deprivation were delinquency, affectionless psychopathy and mental health problems, among other things. In the next section we shall examine some arguments that oppose Bowlby.

LONG-TERM EFFECTS OF MATERNAL DEPRIVATION: ARGUMENTS AGAINST BOWLBY

BOWLBY'S OWN FINDINGS

In a little-quoted study of children who had spent their early life in a TB hospital, John Bowlby found that they had few problems in adolescence: no intellectual retardation, a normal capacity for friendship and only slight maladjustment.

Bowlby had to admit: 'statements implying that children who are brought up in institutions or who suffer other forms of serious privation and deprivation in early life commonly develop psychopathic or affectionless characters are seen to be mistaken ... Outcome is immensely varied' (Bowlby et al 1956).

FOR CONSIDERATION

The work of Michael Rutter is among the most influential in this field. He received a knighthood for it. Do you find his arguments more convincing than those of Bowlby?

KEY DEFINITIONS

DEPRIVATION AND PRIVATION
Deprivation is the breaking of an attachment bond that has been formed, while privation is a failure to ever form an attachment bond.

THE WORK OF RUTTER

Michael Rutter is most famous for arguing against Bowlby's views on maternal deprivation. He makes the distinction between **privation** and **deprivation**. 'Privation' is the failure to form any bonds, which leads to 'an initial phase of clinging, dependent behaviour, followed by attention-seeking, uninhibited, indiscriminate friendliness and finally a personality characterised by lack of guilt, an inability to keep rules and an inability to form lasting relationships' (Rutter 1981). In contrast, 'deprivation' is forming an attachment that is then broken by separation of the child from the attachment object.

In his book *Maternal Deprivation Reassessed*, Rutter summarized the main findings of the maternal deprivation debate:

- Failure to bond (that is, privation) may lead to affectionless psychopathy.
- Disruption of the bond (that is, deprivation) may cause distress and anxiety.
- It is lack of stimulation in infancy that leads to intellectual retardation, not maternal deprivation. However, infants in children's homes are often deprived of both attention and love, and stimulation. Evidence for this is given by Skeels and Dye (1939) – see below.
- Growth retardation is caused by nutritional deficiency.
- Language retardation is caused by not being spoken to.
- Enuresis can be due to the stress of the first few years of any child's life.
- Delinquency is more associated with divorce and family discord than with maternal deprivation. For Rutter, it is the 'discord and disturbance which surrounds the separation' from the parent(s) that is important. For example, children who had lost their mothers through death showed little delinquency.

RESEARCH EVIDENCE

Skeels and Dye (1939). A study of the effects of differential stimulation on mentally retarded children. *Proceedings of American Association of Mental Deficiency*.

Aims

To compare the development of intelligence between children in a children's home and children who have been adopted.

FOR CONSIDERATION

There are ethical concerns today about such research. What do you think these concerns are?

Procedure

A longitudinal study (study over time) compared 12 children placed in a children's home from 2 years old onwards, and 13 similar children cared for by teenage mothers with low intelligence. These particular mothers were chosen to care for the children because they could not directly teach them, just give them stimulation through attention and playing with them.

Findings

The IQs of the two groups were measured at various ages, and then other studies followed them into adulthood. The average IQ scores were as shown below:

	2 years old	3 years old	7 years old
Adopted group	64.3	92.8	101
Children's home group	86.7	60.5	65

Conclusions

It is stimulation of the child that influences their intellectual development. Both sets of children were separated from their parents, but those living in children's homes received little stimulation compared with those adopted and cared for by the teenage mothers.

SUMMARY

Only when separation forms part of a long sequence of misfortunes are children much more likely to be adversely affected (Schaffer 1990). In other words, it is continuing disruption that 'represents a far more serious hazard'. Bowlby tended to emphasize specific stress, whereas research today concentrates on the effects of enduring adversity.

Children can experience short-term separations and show no long-term effects, and contrary to Bowlby's belief, the effects of the separation can be reversed in later childhood. It is privation that has the greatest consequences.

ATTACHMENTS OTHER THAN TO THE MOTHER

SHOULD MOTHERING BE CONFINED TO ONE PERSON?

'The belief that the mother-child unit is basic and unique is long established and deeply ingrained in both popular and professional thinking' (Schaffer 1990). Indeed, John Bowlby believed that the bond to the mother (or permanent mother substitute) was the most important attachment. Research has shown, however, that infants can become attached to individuals other than the mother (either in addition to their attachment to the mother, or even instead of it).

Research since Schaffer and Emerson (see section 4) has shown that children can become attached to many people simultaneously. For Schaffer (1990), 'the necessity of exclusive mothering is a myth'. It is only in modern Western societies that the mother is assumed to be the exclusive caregiver.

Attachment figures other than the mother include:

- The father
- Siblings and peers (for example, as in Freud and Dann 1951; see below)
- Extended family members, for example grandparents
- Childminder; nanny; nursery staff; metapelet (nanny) in kibbutz

Overall, 'mothers are without doubt in an excellent (and usually the best) position to influence their child's development, but the older sibling and the woman next door may well leave their mark too' (Schaffer 1977). Furthermore, 'statements about women inevitably being "better" parents by mere virtue of their femininity appear to be no more than facile generalisations' (Schaffer 1990).

FATHERS

Fig 3.16

Traditionally most research in the area of attachment has ignored the role of the father. It is now felt that the attachment to the father is different to that of the mother: it is based on more intense short interactions. Infants prefer their fathers as playmates, but, in times of stress, seek the mother (Clarke-Stewart 1978).

Parke (1981) observed the different parents playing with their infants. Fathers tended to play more vigorously with the child in more physically stimulating games or unusual and unpredictable types of play. Mothers tended to join in the child's play with toys and read to them.

FREUD AND DANN (1951)

This was a case study of six orphans (three boys and three girls) who had lived in the German concentration camp at Terezin during the Second World War since the age of 6–12 months old. They were cared for by various inmates, but by no particular persons.

After the war, the children (around 3 years old) were brought to England. They showed emotional problems (like temper tantrums). The group was unhappy if one of them was not present. There was evidence of them being attached to each other. (Their problems in later life were not as extreme as expected.)

KIBBUTZ

In a kibbutz, the parents work during the day, and the children are cared for all together by people filling the role of a metapelet ('nanny'). The children see their parents in the evenings. Studies have found that the children are attached both to the nannies and to their own parents (for example, Fox 1977). However, there is some dispute as to whether the children suffer in later life from this arrangement. Some studies find that they do, others that they do not.

Fox (1977)

A total of 122 children between 8 and 24 months old from the Israeli kibbutz system were observed in social situations that involved separation and reunion with the mother, and with the metapelet. The amount of crying on separation, and proximity to the adult, were the key measures of attachment used. The infants showed attachment behaviour in the same way to both the mother and the metapelet.

CONCLUSION

Research, as detailed in this section, has shown that infants can become attached to other people than the mother: father, grandparents, siblings, peers and professional caregivers. This attachment can be in addition to that to the mother, or in some cases even instead of it. Therefore the attachment to the mother seems not to be as exclusive and unique as previously thought.

EFFECTS OF INSTITUTIONAL REARING, ADOPTION AND FOSTERING

A STUDY OVER TIME

Many children separated from their parents on a permanent basis are placed in children's homes and/or adopted or fostered. What are the effects of such experiences on the young child? The only way to answer this question is to follow the children over a long period of their lives.

The most famous longitudinal study to do this was undertaken over 15 years by Barbara Tizard. It is reported in three main stages: Tizard and Rees (1975), Tizard and Hodges (1978), and Hodges and Tizard (1989a & b).

> **KEY DEFINITIONS**
>
> **LONGITUDINAL STUDY**
> A piece of research that follows a small group of people over a long period of time (e.g. many years).

TIZARD AND REES (1975)

The basis of the study was 65 children placed in a residential nursery at around 4 months old. The nursery had a high staff turnover, and a policy discouraging attachment between children and nurses. An average of 24 caregivers had looked after the children by 2 years old, and 50 by 4 years old.

Between the ages of 2 and 7 years old, 24 of the children were adopted, and 15 returned home to their biological parent(s). The remainder of the 65 stayed in the residential nursery. There was also a comparison group of children who lived throughout with their parents in London. The four groups are referred to as follows:

- **Institutional:** lived in residential nursery throughout
- **Returnees:** lived in residential nursery until 2 years old, then returned to biological family
- **Adopted:** lived in residential nursery until 2 years old, then placed with adopted family
- **Control:** lived with biological family throughout

Measurements of intellectual and social development were taken when the children were $4\frac{1}{2}$ years old. The results were as follows:

- **Intelligence:** scores from highest to lowest: adopted group; control; institutional group; returnees.
- **Social development:** the best scores were obtained by the adopted group and the returnees.

TIZARD AND HODGES (1978)

This continuation of the study focused on the adopted group and the returnees when they were in middle childhood (approximately 8 years old). There was no sign of affectionless psychopathy (see section 13) in any of the children, but they did show some deviant symptoms (for example, attention-seeking behaviour). They were naturally over-affectionate to strangers, and there were some difficulties at school.

About half the children had formed an attachment by $4\frac{1}{2}$ years old, and almost all by $8\frac{1}{2}$ years old. Those children adopted at an earlier age had advantages, as well as hard work by the adoptive parents to reverse any early problems. The late adoptees had adjusted well by 7 years old because of the emotional effort of the adoptive parents (Tizard 1977).

Tizard and Hodges conclude that the period of early institutional care can cause some problems, but the children are 'not scarred for life'. There is little support for Bowlby's idea of a critical period during which attachments must be formed (see section 13).

HODGES AND TIZARD (1989A+B)

This was a follow-up of the groups in adolescence. However, it was only possible to find some of the original sample. The main results can be summarized as follows:

- **Attachment to mother:** the adopted group was found to be similar to a new control group (of children living with biological parent(s)), according to ratings by mothers; that is to say, attachment existed.
- **Showing of affection:** the returnees were less affectionate to their mothers.
- **Relations with siblings:** the returnees had most problems in this area.
- **Adults outside family and peer relations:** the adopted group and the returnees had difficulties here in being overfriendly to strangers and keen for adult attention; also they were more quarrelsome and liable to bully other children (as rated by teachers).

Hodges and Tizard talk of a phenomenon they call 'ex-institutional syndrome'. This was only evident in half the children in the adopted and returnee groups. Where it was evident, it was there at ages 8 and at adolescence – thus it was a lasting characteristic.

CONCLUSIONS

According to the research examined in this section, children who had spent their first few years in institutions and then were adopted or returned to their biological parent(s) showed some problems – but rarely to the extreme suggested by Bowlby. The main problems were relations with peers and adults outside the family.

Children adopted at an early age do not necessarily experience major problems in adolescence, with the help of the adopted parents. There are minor problems (with overfriendliness to adults outside the family, for example). The age of adoption is important.

KEY DEFINITIONS

'EX-INSTITUTIONAL SYNDROME'

For Hodges and Tizard, this included:
- Need for adult attention and approval
- Difficulties in peer relations: either difficulties forming relationships, or overfriendliness to all peers
- Lack of special friends
- Not seeking emotional support from peers

CD-ROM

To learn more about the effects of institutions and adoption, see CD-ROM Attachment: Attachment in a children's home.

INTRODUCTION

'It's always tricky being a nursery nurse. Because we are taught all about attachment and bonding you become very aware of the phases children are going through. It's not a good idea to get too emotionally close because you will confuse the child. When a child's crying it's difficult to know whether to cuddle her or not. I remember one child who always screamed when her mum came to collect her. She clung to me as if I was her mum. I felt really guilty.'

FOR CONSIDERATION

Children may be placed in day care for a few hours, or the whole day. Does the length of time matter?

DAY CARE OPTIONS

John Bowlby believed that young children left in day care would suffer maternal deprivation and consequent problems in later life (see section 13). In the next few sections we shall look more closely at day care. There are different forms of day care available:

- **Group based:** day nurseries or playgroups
- **Individual based:** childminders or nannies (though there can be a number of children under the care of the same childminder)

In this section we shall look at day care in nurseries or playgroups.

Fig 3.17 What effects does day care have on young children?

DAY NURSERIES OR PLAYGROUPS

Whether the child will suffer from being in a day nursery or playgroup depends upon a number of factors.

Quality of the substitute care

High-quality day nurseries and playgroups will have a large number of staff compared with the number of children, so that the children will be given individual attention. Also, there needs to be stability in the staff (low turnover), so the children can see the same member of staff each time and bond to them, rather than seeing different staff every day.

Some of the characteristics that make for a good day care centre (based on the recommendations of the National Association for Education of Young Children 1991) are considered below:

- A high-quality day care centre is clean and not crowded, and the children can play both indoors and outdoors (rather than being crowded and having limited areas and facilities for children).
- A good staff-to-child ratio is important: 1:3 for infants, 1:6 for toddlers.
- There should be a variety of activities during the day, including play, nap and meals. Poor facilities and staff shortages will limit the range of activities.
- The staff should be responsive to child's distress and needs – the individual child should not be ignored.
- The parents should be welcome to stay and join in, not encouraged to leave as soon as the child has arrived.

Howes (1990) found that the behaviour of one-year-olds can change depending on the quality of the nursery or playgroup, as shown in the table.

	High quality	Low quality
compliance with adult requests	small improvement	decline
peer relationships	improvement	decline
level of concentration	increase	decrease
hostile behaviour	large decline	increase

Age of the child

Belsky (1988), based on a study of over 400 children, believes that infants who spend more than 4 months (and more than 20 hours per week) in their first year in day care will develop insecure attachments to their parent or parents. Children aged 2 or 3 years or more fare better in day care.

Reunion with parent(s)

It is important that the time spent with the parent or parents is positive: it is the quality of interaction that matters, not the quantity of time spent together. For example, mothers who enjoy their jobs will have a more positive interaction with their infants and strong bonds will form.

CONCLUSION

High-quality day care, which includes the opportunity for infants to become attached to the staff, is not necessarily harmful to the child's development. The length of time in day care and the relationship with the parent or parents outside day care are also important.

KEY DEFINITIONS

COMPLIANCE WITH ADULT REQUESTS
This is used as a measure of children's good behaviour and obedience.

HOT EXAM HINT

You may be asked about day care for children. It is useful to distinguish between high-quality and low-quality care.

POSITIVE AND NEGATIVE DEVELOPMENT

The development of the child in a nursery includes both positive and negative aspects of behaviour:

- Emotional insecurity: the nature of the attachments to parents formed (that is, type A, B or C)
- Sociability: interactions with peers
- Aggressive and non-compliant behaviour
- Intellectual development

KEY DEFINITIONS

EMOTIONAL STABILITY
A measure of the child's mood. For example, children who cry too much (or too little) have relatively low emotional stability.

EMOTIONAL STABILITY

There are a number of factors that influence this aspect of development, the quality and stability of substitution care being the most important (see section 20).

Emotional security is traditionally measured using the **strange situation** (section 5). More children of full-time working mothers show insecure behaviour in the strange situation (compared with children of mothers who work part-time or are not employed). Such behaviour includes not staying close to the mother, or not seeking physical contact on reunion (Clarke-Stewart 1988). However, the child's temperament is an important influence here.

SOCIABILITY

Children in high-quality day care show advances in sociability, social competence (for example social skills in interaction with other children, such as sharing toys, learning to give and take) and self-confidence compared with children who stay at home (Rubinstein and Howes 1979).

This study is further developed in Rubinstein and Howes 1983 (see opposite).

AGGRESSIVE AND NON-COMPLIANT BEHAVIOUR

Children who spend large parts of their young lives in day care can show more aggressive and non-compliant behaviours. These include avoiding mothers on return, disobeying them and bullying peers. However, these behaviours are not found among all children in day care.

Fig 3.18 Children's social skills might benefit from time spent with other children in high-quality day care.

INTELLECTUAL DEVELOPMENT

Children in high-quality day care can show improvements in cognitive development and language development compared with children who stay at home (Rubinstein and Howes 1979). The interaction with other children can speed up cognitive development.

RESEARCH EVIDENCE

Rubinstein and Howes (1983). Social–emotional development of toddlers in day care. *Advances in Early Education and Day Care.*

Aims

To compare the experiences and development of children reared at home with those in group day care.

Procedure

A carefully matched middle-class sample of 30 toddlers aged 17–20 months old was studied. Half of them had been attending high-quality day care for an average of 5 months by the time the study began. The other half had stayed at home all their lives.

Each child was observed for a total of 5 hours at different times. There was a follow-up of the children at 3–4 years old.

Findings

- **Initial assessment:** there was no difference between the groups in degree of sophistication of social behaviour during play, but the day care group showed a more sophisticated level of play.
- **Follow-up:** day care children showed no differences in social and emotional development compared with the home reared group. They were, however, less compliant to their mothers, but also superior in 'spontaneous speech' and language development.

Conclusions

From these results there is no real concern about the effects of group day care.

SUMMARY

Day care can influence the development of children in terms of emotional insecurity, sociability, aggression and non-compliant behaviour, and intellectual development.

In this section we have looked at these positive and negative effects. In the next section we shall look at individual day care.

> ☕ FOR CONSIDERATION
>
> The use of follow-up studies is a good way to see how behaviour changes in the longer term. It may involve months or even years.

CHILDMINDERS/NANNIES

Childminders and nannies can give a more personal relationship between the adult and the child than the day nursery or playgroup. However, this is not true if there are many children with the same childminder. Again, there are important factors that influence the experience for the child; these are dealt with below.

Relationship between minder/nanny and child

This issue includes the level of attention and stimulation given to the child. It is important for the minder or nanny to play with the child and build the relationship over time (so the stability of the relationship is important – as we saw with group day care).

Awareness of child's needs

Often quiet children are seen as ideal! However, it is important to remember that in some children quietness could be a sign of distress.

Insecure children

Insecure children are not suited to separation from their parents in this way.

Fig 3.19 Is a childminder or nanny better for growing children?

VARIATION IN REACTIONS

Bryant et al (1980) observed children at the childminder and at home throughout Oxfordshire. About a quarter of the children thrived well at the childminder, while another quarter were quiet at the minder but happy at home. The third quarter were quiet at home and at the minder, and the final group were clearly distressed at the minder. Evidently childminding is a successful form of substitute care for some children and not others.

CONCLUSIONS ON CHILDMINDING

Leaving a child with a childminder or nanny is a different experience for them to group day care (such as a nursery). There is the obvious advantage of a more personal relationship, but many factors must be considered to ensure the experience is not distressing for the child.

GENERAL EVALUATION OF DAY CARE

Day care for young children is not harmful to their development if it is of high quality, with stable staffing. Home care is not optimal for child development if the home environment is difficult (for example if the caregiver is depressed). Schaffer (1990) believes day care is a positive experience for the child, and believes that children over the age of one year will not necessarily be harmed by day care.

However, there can be problems relating to day care and the development of a secure attachment if:
- The child is not securely attached to the parent(s) before attending the day care.
- The day care is of poor quality.
- There are unstable family relationships outside of day care (for instance stress, or parent(s) unhappy with work); when the child returns home from day care they encounter more insecurity.
- The child spends more than 35 hours per week in day care.
- The child is in the first year of life.

So, in other words, much of the effect of day care depends on the surrounding context of the network of care for the child.

FOR CONSIDERATION

In Britain, in the past, it was common for children of richer families to be brought up by a nanny rather than their parents. In fact, this was the experience of John Bowlby!

CHAPTER 4 | STRESS

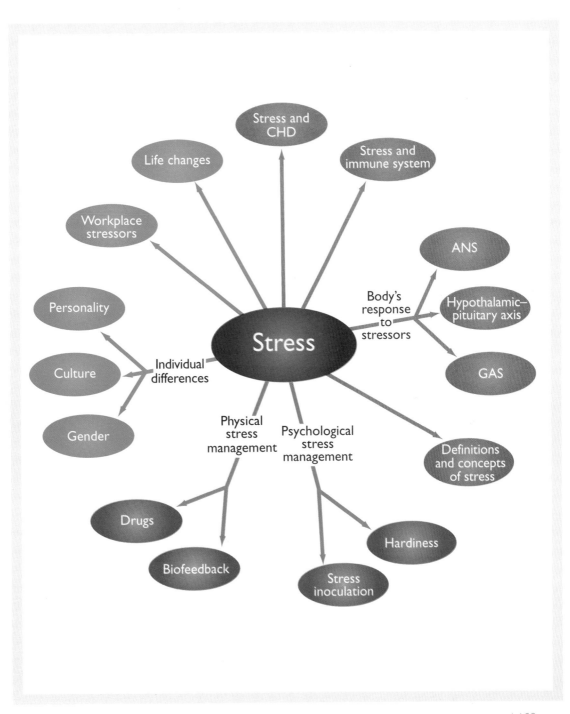

To prepare for the AQA exam you need to know the following things.

Stress as a bodily response

Definitions and concepts of stress

- The body's response to stressors
- General adaptation syndrome (GAS)
- Hypothalamic–pituitary axis
- The role of the autonomic nervous system

Research into the relationship between stress and the immune system

Research into the relationship between stress and cardiovascular disorders

Sources of stress

Life changes (including Holmes and Rahe)

Workplace stressors
- Work overload
- Work role ambiguity

Individual differences in modifying stress
- Personality (Friedman and Rosenman)
- Culture
- Gender

Critical issue: stress management

Physical stress management techniques
- Drugs
- Biofeedback

Psychological stress management techniques
- Stress inoculation (Meichenbaum)
- Increasing hardiness (Kobasa)

The role of control in stress perception

WHAT IS STRESS?

Fig 4.1 *Is this situation stressful?*

INTRODUCTION

Karen couldn't stand it any longer. The pressure of her commitments was weighing down upon her like a suffocating pillow. Why had she agreed to join that committee when she didn't even like meetings? How could she go to this meeting tonight, finish her report and prepare for tomorrow? The worst of it was that next week she had agreed, months ago, to present a talk at a conference. When could she get that ready? She realized, as an overwhelming sense of panic began to rise inside her, that she was cracking up.

Andrew crouched in his familiar stance, feet pressed against the blocks. He felt the muscles tensing in his legs; there was no strain or pain; he somehow knew that all his practice was about to pay off. The words 'Get set' echoed slowly in his ears. It was as though the world had gone into slow motion, everything apart from his legs. They were like coiled springs, about to be released. The crack of the pistol exploded in his head, sending shock waves pulsating through his body. This was it, he was less than ten seconds away from victory.

You have just read two accounts of the human stress response, something that we are all familiar with. It's likely that you recognized the first passage as classic stress, something that the media always portrays as negative. But what of the second passage; is that really stress? As you will see throughout this chapter, psychologists have not had an easy time trying to define and conceptualize this topic. Many theorists have gone back to biology to try to explain what stress is; others have focused on how cognitive factors make situations stressful. Let us now look at some examples.

DEFINITIONS OF STRESS

'Stress is the nonspecific response of the body to any demand'
(Selye 1950)

What Hans Selye is saying is that when put under pressure (demand), the body responds with an ancient and adaptive physiological change. It becomes generally aroused, ready for action. This definition focuses very much on the biology of the person.

'Stress responses are said to arise when demands exceed the personal and social resources that the individual is able to mobilise'
(Steptoe 1997)

Steptoe's more recent definition acknowledges that stress is all about experiencing a deficit. Your body can't deliver, be it in a physical, mental or social way, enough resources to deal with the demand.

Fig 4.2 *Hans Selye*

- The car represents a stressor
- The bridge represents the body

Body coping with the strain

Body not coping with the strain

Fig 4.3 *How does the body deal with stress?*

KEY DEFINITIONS

STRESSOR
Any factor which stimulates the stress response. It could be internal (such as a physical illness) or external (such as a traumatic life event).

RESPONSE
This term applies to the way in which the body responds to a stressor. It can include biological and cognitive responses.

TRANSACTION
This term is used to describe the interaction between a stressor and a person's biological response.

HOT EXAM HINT

You may be asked to define stress in the exam. Try to include in your answer the fact that demands exceed resources. It is always a good idea to give the examiner an example – you could even use not being prepared for an exam!

If you are asked to explain how psychologists have tried to conceptualize stress, remember to include terms such as 'stressor', 'response' and 'transaction'.

CONCEPTS OF STRESS

The engineering model

In the early days of stress research, when psychologists focused primarily on the causes of stress, they borrowed concepts from engineering. Within engineering stress refers to any force (for example weight) pressing on the structure or form of a system. Research within this model attempts to answer the question 'what causes stress?'.

The physiological model

At about the same time (particularly with the work of Hans Selye), psychologists were also looking at biological responses to stress. Research within this model attempts to answer the question 'how does the body deal with stress?'.

One good analogy for combining these two models is to think of a bridge.

This sort of analogy is only partially useful when attempting to explain stress. There are a number of limitations of the engineering and physiological models:
- They are both very simplistic.
- They view all stress as 'bad' – because it's seen as a weight or force. Bridges would be better off with nothing on them.
- They do not provide a detailed explanation why some people can deal with stress better than others. Some bridges are stronger and more effective than others.

Baum (1990) has suggested that in order to understand fully the concept of stress, we should look at the focus of the research. He proposes that research can be categorized in three ways:
1. Research which focuses on the factors which cause stress (**stressors**) – the stimulus
2. Research which focuses on the internal **responses** of the individual
3. A focus on the process itself

3 is interesting because not only does it include 1 and 2, but it also considers the **transaction** between the person and the environment. Its focus is not only on the stimulus and the response. It acknowledges that a person is 'active' in mediating stress through behaviours, thoughts (cognitions) and emotions.

CONCLUSION

There is no one definition for stress. However, most psychologists would agree that it arises when the demands of a situation have exceeded a person's resources to cope (be they cognitive or biological).

Over the years psychologists have studied stress by focusing on different aspects of it. Early research started out by considering things that cause stress and the way in which the body responds to it. These are known as the engineering model and the physiological model respectively. As you will see in other sections of this chapter, subsequent stress research has progressed to focus on the transaction between stressors and biology.

SECTION 3 | CAN STRESS BE GOOD FOR YOU?

INTRODUCTION

Simeon is a young entrepreneur who runs a very successful business in London. Day after day he exposes himself to high levels of stress, chasing deals, closing contracts. Even when he's not at work, he charges around constantly busying himself, making numerous social engagements for his family. He thrives on activity. He gets a kick out of being stressed.

KEY DEFINITIONS

AROUSAL
A physiological change within the body preparing the person to respond to a stressor – a state of readiness.

It's likely that you know a character like Simeon. Relaxation for this sort of person would be torture. So does this suggest that for some people stress can be good? The evidence seems to say yes. In order to understand why, we need to think about stress as one part of **arousal**. It is possible to have too much or too little.

BOREDOM, MOTIVATION AND STRESS

If an organism (in our case human) were hardly aroused, its motivation to do anything would be minimal. We would say that the person was bored. If we increased arousal (perhaps through giving them tasks to perform) we could increase their motivation to some sort of optimal level. Not too much, not too little.

KEY DEFINITIONS

DISTRESS
A term coined by Hans Selye to describe the negative aspects of stress.

EUSTRESS
Selye's term for the positive aspects of stress.

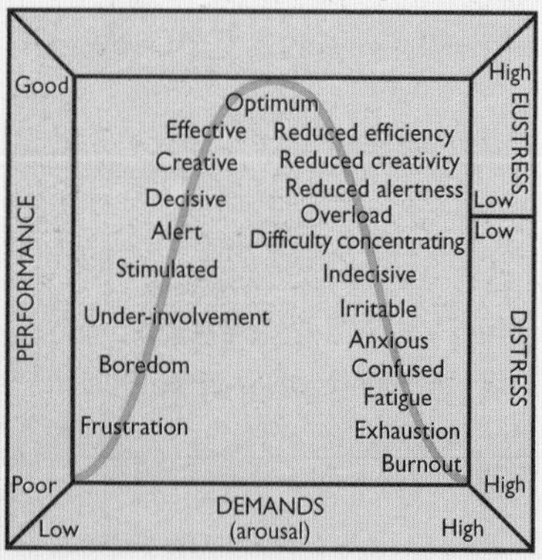

In fact, some of the classic theories of motivation (for example Fiske and Maddi 1961, Hebb 1955) propose that individuals function best and feel at their best at an optimal level of arousal. This level is different for each of us.

If we continued to arouse the person (perhaps by giving them an impossible workload) we would create the classic stress response.

DISTRESS AND EUSTRESS

It was Selye (1974, 1985) who first coined the terms **distress** and **eustress** as a way of showing positions on the arousal curve (see Fig 4.4). He suggested that distress is a harmful and damaging form of stress, whereas eustress (from the Greek 'eu' meaning good) can be beneficial and useful.

As you can see from the graph we all need a certain level of arousal (eustress). It gets us up in the morning and motivates us to achieve things. However, too much arousal and our psychological well being takes a nose-dive. We feel out of control and unable to cope, and our performance on mundane tasks is reduced. So what determines whether we have too much or too little arousal? Once again it is the way we think about a situation (our cognitions). Simeon, in the above example. clearly felt good about his level of activity. He felt challenged rather than threatened.

Fig 4.4 Arousal graph

CD-ROM

Stress: Eustress versus distress

AROUSAL – THE COGNITIVE FACTOR

The way we perceive an event can determine the level of arousal we experience, which in turn can determine whether the stressor is good or bad. Lazarus and Folkman (1984) propose that 'challenged' individuals are more likely to have better morale because of the 'positive' emotions we associate with a challenge. Being challenged is very different to being overwhelmed by a situation. Lazarus and Folkman go on to theorize that the physiological response to challenge is different to a threat. It could be this difference which determines whether a person goes on to develop a stress-related illness or not.

Let's now look in more detail at how cognitive appraisals are made.

HOW DO WE JUDGE WHAT IS STRESSFUL?

The ancient Greek philosopher Epictetus (circa AD 55–135) had a good idea what stress was when he said 'Men are disturbed not by things, but by the views which they take of them'.

His astute pondering suggests that in order for the physiological changes of the stress response to begin, an individual has to perceive something as stressful. Contemporary psychology tends to use the term **cognitive appraisal**, as introduced by Richard Lazarus and others (for example in Cohen and Lazarus 1983). It is a mental process in which people assess two factors:
- Whether a situation threatens their well-being.
- Whether they have the resources to deal with it.

Lazarus and colleagues refer to these assessments as 'primary' and 'secondary' respectively. Let us briefly consider each in turn.

Primary appraisal

This is our initial judgement of a situation. What does it mean for us? Is it a threat, and if so how much of one? Frequently, individuals who are experiencing a minor stress 'catastrophize' it, increasing its personal impact, therefore making it appear much more stressful (Ellis 1987). How information is presented to us can affect the perceived stress levels.

Secondary appraisal

This is an ongoing judgement of the resources we have to cope. In a way these judgements can be real or imagined. Brown (1986) suggested that stress is only viewed as a threat because we don't believe we have the ability to deal with it. It is the prediction about future coping that is creating the stress.

CONCLUSION

In order to decide whether stress is good for us, we have to view stress as one extreme of arousal. Extreme stress (arousal) is not good for us, but neither is minimal stress (boredom). As Selye points out, the optimal arousal level is somewhere in the middle.

SECTION 4 | THE FLIGHT OR FIGHT RESPONSE

INTRODUCTION

In 1929 Walter Cannon published a book entitled *Bodily Changes in Pain, Hunger, Fear and Rage*. In it he talked about the flight or fight response, an evolutionary mechanism (that increases our chances of survival) designed to arouse the body to bring about some sort of action. As its name implies, Cannon believed the two most useful types of action were running (flight) or preparing to fight (fight).

KEY DEFINITIONS

FLIGHT OR FIGHT RESPONSE
A term coined by Walter Cannon (1929) to describe the alarm reaction of the body to stress. This physiological preparedness allows the individual to either stay and fight or run away.

AN ANCIENT SCENARIO

Imagine the scene. One of our ancient ancestors has just noticed a rather threatening creature emerging from the undergrowth. Immediately, he feels a pounding sensation in his chest and a tensing and tightening of all his muscles. Now he has to think. Does he use this increased arousal to stand his ground and fight, or should he run?

His decision is made almost instantaneously. This creature looks angry, hungry and almost twice his size – he had better run.

Fig 4.5 Flight or fight?

WHAT IS THE FLIGHT OR FIGHT RESPONSE?

What physiological changes underlie the flight or fight response? In his work with animals, Cannon demonstrated that 'great emotional stress' (as he termed it) produced powerful biological changes. He showed that adrenaline (or epinephrine) and noradrenaline (or norepinephrine) played an important role in the body's emergency response.

Cannon argued that adrenaline arouses the individual, allowing them to be more responsive to potentially dangerous situations. These increases in stress chemicals are initiated by a part of the nervous system known as the autonomic nervous system (ANS) (see section 5 for more details).

Some of the functions of adrenaline/noradrenaline during the flight or fight response are as follows.

Adrenaline helps in the following ways:
* Dilates airways, thereby increasing oxygen intake
* Increases the heart rate, thereby increasing the blood supply to certain organs
* Fat and glucose mobilized from the liver and other fat stores, which provides energy for the body

KEY DEFINITIONS

ADRENALINE (EPINEPHRINE)
A hormone and neurotransmitter produced by the adrenal medulla (see section 6). It has an arousing effect on the body.

NORADRENALINE (NOREPINEPHRINE)
A neurotransmitter and hormone involved in activating the sympathetic division (see section 5) of the autonomic nervous system (ANS).

Noradrenaline helps in the following ways:
- Increases the sharpness of senses, for example pupils dilate to let in more light
- Increases the rate at which blood clots, which in turn reduces the blood lost through bleeding if you are injured
- Fat and glucose mobilized from the liver and other fat stores

EVIDENCE SUPPORTING THE FLIGHT OR FIGHT RESPONSE

The most obvious support for the flight or fight response comes from physiological research. It is well documented that stimulation of the ANS increases the production of adrenaline and noradrenaline.

Studies have provided support for the evolutionary argument of increased adrenaline/noradrenaline. Frankenhaeuser et al (1961) showed that participants showed superior performance on certain tasks when injected with adrenaline.

Lord et al (1976) demonstrated that rats showed poorer escape responses from an electric shock when the arousal part of their AN was blocked using drugs. This would support the argument that the flight or fight response was designed (in part) to enhance escape (avoidance) behaviour.

EVALUATION OF THE FLIGHT OR FIGHT RESPONSE

Evans (1978) points out that not all research shows superior task performance with increased adrenaline. Often the more complex the task, the more impaired performance becomes. Under these circumstances increases in adrenaline can hamper performance.

In his later work, Cannon identified limitations associated with the flight or fight response. If it occurs too frequently or goes on too long (usually referred to as 'chronic stress'), it begins to have adverse effects on physical health (Cannon 1935). This indicates that the flight or fight mechanism was designed, through evolutionary adaptation, to be generally arousing but short lived.

Both Cannon and Frankenhaeuser used animals in their research. To what extent can we (or should we) generalize their findings to humans?

Fig 4.6 Walter Cannon

🔥 HOT EXAM HINT

It is likely that you will be asked direct questions regarding the flight or fight response. You need to be able to describe what it is and evaluate it.

CONCLUSION

- The flight or fight mechanism is an evolutionary response.
- It arouses the individual to help them prepare to either run or fight.
- It is initiated by the ANS, and designed to be a short-term reaction to stress.

SECTION 5 | THE AUTONOMIC NERVOUS SYSTEM

KEY DEFINITIONS

AUTONOMIC NERVOUS SYSTEM (ANS)
Part of the nervous system that controls involuntary muscles and the release of hormones from glands.

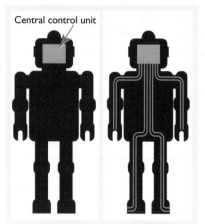

Central control unit

Fig 4.7   Fig 4.8

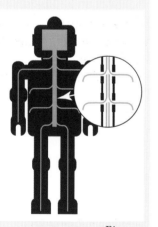

Fig 4.9

INTRODUCTION

The autonomic nervous system (ANS) has a major role to play in the production of the stress response. However, before we look specifically at this part of the nervous system it is worth seeing how the ANS fits into the nervous system as a whole.

A ROBOT EXAMPLE

Imagine you were asked to design a robot that looked and acted very much like a human. You would probably start with some sort of control centre (a central processing unit) (Fig 4.7).

Now how would you get messages to the rest of the body? Clearly, you would need to run wires throughout the robot, to the extremities (Fig 4.8).

However, if you use the long support shaft you built in to help your robot stand, you could pass the wires inside, thereby making them more protected. If you create gaps all the way down the support shaft, the wires can exit at different points down the robot's back. They could then travel in all directions throughout the robot's body (Fig 4.9).

The sorts of message you would need the robot to 'relay' if you were trying to mimic a human would include information about sensations such as pressure, pain and temperature, and also messages that instructed muscles to move.

However, if the robot were to be truly like a human you would want it to control its internal organs. It would need to control its temperature, digestion and heartbeat. Part of these functions could be achieved by running wires directly to the various organs and structures within your robot. These would be part of a different wire network to those involved in movement and sensation.

Finally, you would need this internal control network to work without conscious effort. The robot could then use its information processing capacity to solve problems and learn. In order for this to work effectively, you would need two 'divisions' of this network, one to speed internal processes up and one to slow them down, so that systems could be regulated accordingly.

THE HUMAN NERVOUS SYSTEM

CD-ROM

Stress: the human nervous system

You have just seen how we could design a robot nervous system. It shouldn't surprise you to learn that the human system is designed in an almost identical way. Fig 4.10 shows the major divisions.

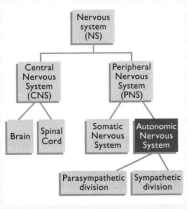

Fig 4.10 *Divisions of the nervous system*

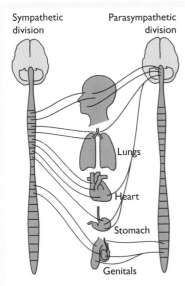

Fig 4.11 *The ANS*

HOW DOES THE ANS WORK?

As you can see from Fig 4.10, the ANS is part of the peripheral nervous system. 'Peripheral' refers to the nerves that branch off from the spine and travel throughout the body, from the head to the tips of the toes. Some of these nerves control movement, temperature and touch (including pain) – these are part of the **somatic** division. The ANS also consists of nerves fed from the spinal cord; however these supply organs and glands such as the heart, stomach and blood vessels (see Fig 4.11). You will also see from Fig 4.10 that the ANS is further divided into two sections (usually referred to as divisions), the sympathetic and the parasympathetic.

The sympathetic division

The sympathetic division speeds bodily activity up, including increasing heart rate and stimulating certain glands (including the adrenal medulla) to secrete hormones (adrenaline and noradrenaline) which further increase arousal. This is the flight or fight response (see section 4). It is an immediate arousal response to a stressor.

During the flight or fight response the sympathetic division is responsible for the following bodily changes:

- Increased heart rate
- A reduction in digestive activity and saliva
- A release of sugar and fat (to generate energy)
- A dilation (expansion) of the airways
- A dilation (expansion) of the pupils
- Production of adrenaline and noradrenaline

The parasympathetic division

When the stressor has subsided the body needs to return to its original state. The parasympathetic division takes over again and relaxes the individual. By doing this, the body calms itself down. The parasympathetic division is responsible for the following bodily changes:

- Decreased heart rate
- An increase in digestive activity and saliva
- A conservation (storing) of sugar and fat
- A contraction of the airways
- A contraction of the pupils

THE ROLE OF THE BRAIN AND THE ANS DURING STRESS

The ANS is an involuntary, self-regulating system, which doesn't require direct instruction from the higher centres of the brain. Think how terrible life would be if every second or so we had to tell our heart to beat, or our armpits to sweat. However, our brain must interpret something as a stressor for the ANS to begin the flight or fight response. This stress recognition activates a brain structure known as the hypothalamus. Many psychologists refer to this as the 'stress centre' because it is through its activation that the ANS becomes aroused. However, the hypothalamus also sets into motion a parallel bodily response to stress – the hypothalamic–pituitary link. Section 6 looks into this in more detail.

THE HYPOTHALAMIC– PITUITARY LINK

HYPOTHALAMIC–PITUITARY LINK
The name given to the hormonal process in which the hypothalamus communicates with the pituitary gland which in turn communicates with the adrenal glands. The result is the secretion of cortisol.

INTRODUCTION

As you saw in the previous section, the hypothalamus (a region within the brain) is regarded by most psychologists as the starting point for the stress response. The hormonal process that it initiates is known as the **hypothalamic–pituitary–adrenal axis**.

HOW DOES THE HYPOTHALAMIC–PITUITARY– ADRENAL AXIS WORK?

Higher centres within the brain interpret events within the environment. If they are perceived as threatening or anxiety provoking, they activate a 'primitive' area of the brain known as the hypothalamus. This structure was probably present in our earliest ancestors, for its benefits to aid survival. The hypothalamus then stimulates the release of a hormone known as corticotropin-releasing factor (CRF). All hormones released into the blood have a target organ; in the case of CRF the target organ is the pituitary gland.

Fig 4.12 The pituitary gland

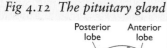

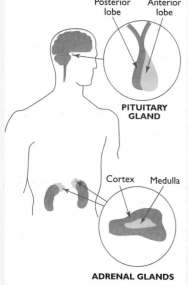

Fig 4.13 The adrenal glands

THE PITUITARY GLAND AND BEYOND

The pituitary gland is often referred to as the 'master gland', because it secretes a wide range of hormones that considerably influence bodily functions and behaviour. Anatomically speaking, it is no larger than a pea and is divided into two parts, the anterior (front) and posterior (back). When the anterior part of the pituitary gland detects CRF it begins to release a hormone known as adrenocorticotropic hormone (ACTH). This travels in the blood, again, to its target organ: the adrenal glands.

THE ADRENAL GLANDS

As you can see from Fig 4.13, the adrenal glands curve over the top of both of our kidneys. The adrenals appear to be just one structure; however, like the pituitary gland they actually comprise two. The outer part of the gland is known as the **adrenal cortex** and the centre or inner part is known as the **adrenal medulla**. It is the adrenal cortex that is involved in the hypothalamic–pituitary–adrenal axis. This part of the gland secretes hormones known as **corticoids** – mineralocorticoids and glucocorticoids.

CORTISOL
A hormone which reduces inflammation in any part of the body. It also converts fat into energy.

Cortisol

Cortisol (or hydrocortisone) is the chief glucocorticoid. One of its primary functions is to convert stores of fat into energy. It also acts as an anti-inflammatory substance, particularly if any part of the body becomes injured during fight or flight.

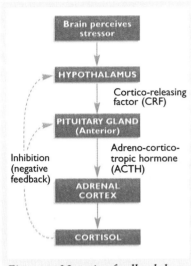

Fig 4.14 Negative feedback loop

NEGATIVE FEEDBACK INHIBITION

The brain cannot continue to secrete ACTH, or during times of stress we would overdose and ultimately die. As with many hormonal systems, the hypothalamic–pituitary–adrenal axis has a 'feedback inhibition loop' which acts as shown in Fig 4.14.

Laboratory studies have shown this negative feedback inhibition process in action. If you inject a person with large amounts of a synthetic glucocorticoid (for example dexamethasone), their brain detects the massive increase and stops the production of CRF, ACTH and glucocorticoids. If negative feedback regulation is not working well, these hormones will continue to be secreted. This is exactly what is seen in old humans, old primates and old rats. Even when they are not exposed to a stressor, or the stressor has been removed, they continue to secrete excessively high amounts (cited in Sapolsky 1998).

EVALUATION OF THE HYPOTHALAMIC–PITUITARY–ADRENAL AXIS

As with all biological explanations of stress, this process provides objective measurements. CRF, ACTH and glucocorticoids can all be measured precisely.

Just because this process can be objectively measured does not mean the underlying psychological causes of stress can be explained. There is much debate whether hormonal measures correlate with emotional experience.

Mason (1975) found that levels of adrenaline and noradrenaline varied in individuals when exposed to the same stressors. As you might expect there are physiological variations between individuals when exposed to the same stressful experience.

However, even though hormonal amounts may vary, scientists will argue that there is strong evidence to link certain hormones with certain behaviours/emotions.

Looker and Gregson (1989) summarize the links that research has identified between emotions and stress hormones. The table gives three examples.

Emotion	Hormone	Change from normal levels
Aggression	Noradrenaline Cortisol	Large increase Little or no change
Fear/flight	Adrenaline Cortisol	Large increase Increase
Depression	Cortisol Adrenaline Noradrenaline	Large increase Little or no change Little or no change

THE GENERAL ADAPTATION SYNDROME

INTRODUCTION

During the 1930s a young scientist was embarking upon his career in endocrinology (the study of hormones). A colleague up the corridor had managed to isolate a substance obtained from the ovaries, and both men were keen to know what it was and what it did to the body. The young scientist began by injecting the substance into laboratory rats. He was clearly not very skilled at this task, because daily he would drop them or they would wriggle out of his hands. Great commotion ensued while he recaptured them.

After a few months the scientist examined the rats and found they had peptic ulcers, greatly enlarged adrenal glands and shrunken immune system tissues (the thymus). Being a good scientist, he had simultaneously been injecting a control group of rats with a saline solution (salt water), which should have had no effect on them whatsoever. Imagine the scientist's amazement when the control group showed the same symptoms. It was clearly nothing to do with the ovarian extract.

Most scientists would have probably changed career at this point, but this one persisted in trying to find an explanation. In the end he did – this young scientist was called Hans Selye and he developed the theory of the general adaptation syndrome. The effects observed in the rats had been caused by the stress to which they were exposed.

KEY DEFINITIONS

GENERAL ADAPTATION SYNDROME (GAS)
A sequence of stages proposed by Hans Selye explaining how the body reacts to stressful situations.

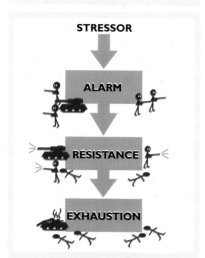

Fig 4.15 General adaptation syndrome

WHAT IS THE GENERAL ADAPTATION SYNDROME?

This is the name given to a process that describes the bodily changes a person or animal experiences when confronted with stress. It was detailed in a book called *The Stress Of Life* written by Selye in 1956. He proposes two main ideas:

* The body responds in a surprisingly similar way to a wide variety of stressors (this is what he calls the general adaptation syndrome (GAS)).
* Under certain conditions stressors will make you ill.

PHASES OF THE GAS

Selye argues that the body responds to stress in three distinct stages or phases (see Fig 4.15).

One simple way of understanding the phases is to liken them to a battle.

Phase 1: alarm

The troops are prepared and placed in position. The enemy starts firing and your soldiers respond swift and hard.

This is where the brain perceives a threat and starts the process of 'flight or fight' (see section 4). Both the autonomic nervous system (ANS) (see section 5) and the hypothalamic–pituitary link (see section 6) are activated. Research has shown that even brief exposure to a stressor can initiate a full-blown stress response (Cacioppo et al 1995).

Phase 2: resistance

As the battle progresses there are casualties on both sides. You have to bring in reserve troops to ensure that the enemy does not gain the upper hand.

As in the alarm stage, the ANS and the hypothalamic–pituitary system work together to mobilize energy and deliver it to whichever muscles require it. If the stressor remains then the body continues to produce hormones such as adrenaline and cortisol. These elevated levels eventually start to take their toll on the body and its ability to resist diminishes.

It is very common for people to use denial as a coping strategy during this stage ('There's nothing wrong with me, I can cope very well thank you'), as their body heads towards Selye's last phase.

Phase 3: exhaustion

By now things are going wrong. Many of your troops are dead and those that remain are very weary. You have used up all your reserves and the enemy appears unrelenting. If things carry on this way you will go down in the history books as the side that put up a gallant fight but ultimately lost.

Selye proposed that eventually, if the stressor persisted, the body would show symptoms of wear and tear. Organs and systems particularly vulnerable to this are the heart, blood vessels and (as Selye found with his rats) the adrenal glands and immune system tissue. Many of Selye's rats were literally stressed to death. Selye referred to illnesses that are caused or worsened by stress as 'diseases of adaptation' (see section 8).

EVALUATION

The GAS has been a very influential model, acting as the foundation for further research.

As a biological explanation it has been criticized for not detailing the emotional and cognitive elements of the stress response. Viewing something as a threat or a challenge can determine the impact it will have on the body (Lazarus and Folkman 1984). Many researchers argue that psychological stressors can simulate physical ones, in terms of how the body responds. Feeling incompetent or unloved can generate the GAS, as can being threatened with a gun (Cacioppo et al 1995).

There are ethical considerations to bear in mind when looking at Selye's work. Many of his rats died. Some would argue that what we learnt about human illness and stress made the research worthwhile.

The fact that Selye based his theory on evidence from rats has raised questions about how far we should go in applying it to humans.

HOT EXAM HINT

Be ready to describe the three stages in Selye's model. You need to know their names and also the key features of each stage.

INTRODUCTION TO STRESS AND ILLNESS

INTRODUCTION

Dominic knocked, then pushed open the door and walked into the office. He was greeted by a polite hello and wafts of sterilizing fluid and disinfectant. He knew as he sat down in the chair that this time he would be referred for tests. His ulcer if anything was getting more irritated. Why do doctors always ask how stressed you feel? He felt fine, busy, but fine. It wasn't his brain that had the problem with the ulcer, it was his guts.

CD-ROM

To learn more about how stress presents to the doctor, see CD-ROM Stress: GP corner: stress and anxiety.

Fig 4.16 Patient in consultation with GP.

KEY DEFINITIONS

PSYCHONEUROIMMUNOLOGY (PNI)
A branch of medicine that investigates the links between behaviour, the nervous system and the immune system.

It has been estimated that at least 75% of GP consultations are associated with stress. The interesting thing is, not every patient realizes it.

As you have seen in the previous pages, sophisticated biological processes underpin the experience of stress. Many of the bodily responses are useful in the short term (remember the **flight or fight** mechanism). However, when the stress response persists (chronic stress), or is excessively strong, the individual risks developing illness.

Since ancient times physicians have observed links between a person's mental state and their physical health. In simple terms, the way you think has the potential to make you ill. This may sound quite a logical presumption; however, the medical profession has only recently dedicated a discipline of investigation to it. This field is known as **psychoneuroimmunology (PNI)**.

PSYCHONEUROIMMUNOLOGY

Prior to the last forty or so years, psychologists and doctors worked mostly in separation, publishing papers in their specialized fields. Immunologists rarely exchanged ideas with neurologists or endocrinologists. Then in the 1960s, collaborative teams started to work together on projects. The specialism known as **psychoneuroimmunology** was born ('psycho' referring to the mind, 'neuro' referring to the nervous and hormonal systems, 'immuno' referring to the immune system). In recent years it has provided empirical evidence to show direct links between all four bodily systems. It has shown that the mind–body interaction is direct and powerful. The links between stress and illness are primarily studied within this field.

MIND–BODY DISORDERS

Most scientists would argue that every physical illness has a psychological component. The last time you had a cold or flu, your primary symptoms were physical, but it is likely you experienced psychological discomfort as well. However, if you think about it, this could get quite complicated. Did

Fig 4.17 'It's alright Mr Smith, the doctor's just praying it's all in your mind'.

your stressed mental state prior to catching the cold make you more susceptible to it? Did your stressed mental state make you interpret the symptoms of the cold as more severe?

PNI researchers tend to make distinctions of mind–body involvement in the following way.

Psychogenic disorder

A disorder that is psychological in origin, but presents with physical symptoms. A good example is psychogenic pain, in which doctors can find no physical reason for a person's pain.

Somatogenic disorder

A disorder that is physical in origin, and presents with physical symptoms; for example a blister on the foot caused by badly fitting shoes.

Psychosomatic disorder

A disorder that is both physical and psychological in origin. For example, a 'tension' headache may have been caused by both excessive anxiety and changes in blood flow to the scalp.

SOME ILLNESSES ASSOCIATED WITH STRESS

It is very unlikely that stress is the **sole cause** of any illness. However, there is no doubt that its occurrence exacerbates the development of any underlying illness. Below is a list of primary psychosomatic disorders that have been linked to stress.

- Duodenal and stomach ulcers
- Inflammatory bowel disease
- Asthma
- Headaches
- Hypertension (high blood pressure)
- Coronary heart disease (CHD)

Stress can be linked to illness in two ways:

- **Direct effects** – experiencing stress can alter or damage biological processes, which in turn can lead to illness.
- **Indirect effects** – experiencing stress may affect a person's behaviour. They might skip meals or eat more junk food. They might smoke or drink more.

STRESS AND CARDIOVASCULAR DISORDERS

The two most common cardiovascular disorders in modern society are CHD and hypertension. Most researchers admit that stress plays a contributory role in the development of these disorders; however, there is still some debate as to how significant stress actually is.

Sections 9 and 10 look at hypertension and CHD in more detail.

SECTION 9 | STRESS AND HYPERTENSION

INTRODUCTION

Mrs King grabbed the overflowing washing basket from the table, knocking a hot mug of coffee flying in the process. It smashed onto the floor. Her three children were still fighting, taking it in turns to see who could scream the loudest. 'That's it,' she shouted, momentarily slipping into hysteria. 'My blood pressure can't take any more!'

KEY DEFINITIONS

SPHYGMOMANOMETER
A device used to measure blood pressure.

SYSTOLIC BLOOD PRESSURE
Blood pressure taken when the heart is contracting (this is when the blood is flowing at the highest pressure).

DIASTOLIC BLOOD PRESSURE
Blood pressure taken when the heart is resting and the chambers are filling with blood.

Fig 4.18 A sphygmomanometer

FOR CONSIDERATION

There are cultural variations in what are regarded as normal levels of blood pressure. African and Japanese people tend to have lower than average levels, while Afro-Americans tend to have higher than average levels.

KEY DEFINITIONS

ESSENTIAL HYPERTENSION
Elevated blood pressure due to unknown causes.

I'm sure many of you have had experiences similar to the one presented in the case study above. But how many of us consider what effect the stressor is having on our body? One of the symptoms of the stress response is elevated blood pressure. This is fine as long as the stressor is short lived. If it persists, the raised blood pressure becomes a health risk.

HOW IS BLOOD PRESSURE MEASURED?

As blood travels through the arteries its pressure varies as the heart beats. The most common method of measuring blood pressure is to use a **sphygmomanometer**. This consists of a cuff connected to a device designed to measure pressure using a column of mercury (called a mercury manometer). The cuff is placed around the upper arm and inflated until the blood supply to the lower arm is cut off. A stethoscope is positioned over the blood vessels at the elbow and a rushing sound is listened for (indicating that blood has begun to flow back into the lower arm). This is blood flowing at the highest pressure – namely when the heart is **contracting strongly**. This will give a reading of mercury known as the **systolic blood pressure**. When the pressure returns to the minimum level that allows blood to flow, this gives a reading of mercury known as the **diastolic blood pressure**. In an average healthy adult the reading is approximately 120 mmHg (millimetres of mercury) **systolic** and 80 mmHg **diastolic**. This is usually expressed as a fraction: '120/80'.

HYPERTENSION

Hypertension is persistently high blood pressure over several weeks or more. It increases a person's risk of developing coronary heart disease (CHD), stroke and kidney disease.

About 85% of hypertensive cases are classified as **essential hypertension** – this means the underlying causes are categorized as unknown. Even though this label is used, certain risk factors have in fact, been known for many years: obesity; poor diet (including cholesterol-rich food and excessive salt); alcohol; lack of exercise; genetic factors (a family history of hypertension).

A much more controversial and possibly more worrying risk factor is chronic stress. Let us now examine the evidence for this connection.

RESEARCH EVIDENCE LINKING STRESS WITH HYPERTENSION

Some of the earliest research linking stress to hypertension was published in the1940s and 1950s under the banner of psychoanalysis. This work built on the theories of Sigmund Freud (1856–1939) that certain physiological conditions were an outward manifestation of some emotional trauma from childhood. He had suggested that asthma was symptomatic of a problem of communicating with others. Hypertension was caused by the repression of hostile emotions and gut ulcers were the result of frustrated desires to seek help. Hypertension had found itself branded as an 'illness of repressed hostility'.

Cobb and Rose (1973) looked at the medical records of thousands of men employed as air traffic controllers and compared them with other air traffic personnel. After the sample was controlled for age (as blood pressure tends naturally to increase with age), air traffic controllers showed significantly higher levels of blood pressure (more hypertension) in high-stress locations than other air traffic personnel.

Research such as this would suggest that certain occupations are more prone to stress-related hypertension than others. Also, levels of stress experienced correlate with the severity of the hypertension.

UNDERLYING MECHANISM

So how does stress affect blood pressure? Studies have shown that the emotional expression of anger can affect resting blood pressure. Goldstein et al (1989) demonstrated that when experienced anger is not expressed, blood pressure rises. There are many stressors which make us angry: it is frequently a side effect of stress. The physiology behind anger is quite easily understood. Anger increases the heart rate and constricts blood vessels in the skin and viscera (the internal organs of the body, especially the abdomen). Because blood vessels have constricted, blood can now be delivered with greater speed to muscles where it is needed. These changes have the effect of increasing blood pressure.

CONCLUSION

Essential hypertension can be caused by a variety of things. However, the evidence linking it to stress is very convincing.

FOR CONSIDERATION

Some studies have focused on environmental stresses and hypertension. Overcrowding within prisons has been shown to increase the risk of hypertension (D'Atri and Ostfield 1975). Long-term exposure to noise within the work environment has also been shown to elevate blood pressure (Johnsson and Hanssen 1977).

CD-ROM

Stress: some interesting facts about stress

HOT EXAM HINT

Often you will be asked to demonstrate the link between hypertension and stress. It is always a good idea to include technical terms in your answer, such as 'essential hypertension'.

STRESS AND CORONARY HEART DISEASE

INTRODUCTION

Coronary heart disease (CHD) is the biggest single cause of death in modern industrialized nations. In Britain, almost 50% of all deaths result from heart disease, compared with 25% from the second biggest killer, cancer. As we saw at the end of section 8, scientists are still unsure about the importance of the role stress plays in the development of CHD.

WHAT IS CHD?

Fig 4.19 *'My life's so stressful at the moment. I don't know which cocktail to order'.*

CHD describes a number of conditions caused by a blockage of the arteries which prevents oxygen reaching the heart muscle (myocardium). These could include:

- **Angina pectoris** –a sensation of tightness or chest pain due to a restriction in an artery
- **Heart attack** (myocardial infarction (MI)) –where part of the heart muscle dies because of a lack of oxygen

HOW CAN STRESS BE LINKED WITH CHD?

Decades of intense research have identified certain risk factors for CHD. Some of the most common are:
- Smoking
- High blood pressure
- Obesity
- Family history of CHD
- High cholesterol
- Diabetes
- Lack of exercise

However convincing the above factors may be, even combined they can only explain half the overall pattern of heart disease within any population. This has led researchers to look for answers to the remaining 50% in other areas. The psychological makeup of the individual has been their primary choice. As will be discussed in the next section (section 11), personality types have been heavily implicated. Characteristics of the personality known as Type A (particularly hostility) have been most associated with increased risk of CHD. But what exactly is the process that links stress with CHD?

PHYSIOLOGICAL REACTIVITY

One avenue of research has suggested that people who show Type A characteristics also tend to have a more reactive physiology than Type Bs. This means Type As, on average, respond more vigorously to stressors (Wright 1988). This has implications on the wear and tear of their bodies, particularly the cardiovascular system.

To help you understand these processes, think of two car drivers. Both drive average saloon cars every day. One takes it steady, accelerating

KEY DEFINITIONS

TYPE A PERSONALITY
A group of personality characteristics first described by Friedman and Rosenman (1959). They include an overriding need to achieve, a highly competitive nature and a tendency to show anger or hostility (see section 11).

TYPE B PERSONALITY
The opposite of Type A. Type B individuals tend to be more relaxed and show lower levels of hostility (see section 11).

PHYSIOLOGICAL REACTIVITY
The extent to which the body responds to a stressor. This can be measured in terms of duration and intensity.

gently and changing the gears slowly. The second is much more erratic; they accelerate away from traffic lights by slamming the pedal to the floor, and crash the gears into place. Which car would you rather pay for after a service? In the second car, all the components are frequently pushed to their limits – just like the Type A body.

As you saw in earlier sections, when the body is pushed to its limits it produces large quantities of hormones such as adrenaline and cortisol. Long-term exposure to these chemicals appears to increase atherosclerosis (the development of fatty deposits in artery walls). But can social and psychological factors really push the body to its limits?

Manuck et al (1983) conducted a study into the link between social stress and atherosclerosis, by considering the social hierarchies of monkeys. Primates tend to live in highly structured societies where social interaction is highly important for physical and psychological well being. The researchers deliberately stressed some of the monkeys by regularly breaking up their social groups (monkeys were removed from one group and placed within another). Regardless of whether the monkeys had high- or low-cholesterol diets, those who had been separated showed greater levels of atherosclerosis than those who were left alone (see Fig 4.20). It appeared that social stress was associated with increased atherosclerosis.

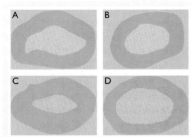

Fig 4.20 Manuck's atherosclerosis diagram. A, B and D: these monkeys were living in stable groups, or were subordinate, and their coronary arteries show less occlusion. Greatest occlusion was found in C, dominant monkeys whose social groupings regularly broke up.

HIGH BLOOD PRESSURE

One way in which this increased physiological reactivity to stressors manifests itself is in high blood pressure (see section 9). The characteristics of the Type A personality (particularly the hostility element) have been associated with hypertension. Chronic hypertension puts strain on both the heart and the arteries.

BEHAVIOURAL FACTORS

Many researchers believe the relationship between stress and CHD is not a direct one. It is mediated through our behaviours. For example, stressed individuals tend to smoke and drink more alcohol (Baer et al 1987). They may also skip meals and eat more junk food. Interestingly (particularly if you think back to the analogy of the over-worked car), studies have shown that stressed individuals are more likely to push themselves to the limits, even when they are injured or fatigued (Carver et al 1981).

EVALUATION

As you will see in much more detail in section 11, Type A personality characteristics (always pushing oneself, easily roused to hostility) appear to be the mechanism linking stress to CHD. Having a Type A personality means you:
- Tend to be more physiologically reactive to stressors (increasing wear and tear on the body)
- Tend to have elevated blood pressure (increasing pressure on the cardiovascular system)
- Tend to engage in unhealthy stress-related behaviours (smoking, drinking alcohol and eating irregularly – often junk food)

SECTION 11 | STRESS AND THE TYPE A PERSONALITY

INTRODUCTION

Stress has frequently been cited as a contributory factor in the development of coronary heart disease (CHD). However some investigators within this area point out that it was not stress as such which contributed to the development of CHD, but the personality of the person. Personality was acting as a mediating factor. In the 1950s in San Francisco, Ray Rosenman and Meyer Friedman began the first systematic research programme into personality characteristics and CHD. Through their research they identified two major personality types: Type A and Type B.

KEY DEFINITIONS

TYPE A AND B PERSONALITY CHARACTERISTICS?
Friedman and Rosenman (1959) defined the characteristics of Type A and Type B personalities as follows.

Type A:
- Overriding need to achieve
- Work under time pressures
- Highly competitive
- Quick to show hostility, particularly if their progress is blocked

Type B:
Complete opposite characteristics to Type A. Much more relaxed about life and show lower levels of hostility.

PROBLEMS IN IDENTIFYING A TYPE A PROFILE

As you can see (within the criticisms of their original study, below) even Rosenman has more recently admitted that Type A is very difficult to define.

Further work in this field has suggested that Type A personalities have a number of less obvious underlying traits. They possess a strong sense of duty; they are often over-controlling and appear to be driven, almost to the point of having to prove something to the world (Totman 1990).

However, whichever characteristics we choose to represent Type A, the idea that people with this personality type are always striving to progress is a recurring, common theme.

RESEARCH EVIDENCE

Friedman and Rosenman (1975). Coronary heart disease in the Western Collaborative Group Study. *Journal of the American Medical Association.*

Fig. 4.21 'Don't worry, my wife just has a Type B personality.'

Aims

To investigate the association (correlation) between previously identified high-stress personality characteristics (impatience, hostility and competitiveness – which they called Type A), and CHD.

Procedure

Over 3000 Californian men aged between 39 and 59 volunteered to take part in the study. They were assessed over a period of eight and a half years, making it a longitudinal design (a study that takes place over a period of time). All the participants were healthy at the start of the study.

The first part of the study involved categorizing the participants into high-stressed personalities (Type A) or non-stressed (Type B). This was done using structured interviews. However, the researchers were not only interested in the participants' responses to specific questions (such as 'How do you react when you have to wait in a queue?'), but also in how they behaved during the interview situation. The whole experimental procedure was set up in such a way as to antagonize the participant. Participants were kept waiting by the interviewer, who then proved to be unfriendly and often seemingly incompetent. The behaviour characteristics of each participant counted for 75% of the overall score that determined their personality type, whereas answers to the questionnaire were worth 25%.

Findings

Nearly twice as many Type A participants developed CHD during the duration of the study (257 participants). When physiological measures were assessed they were found to have significantly higher levels of adrenaline (epinephrine), noradrenaline (norepinephrine) and cholesterol.

Conclusions

This study demonstrated that there is a significant relationship between Type A characteristics and CHD. The physiological measures suggest that there are biological differences between Type A and Type B.

Criticisms

- The study used the **correlation** method. As always with correlation you must not infer a causal relationship: we cannot say that 'Type A personality characteristics have caused CHD'.
- The study used volunteers – a self-selecting sample. This is always questionable as certain types of people tend to volunteer for studies.
- The study used men – can the findings be generalized to women?
- The study used interviews – even if interviews are highly structured they are always open to the criticism of being subjective. It is impossible for the interviewer to be totally consistent. No two interviews are ever the same.
- Type A characteristics are a collection of behaviours. The concept is not specific enough to determine which aspects of Type A are associated with CHD.
- In fact, more recently Rosenman published in the journal *Stress Medicine* (1991) a paper questioning how significant each factor of the Type A personality was. He suggests that competitiveness may be the so-called 'toxic factor' because it leads to impatience and hostility. He concludes by pointing out that it is unlikely 'that intercorrelated emotional and behavioural aspects of a human being can ever satisfactorily be subdivided into single component parts'.

STRESS AND THE IMMUNE SYSTEM

KEY DEFINITIONS

PATHOGEN
A 'foreign substance' entering the body.

ANTIGENS
Proteins present on a pathogen's outer surface. They enable it to be recognized.

T-LYMPHOCYTES
A specialized type of white blood cell (leucocyte). They recognize antigens, attach themselves to them and destroy them.

PHAGOCYTES
(Another type of white blood cell). Destroy invaders by engulfing them.

NATURAL KILLER (NK) CELLS
Cells within the immune system that target potential tumours and destroy them before they can grow.

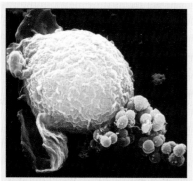

Fig 4.22 Natural killer cell

INTRODUCTION

The human immune system is designed to deal with outside invasion. In order to be effective it needs to recognize an intruder and take the correct course of action. Usually the correct course of action involves destroying the invader.

Under normal circumstances, with the system working at optimum efficiency, it is able to destroy the majority of invaders and cell mutations. But if the system is put under pressure (usually referred to as being **suppressed**) then its efficiency becomes compromised.

HOW STRESS SUPPRESSES THE IMMUNE SYSTEM

A growing number of psychologists and other scientists have been saying in recent years that stress can have a compromising effect on immune system functioning. In the long term the physiological changes accompanying the stress response can damage the immune system. The process of damage can occur in two ways:
• Direct nerve links (neural pathways)
• Chemical (involving hormones and other chemical messengers)

Neural pathways

Immune system tissues are connected to the nervous system via a rich network of nerves. The peripheral nervous system provides an extensive branching of nerve fibres into all the major structures of the immune system, including the spleen, thymus, tonsils and gut. In fact, at least half the nerve connections in the spleen are involved in sending messages to and from the brain. As you saw in section 5 the sympathetic division of the autonomic nervous system (ANS) has in general a stimulating effect on the body. Chronic stress can create an over-stimulation of immune system organs. This can accelerate potential damage of immune system tissue.

Chemical damage

As you saw in section 7, it was Hans Selye who first observed that when rats were exposed to severe stressors their thymus gland shrank while their adrenal glands enlarged. Both glands are important structures within the immune system. Under normal circumstances the thymus is responsible for the production of white blood cells (lymphocytes), and would generate them in a plentiful supply. However, the stress hormone cortisol blocks the production of new lymphocytes, causing the gland to shrink (explaining Selye's earlier observation). Therefore chronic exposure to cortisol suppresses the immune system.

The direct effects of adrenaline and noradrenaline produce another link between stress and the immune system. Both these chemical messengers are known to suppress the immune system, and the amount of suppression is related to the quantity released (Martin 1997).

RESEARCH EVIDENCE

Kiecolt-Glaser et al (1984). Psychosocial modifiers of immunocompetence in medical students. *Psychosomatic Medicine*.

Aims

The aim of this study was to establish a link between the experience of negative life events (primarily in the form of end-of-year medical exams) and immunosuppression.

Procedure

49 male and 26 female first-year medical students volunteered to participate in the study. It was divided into two sessions: session 1 (blood samples and a stress questionnaire) was conducted both 1 month before their final exams and 1 month after their last major exam. The researchers labelled this the lower-stress condition. Session 2 was labelled the higher-stress condition, and took place just after the student's second exam, during the final exam week. Only blood samples were taken during this session. Blood samples were analysed for antibody concentrations and NK cell concentrations (the lower the NK activity, the more suppressed the immune system).

Findings

Antibody concentrations did not appear to be related to the stress variables; however, NK activity was significantly lower in the higher-stress session. Also, those students who showed that they were experiencing other stressful events (such as loneliness, as measured by the stress questionnaire) showed significant extra NK reduction.

Conclusions

This study demonstrated that there is a significant relationship between life events (in the form of examinations and loneliness) and immunosuppression.

Criticisms

- You must remember that the sample was quite small and the participants were a very specific group (medical students). The extent to which the findings can be generalized to the wider population is open to debate. Also, bear in mind that the participants were all volunteers. As we mentioned in section 11, certain types of people tend to volunteer for studies.
- It appears that the physiological changes that accompany stress have a highly detrimental effect on the immune system, but could the opposite be possible? Could behaviour such as laughter have a beneficial effect?

STRESS AND LIFE EVENTS

INTRODUCTION

Giles had done it again. He had just accepted a new job that would require him to move town. He had only moved nine months ago. Now he was going to have to pack up his things and start all over again. What made it worse was, this time, he hadn't got a girlfriend to move with. He would have to do it all on his own. Giles began to question whether promotion was worth it after all. Money wasn't everything – what had happened to his quality of life?

KEY DEFINITIONS

LIFE EVENT
Something that occurs in our life that has an effect on us.

LIFE TRANSITION
The process of moving from one stage in life to another (for example from work to retirement).

FOR CONSIDERATION

Life transitions are unavoidable stressors that affect all of us at some stage in our lives. They tend to be age related and culturally dependent; for example, in a Westernized culture you would expect to encounter:
- Birth
- First day at school
- Adolescence
- First job
- Leaving home
- Marriage/cohabitation
- Parenthood
- Retirement
- Bereavement
- Death (or the anticipation of it!)

Lifestyle changes can have quite profound effects upon us. Giles, in the above case study, was experiencing three lifestyle changes simultaneously – he had a new job, was moving area and had just split up with his girlfriend. Clearly these events were causing him stress, as he was beginning to question the wisdom of pursuing a successful career. The first question we need to ask is: what do we mean by life events?

LIFE EVENTS

Life events can take three distinct forms: **life transitions** (changes from one stage of life to another), **life traumas** (perceived as 'bad') and **positive life events** (perceived as 'good'). Let us look at each in turn.

LIFE TRAUMAS

Other life events are experienced as one-offs, either as traumatic events such as illness or bereavement (which affect the individual), or as group traumas such as earthquakes, nuclear accidents or terrorist attacks. In both cases the trauma is perceived as stressful because the individual feels out of control; the event was not predictable and it completely challenges their view of the world.

From an individual perspective, the event could be the death of your mother. If you are young, it was not predictable (on the whole people tend to die when they are older); it challenges your view of a fair or just world and there was nothing you could do about it (you have a sense of being out of control).

POSITIVE LIFE EVENTS

These are life events that are viewed as having a positive outcome. Getting a dream job or winning the lotto would be examples of this. One thing that all three types of life event have in common is that they involve change.

Fig 4.23 What kind of life events are these?

CHANGE

Any change, whether it is viewed as desirable or undesirable, whether an individual or a large group of people experience it, initiates the stress response (Holmes and Rahe 1967). Many psychologists suggest our body responds to change or transition in our lives by preparing itself to act. If you remember, Cannon refers to this evolutionary mechanism as the 'flight or fight' response (see section 4). Our bodies cannot distinguish between a 'good' change and a 'bad' change – it is the change itself that poses the potential threat.

DAILY HASSLES

Some psychologists suggest that it does not always have to be major life events or transitions that initiate the stress response; it could be daily irritations, or as we might call them, 'hassles'. It was Richard Lazarus and his colleagues who first proposed this idea, in 1981. They developed a 'hassle scale' (Kanner et al 1981) which listed 117 questions designed to identify the level of hassles someone had experienced over the past month. In their initial research, based upon 100 middle-aged adults, assessed over a 9-month period, three of the most common hassles reported were:

- Concerns over weight
- Concerns over the health of a family member
- Too many things to do

As a development of their initial research they suggested that experiencing 'pleasant events' could reduce stress and cushion its impact. So they developed another instrument, the 'uplifts scale', which identifies 135 events that bring joy or satisfaction to individuals.

EVALUATION

Life events can be related to stress; however, the link between them is highly complicated. The ways in which life events are interpreted determine how stressful their impact is. Some people may view a life event as a threat, others may see it as a challenge (Cohen and Lazarus 1983).

Life events are culturally determined. For example, it is naive to think that the transition from boy to manhood (adolescence) is always stressful. In some cultures this process is valued and its implications are seen as highly important. At puberty, it is believed that Zulu boys are introduced ritually to their ancestral spirits and become a full member of their family – rather different to a modern Westernized view of adolescence (Elliott 1978).

Where hassles are concerned, studies have shown that the relationship between hassles and health is weak. There appears to be no relationship between uplifts and health (DeLongis et al 1982).

THE SOCIAL READJUSTMENT RATING SCALE

INTRODUCTION

As you saw in section 13, life events initiate the stress response because of the very fact that they represent change. Some researchers have gone as far as attempting to quantify (express as a quantity) the impact life events have on the health of an individual. Two of the pioneers in this field were Thomas Holmes and Richard Rahe (1967) at the University of Washington. They developed a scale to assess the impact of stressful life events on health, called the social readjustment rating scale (SRRS).

KEY DEFINITIONS

SOCIAL READJUSTMENT RATING SCALE (SRRS)
A hierarchical scale devised by Holmes and Rahe to identify the most common stressful life events.

KEY DEFINITIONS

LIFE CHANGE UNITS
The scores obtained from a particular life event, which are usually weighted and added together.

CD-ROM

Stress: The social readjustment rating scale

WHAT IS THE SRRS?

Based upon their clinical experience of working with patients suffering from stress and anxiety, Holmes and Rahe constructed a list of life events that they believed precipitated their patients' stress. They then asked hundreds of men and women of various ages and backgrounds to rate the 'average amount' of adjustment that they felt would be required to accommodate the change. On the basis of these responses, values were assigned to the different life events and a hierarchy was produced (see Fig 4.24).

As you can see, top of the table is the death of a spouse (with a mean value of 100 points). Pregnancy appears 12th, with a mean value of 40 points. Vacation (holidays) are 41st, with a mean value of 13 points, and 42nd is Christmas (something we all experience once a year) with a value of 12 points.

When the SRRS is used to assess an individual's level of stress, the person is asked to select the life events from the list that have occurred to them within a specified period of time (not usually more than the past 24 months). The scores (or as they are more correctly known, 'life change units' (LCUs)) are then added together to provide an overall stress score.

Look back at the case study in section 13. Giles arguably could have notched up an LCU score of at least 121:

Marital separation (splitting up with girlfriend) = 65 points
Change to a different line of work   = 36 points
Change in residence   = 20 points

If we then started adding assumed events to the case study, such as Christmas (12 points), a mortgage over $10 000 (31 points), and so on, we could soon take Giles's LCU score to at least 164.

Rank	Life event	Mean value
1	Death of a spouse	100
2	Divorce	73
3	Marital separation	65
4	Jail term	63
5	Death of close family member	63
6	Personal injury or illness	53
7	Marriage	50
8	Fired at work	47
9	Marital reconciliation	45
10	Retirement	45
11	Change in health of family member	44
12	Pregnancy	40
13	Sex difficulties	39
14	Gain of new family member	39
15	Business readjustment	39
16	Change in financial state	38
17	Death of a close friend	37
18	Change to different line of work	36
19	Change in number of arguments with spouse	35
20	Mortgage over $10,000	31
21	Foreclosure of mortgage or loan	30
22	Change in responsibilities at work	29
23	Son or daughter leaving home	29
24	Trouble with in-laws	29
25	Outstanding personal achievement	28
26	Wife begins or stops work	26
27	Begin or end school	26
28	Change in living conditions	25
29	Revision of personal habits	24
30	Trouble with boss	23
31	Change in work hours or conditions	20
32	Change in residence	20
33	Change in schools	20
34	Change in recreation	19
35	Change in church activities	19
36	Change in social activities	18
37	Mortgage or loan less than $10,000	17
38	Change in sleeping habits	16
39	Change in number of family get-togethers	15
40	Change in eating habits	15
41	Vacation	13
42	Christmas	12
43	Minor violations of the law	11

Fig 4.24 The SRRS

HOT EXAM HINT

Evaluation of the SRRS is always a good way to criticize research into life events. However, remember only to evaluate if the question asks for it.

HOW ARE THE SCORES INTERPRETED?

Holmes and Rahe (1967) proposed that there was a relationship between a participant's LCU score and their health (either illnesses experienced within the last two years, or yet to come!). They concluded that an LCU score of 150 or over increased the chances of developing a stress-related illness by 30%, while an LCU score of 300 or more increased the odds by 50%.

EVALUATION

Holmes and Rahe worked hard to ensure that their list covered a very wide range of events, including occupational, relationship, financial and so on. However, it could still be criticized for only providing events from American culture.

Hough et al (1976) argued that some items in the list are too vague or ambiguous. When we related the SRRS to Giles (in section 13), we had to select the item that said 'change to a different line of work'. If you remember, Giles was actually moving job; however there is no item in the SRRS that matches this exactly.

The SRRS does not recognize the role of subjective appraisal within the items (Lazarus and Folkman 1984). Death of a spouse would, for most people, be one of the most traumatic events in their life. However for some it might represent a happy release from an abusive relationship, not to mention the life assurance money!

The evidence that links scores on the SRRS and physical illness is correlational (that is, we cannot tell what caused what). It may well be that the stressful life events do not cause illness, but rather the illness manifests itself in life events (Brown 1986). For example, if someone was developing a physical illness, initially they might feel generally under the weather. This might have an adverse effect on their personal relationships – they might behave more grumpily than usual. This could break up their relationship with a partner. Equally they might start to under-perform at work, which could cost them their job. Soon after these two life events, the person might develop the symptoms of the full-blown illness. It would be impossible to tell whether the life events preceded the physical illness, or vice versa.

The SRRS paved the way for many similar scales – the life experiences survey (Sarason et al 1978), the unpleasant events schedule (Lewinsohn et al 1985) and even scales designed to be used with children (Johnson 1986).

The life experiences survey (Sarason et al 1978) allowed participants not just to identify stressful life events, but how they perceived them – either as negative or positive. Not too suprisingly, it was found that negative life events were better predictors of illness than positive events (DeBenedittis et al 1990).

STRESS AND THE WORKPLACE

INTRODUCTION

Most of us spend a large proportion of our lifetime at work. Work is usually seen as a means to an end (a way of acquiring money). People often complain how stressful their job is. All work creates a certain amount of stress. As we saw in section 3, we need enough **eustress** to reach our optimal performance. However, job performance, job satisfaction and physical health all suffer if workers experience excessive stress.

FOR CONSIDERATION

- It is estimated that at least 6.7 million working days a year are lost in Britain through work-related stress.
- Approximately 1 in 5 workers in Britain are affected by stress-related illness (around 5 million people).
- Estimates suggest that workplace stress is costing Britain's economy about £3.8 billion a year.

Fig 4.25 Cramped or disorganized work spaces can cause stress.

KEY DEFINITIONS

WORKPLACE STRESSOR
Any part of our work that is perceived as stressful and initiates the stress response.

FACTORS THAT CAN MAKE WORK LIFE STRESSFUL

Cooper et al (1988) identified five major categories of work stress. Within these groups are a number of sub-categories. The categories are as follows.

Factors intrinsic to the job

- Working conditions

Obviously, the physical surroundings in which work takes place have a direct effect on the amount of stress experienced in the job. For example, Glass et al (1969) found that unpredictable noise caused stress. However, predictable noise also increases stress levels. Cooper and Smith (1985) found that de-humanizing environments and repetitive tasks such as in assembly lines can generate high levels of stress. Telephonists in call centres report high levels of stress because sitting in one place with a headset on is restricting. Also, having to achieve a target number of calls per hour is pressurizing (Spires et al 2001).

- Shift work
- Long hours
- Risk and danger
- New technology
- Work overload
- Work underload

Role at work

- Role conflict

This is a term used to describe a serious difference between the needs of the organization and the needs of an individual. For example, a working mother may need to leave work at 3.00 pm to collect her children from school; however the organization requires her to be at her desk. This will inevitably lead to a conflict of interests. Studies have shown that white-collar foremen were seven times more likely to develop gastric ulcers than blue-collar workers – perhaps indicating middle management have more opportunities for conflict than shop-floor workers.

CD-ROM

Stress: Stress and the workplace
Stress: A certain type of manager

- Role ambiguity
- Responsibility

Relationships at work

- Superiors

You do not need to be a psychologist to appreciate that the relationship between a worker and their boss can have serious implications on the overall effectiveness of an organization. Buck (1972) found that when an employee's immediate boss was perceived as considerate there was friendship, trust and respect from the subordinate. Perceptions such as these have a tendency to reduce stress in social encounters.

- Subordinates
- Colleagues

Career development

- Job security

We all like to feel that our life has purpose and progression. However, within the work arena we may reach a point where progress is halted, because of lack of qualifications or because of age. Whatever the cause we feel thwarted and frustrated. This can lead to stress.

- Retirement
- Job performance

Organizational structure and climate

- Involvement

Being part of an organization can potentially threaten an individual's sense of freedom and autonomy. If the organization never listens to its workers' views and opinions it can take away their sense of belonging (Arnold et al 1995). Being part of an organization that you don't feel you belong to leads to stress.

- Unemployment

 **FOR CONSIDERATION**

The **status** of a job may influence how stressful it is. It seems logical that mundane repetitive jobs are more stressful than work with a lot of variety. However, as we have seen before change itself can be stressful. Lower-status jobs are more stressful because you have little control. However, senior management positions can be stressful because you have to make important decisions – the buck stops with you. Research has shown that stress can be found in both high- and low-status workers (McClean 1979).

 CD-ROM

To learn more about management styles, see CD-ROM section 4l.

 HOT EXAM HINT

It is quite common for examiners to ask you to describe a study into workplace stress. Make sure you learn at least one from the CD-ROM.

EVALUATION

Like most stress research, research into stress in the workplace tends to be correlational. This means we cannot be sure which element has caused which. Clearly a person's home life will impact upon their work life. Organizations need to take stress seriously, if for no other reason than the cost to them per year. Different styles of management and organizational ethos either increase or reduce workers' stress.

SECTION 16 | STRESS AND GENDER

INTRODUCTION

John had just had a very bad day. A deal he had expected to close was still being decided upon, and to top it all his brand new car had been scratched. The traffic was so bad driving home he pulled over and phoned a mate who lived nearby to see if he wanted to meet for a drink. He concluded that by the time he had a drink the roads might be clearer. John briefly told his mate about his terrible day, then they played pool.

Jane had just had a very bad day. A deal she had expected to close was still being decided upon, and to top it all her brand new car had been scratched. The traffic was so bad driving home she pulled over and phoned a mate who lived nearby to see if she wanted to meet for a drink. She concluded that by the time she had a drink the roads might be clearer. Jane explained in detail how the day had made her feel and her friend shared her equally unpleasant day. They had a drink and ended up going on to a restaurant, still talking about their feelings and life in general.

FOR CONSIDERATION

Before looking at stress differences between men and women, it is worthwhile considering the **general health differences** between the sexes.
- Women consult doctors more often than men do.
- Medical professionals tend to attribute stress-related symptoms differently to men and women. In men, stress is frequently attributed to external factors (such as their job or their lifestyle) whereas in women they are frequently viewed as being part of their personality.

KEY DEFINITIONS

SOCIAL SUPPORT
Using social interaction with people to provide emotional and/or practical help.

FOR CONSIDERATION

The three possible positions we could adopt are:
- Yes, there are differences and they appear to be cognitive, emotional and behavioural in nature.
- Yes, there are differences and they appear to be physiological in nature.
- No, there are no gender differences and any difference is down to individual variation rather than gender.

The case study above is a fine example of 'spot the difference'. Jane and John had identical experiences, but there were differences in the way in which they handled it. Could this imply that men and women deal with stress differently?

THE POTENTIAL DIFFERENCES WITH STRESS

Where stress is concerned, there are three positions that research could adopt when answering the question 'do men and women deal with stress differently?' (See left.)

Let us now consider the evidence with regard to each of these positions.

Social support

There is considerable evidence within the scientific literature that social support can act as a buffer in reducing some of the harmful effects of stress. In California, in 1984, a community education project was started entitled 'Friends can be Good Medicine'. It was designed to promote the physical and psychological health benefits of having friends around. We all tend to seek the company of others when we are anxious or stressed, and it is far more effective if we have a deep meaningful relationship with that person in the first place.

A number of studies suggest that females tend to use social support more effectively in times of stress. Henderson et al (1979) found that males reported using more social interaction during times of stress; however, females scored higher on the quality of the social interactions (think of Jane and John in the case study above).

Fig 4.27 Men and women have different ways of coping with stress

Coping strategies

Vingerhoets and Van Heck (1990) showed that men preferred 'problem-focused' coping but women preferred 'emotion-focused' coping.

Life events

It may be tempting to believe that if there are differences between men and women, these are due to exposure to life events. Perhaps men experience more stress-inducing life events than women, or vice versa. In fact, many of the studies suggest that there are no differences in the frequency or severity with which men and women experience stressful life events (Henderson et al 1980).

Women in the workplace

It has long been argued that the working environment places more stress on women than men, because they have a dual role as career woman and homemaker. On the other hand, being at home (particularly with young children) can potentially be very lonely and isolating. Cochrane (1995) believes that the stress of living in daytime isolation with a young child or children predisposes women to anxiety and depression.

Physiological differences

Studies have shown that men and women differ in physiological reactions to stress. Stoney et al (1990) demonstrated that men show a larger rise in blood pressure than women when given stressful tasks. Frankenhaeuser et al (1986) showed that heart rate and adrenaline concentrations both increase in men and women under stress, but cortisol levels and other physiological measures were very different.

WHAT HAS THE EVIDENCE TOLD US?

Social support – women are different to men (and the difference is psychosocial in nature).

Coping – men are different to women (and again the difference is psychosocial).

Life events – there appears to be no difference.

Workplace – women appear to suffer from stress more (because of the dual role they often have to take, as homemaker and career woman).

Physiological – men and women are similar in some physiological responses but different in others.

SECTION 17 | STRESS AND CULTURE

INTRODUCTION

The !Kung Bushmen of Southern Africa seek to take the stress response to its limits. They believe deliberately pushing the body and mind past normal experiences restores balance and harmony within the individual and the community. A tribesman achieves this 'therapy' by dancing, usually for at least 12 hours. By continually moving the dancer creates stress through sensory overload. The rhythm of the drums and hyperventilation in breathing creates an altered state of consciousness (Katz 1982).

CD-ROM

For more on the role of endorphins, see CD-ROM Stress: Some interesting facts about stress.

KEY DEFINITIONS

CULTURAL RELATIVISM
(As applied to stress) The idea that the experience of stress is shaped by a person's cultural background.

The 'paranormal' experiences described above may be due to a major release of endorphins from the excessive exercise. Dancing to the point of exhaustion creates a euphoric trance-like state (Jilek 1982). However, the most interesting point about this tribe is not the physiological explanation of the phenomenon, but their interpretation of stress.

IS STRESS CULTURALLY RELATIVE?

Stress occurs in every culture. However, the sources of and tolerance to stress vary between cultures. This is often a function of environment and upbringing. A young person growing up in a modern Westernized society may feel immense pressure to pass exams, go to university and then get a high-flying job. A young person growing up in a rural African tribal community may feel pressure (if they were a boy) to prove he had outstanding hunting skills. These are very different achievements, but both are potentially stress-inducing. So if stress is culturally relative, what are the implications for researchers?

IMPLICATIONS OF STUDYING STRESS

The anthropologist Allan Young (1980) views the concept of stress as 'culture bound' as well as class related. He argues that researchers (particularly Western scientists) frequently see stress as a disease caused by factors defined by middle-class white populations. As we saw in section 14, one criticism of the SRRS was that it failed to recognize different cultural stressors. All of the 43 life events were taken from American culture. Suggesting that there are 'universal life stressors' which produce a consistent response in humans is only acknowledging part of the story. Different cultures have many ways of experiencing stress that may not be easily understood by others. When trying to understand stress and cultural differences, scientists have tended to pursue three avenues of research:
- Comparisons within a culture
- Acculturation
- Presentation and management of stress

KEY DEFINITIONS

ACCULTURATION
The reorganization of a society to accommodate the presence of another cultural group.

COMPARISONS WITHIN A CULTURE

One interesting way of understanding the effects of stress on different cultures is to look at sub-groups within a culture. One area that has been well researched is the comparison of rural populations with urban.

Sutter (1980) found that urban Samoan children recorded higher stress hormone levels compared with rural children. Urban school children showed a steady decline in levels of stress throughout the year. It was suggested they were adapting to school life, therefore gradually finding it less stressful. Another interesting finding from this study was the difference in stress levels between urban (school-going) and rural (non-school-going) children at different times of the week. School children had highest levels of stress during the week, whereas rural children showed higher levels at weekends. This was the time most villages participated in rituals and feasting.

Evaluation

Studies such as these are quite well controlled in two ways:
1. They make comparisons within a cultural or racial group. Sutter compared two groups of Samoan children.
2. They use objective (physiological) measures of stress hormones to assess stress levels.

Studies such as Sutter's suggest that Samoan children's stress levels can be influenced by the type of environment they live in.

PRESENTATION AND MANAGEMENT OF STRESS

Some cultures view mental disorders not as a medical condition but as a family or spiritual issue (Rack 1982). The statistical medical incidence of certain disorders such as depression and anxiety will therefore be lower within these cultures. Sometimes stress can present in quite dramatic ways and still be culturally viewed as 'normal'. Guarnaccia et al (1990) proposed that it is quite normal in Puerto Rican culture to respond to stressful events with increased heart rate (tachycardia), fainting and seizures. In Britain this might be viewed as a little excessive!

Stress is also managed differently within different cultures. Many societies do not value consulting medically qualified practitioners about stress symptoms. They prefer to use the services of a healer or a spiritual leader.

Evaluation

The way in which stress symptoms present to a medical practitioner (or not) is often a direct reflection of how stress is viewed by that particular culture. Whether stress is seen as an illness or not will determine whether treatment is 'medicalized', or dealt with by family and spiritual leaders.

FOR CONSIDERATION

ACCULTURATION
This is a term used by anthropologists to describe the reorganization of a society to accommodate another cultural group. The stress upon both the immigrants and the indigenous population can be great. Stress researchers often find it useful to compare groups at different levels of acculturation within a population. Hobart (1975) found that Inuit (Eskimo) infant mortality was greater where parents had not adjusted well to a new culture. Nutrition and medical care were factors in this finding, but increased stress was also implicated.

To evaluate: changing culture is stressful in itself, but it also brings with it practical day-to-day stressors.

Acculturation studies do not provide direct evidence that the stress of integrating into another culture has adverse effects on the individual.

HOT EXAM HINT

You can always relate cross-cultural evaluation to a wide range of questions. For example, stressful life events vary across cultures; so too does the presentation and management of stress.

INTRODUCTION

There are of course many ways in which stress can be treated. Basically they fall into two categories: physical and psychological. Physical approaches focus on directly changing the underlying biological effects of stress, whereas psychological techniques focus on changing the thinking and emotion accompanying the stress response. This section is the first of five looking at different stress management techniques. Here we are going to look at prescription drugs.

KEY DEFINITIONS

ANXIOLYTIC
The name give to any drug that reduces the symptoms of anxiety. Anxiolytics can be grouped into three types of drug:
- Benzodiazepines
- Other (non-benzodiazepine) drugs
- Beta-blockers

CD-ROM

To learn more about how doctors approach stress, see CD-ROM Stress: GP corner.

KEY DEFINITIONS

GAMMA-AMINOBUTYRIC ACID (GABA)
A neurotransmitter of the central nervous system, believed to have a major inhibitory effect on neural signals.

BENZODIAZEPINES
A group of drugs that encourage the activity of GABA, thereby quietening down (or sedating) the central nervous system.

KEY DEFINITIONS

BETA-BLOCKERS
A group of drugs that block the action of noradrenaline, thereby reducing the physical symptoms of anxiety.

WHY ARE DRUGS USED?

One of the most effective ways of managing stress is to directly change a person's physiology. If the biological changes associated with the stress response can be reversed, stress will be reduced. Drugs provide the most direct method. Psychiatry attempts to treat stress by reducing anxiety, therefore anti-stress drugs are also anti-anxiety drugs (the more technical term being **anxiolytic**.) Before recommending counselling or psychotherapy (psychological interventions), family doctors seeing a 'stressed' patient may prescribe anxiolytic drugs as a starting point.

HOW DO THEY WORK?

Benzodiazepines

This group of drugs reduces the activity in the part of the brain that controls emotion. They enhance the action of a neurotransmitter (a chemical messenger in the nervous system) called gamma-aminobutyric acid (GABA), which blocks neural signals, thereby preventing excessive brain activity.

Other (non-benzodiazepine) drugs

Other non-benzodiazepine drugs include zolpidem and buspirone. Zolpidem does not work in quite the same way, biochemically speaking, as benzodiazepines; however its overall effect is the same. Buspirone helps by focusing on a different neurotransmitter, namely serotonin. By maintaining levels of serotonin within certain areas of the brain, feelings of anxiety are minimized.

Beta-blockers

Beta-blockers benefit by acting on the sympathetic division of the autonomic nervous system (ANS) (see section 5). As the name implies, they block the action of noradrenaline (norepinephrine), thereby reducing many of the physical symptoms of anxiety (for example racing heartbeat and sweaty hands).

HOW EFFECTIVE ARE THEY?

Drugs are a quick and cheap method of reducing stress (only the cost of a prescription). However, as they do not provide ways of coping with stress they are only a treatment and not a cure. Other pros and cons are listed below.

Benzodiazepines

Advantages:

- They reduce agitation and produce an overall calming effect on the individual.
- There is research evidence (for example Koenigsberg 1994) to suggest that anxiolytics can help facilitate psychotherapy interventions.

Disadvantages:

- In large dosages they can cause apathy and a slowing of mental awareness.
- Because the brain develops a tolerance to the drugs, they are usually only effective for a few weeks at a time.
- Benzodiazepines carry the risk of being abused, because of the 'chilled-out' effects they produce. This can result in both physical and psychological dependence.

Other (non-benzodiazepine) drugs

Advantages:

- They reduce agitation and produce an overall calming effect on the individual.
- Buspirone does not cause drowsiness.

Disadvantages:

- Buspirone's effects are not evident for at least two weeks after starting the treatment. During this time some people may stop taking the drug.
- There is some evidence suggesting that buspirone has the side effects of depression and headaches (Goa and Ward 1986).

Beta-blockers

Advantages:

- They reduce the physical symptoms of stress.
- They do not cause drowsiness.

Disadvantages:

- There is a risk of provoking breathing problems, particularly in people who suffer from respiratory disorders.
- Beta-blockers should not be withdrawn rapidly, particularly after prolonged use. This can cause a recurrence of the stress and anxiety, often in a more severe form.

HOT EXAM HINT

Frequently exam questions within this area assess your knowledge of anti-stress drugs (their names, and so on), but they also require you to evaluate the pros and cons of drug treatments.

SECTION 19 | BIOFEEDBACK

INTRODUCTION – WHAT IS BIOFEEDBACK?

Biofeedback is a stress reduction technique that, arguably, sits in between physical and psychological techniques. It is physical in the sense that individuals are connected to a variety of biological measuring devices, which provide them with readings of what is happening to their body. It is psychological in the fact that they learn (through operant conditioning) to control adverse feedback. Miller (1969) argued that contrary to previous beliefs, even the autonomic nervous system (ANS) (which is always defined as an involuntary system) can be brought under voluntary control, by applying operant conditioning, through biofeedback.

KEY DEFINITIONS

OPERANT CONDITIONING
The use of rewards to shape desired behaviours.

ELECTROMYOGRAM
A device used to amplify and measure the electrical currents generated in active muscle.

THERMISTOR
A device used to measure body temperature.

HOW DOES IT WORK?

The type of physical feedback instrument used depends upon the individual and the specific problem. Biofeedback can be used for specific conditions such as migraine and tension headaches as well as generalized stress symptoms. The two most common and effective instruments are:

- **Electromyogram (EMG)** – which measures the electrical activity of the muscles. Often it is connected to a tone machine which produces a high-pitched tone when the muscle is contracted and a low tone when it is resting. The objective of biofeedback is to learn to keep the tone low, thereby keeping muscles relaxed. The most commonly used muscle in generalized stress is the frontalis muscle (forehead).
- **Thermistor** – which measures body temperature. During tension the skin temperature drops due to peripheral vasoconstriction (a reduction of blood away from the skin to more vital organs such as the heart and brain).

THE PROCEDURE

Stage 1

An individual is connected to both an EMG and a thermistor. The EMG registers using a tone, and the thermistor uses a digital readout. The initial reading is high, due to the anxiety of the situation.

Stage 2

The psychologist instructs the individual to focus their thoughts on reducing particular bodily tensions. They provide the participant with a variety of progressive relaxation techniques.

Stage 3

Gradually, the readings reduce and the participant obtains a reward through observing that their stress was less. The procedure reinforces the person's sense of control over their bodily state.

Fig 4.27 'Did you say you could get Radio 1 as well, Mr Hawthorne?'

Stage 4

Once a conditioned response has been set up, the participant should
- Be able to recognise symptoms of stress
- Be able (through progressive relaxation techniques) to reduce any stress experienced **without the use of the machine**.

Evaluation

Advantages:

- It is a widely used and versatile technique. It can be used in isolation or in combination with other relaxation techniques (Phillips 1979).
- There is evidence that biofeedback is particularly effective with children. They are perhaps more open to try techniques such as these, and view them more as a game.

Disadvantages:

- There is very little evidence to support an overall muscle relaxation. For example, Alexander (1975) found that even though frontalis muscle relaxation occurred during biofeedback, there was no comparable relaxation in the arm or leg muscles.
- Shedivy and Kleinmann (1977) demonstrated that even though specific muscles can be trained to relax, this does not always lead to a subjective feeling of relaxation in the individual. It is no good having a very relaxed frontalis muscle if you still feel very stressed.
- There are problems with time, expense and location. The equipment required makes home use more difficult
- Silver & Blanchard (1978) concluded in a review that there was no consistent advantage of biofeedback over more conventional relaxation techniques.

HOT EXAM HINT

You may be asked to describe a physical approach to stress management, or biofeedback itself. Sometimes a question may ask you to evaluate physical approaches to stress management. Read what is required carefully.

STRESS INOCULATION TRAINING

INTRODUCTION

Stress Inoculation Training (SIT) was developed by Donald Meichenbaum and colleagues in the early 1980s. It is generally viewed as a cognitive–behavioural approach to stress management as it involves training an individual to recognize stress symptoms (hence 'cognitive') then teaching certain skills to alleviate that stress (hence 'behavioural').

HOW DOES IT WORK?

The training programme consists of three stages.

Conceptualization

This is where the participant discusses past stressful events (either individually or in a group setting). They consider what circumstances cause them stress and assess how they have tried to cope with it in the past. It encourages them to explore their cognitive appraisal of stress.

Skills acquisition and rehearsal

During this stage the therapist trains the participant in a variety of coping strategies. These usually include general skills such as relaxation techniques, as well as specific ones targeted at the individual. For example, if a single mother was finding looking after her child stressful, the therapist might well introduce a variety of parenting skills as well as teaching more general relaxation. The participant rehearses these skills under the supervision of the therapist.

Application

In this final stage the participant is encouraged to try out their newly acquired skills in a variety of settings. The therapist gradually introduces simulated stressors to test the participant's ability to cope. Follow-up sessions are scheduled to monitor their progress.

APPLYING SIT TO A CASE STUDY

John had never had much success at examinations. The thought of walking into the exam hall, sitting for an hour or so, trying to recall names and studies filled him with dread. His biggest anxiety, though, was letting his parents down. He knew how much they wanted him to do well.

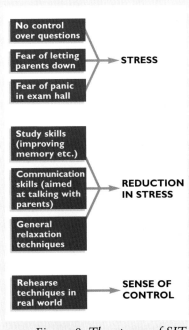

Fig 4.28 *The stages of SIT.*

Stage 1

John discusses with the therapist his past examination experiences. He identifies specific factors that cause him anxiety (for example, feeling he has no control over the questions), then he might explain his fears about letting his parents down.

Stage 2

The therapist might begin to implement a series of general relaxation techniques, including breathing exercises. These may be used in general anxiety situations. Then more specific skills are introduced. John may possibly benefit from study skills (including memory techniques). He may also gain confidence learning some communication skills, specifically aimed at sharing his feelings with his parents.

Stage 3

The therapist may want to try out some simulated exam experiences with John. They begin gradually – perhaps initially getting John to sit in a large room in silence for a few minutes (practising breathing exercises). It may also help if John discusses with his parents his worries over failing and letting them down.

HOW EFFECTIVE IS IT?

Advantages:

- Because SIT has a behavioural element, it provides practical skills that are directly applicable to real life.
- Compared with many other stress management techniques there has been limited research conducted into its effectiveness. However, the few studies that have been done suggest that SIT is an effective technique, and particularly useful for long-term change (Meichenbaum and Turk 1982).
- The strategies taught in SIT can be effective over quite long periods of time. As long as the participant continues to practise, the benefits can last years.

Disadvantages:

- SIT takes time, and willingness by the person to participate. It is also expensive.
- Because SIT combines a number of techniques (relaxation, cognitive appraisal, practical life skills and so on) it is very difficult to identify which specific component is contributing most to its overall effectiveness.

SECTION 21 | HARDINESS

INTRODUCTION

Tamsin was worried when she had to re-apply for her own job, but her concern only lasted for a few days. Tamsin was one of the successful ones. In fact she was relocated to London, something she had always wanted. Her move was far from easy, but as always she laughed her way through it, and still managed to go clubbing even though half of her furniture was still in storage. All in all it took six weeks to settle in, but in that time she acquired a new boyfriend, secured a promotion and gained a £5000 pay rise. Tamsin had always been resilient!

KEY DEFINITIONS

HARDINESS
A term introduced by Kobasa to describe personality characteristics that appear protective against stress.

The term **hardiness** refers to a group of characteristics that predispose individuals to resist the adverse effects of stressors. As the case study suggests, Tamsin had experienced a number of stressors recently; however, her personality was such that she was able to effectively deal with their adverse effects.

WHAT IS A 'STRESS-HARDY PERSONALITY'?

Kobasa (1979) suggested, from the findings of her study, that some individuals were not adversely affected by stress; in fact in some cases it gave them the opportunity to flourish (as with Tamsin in the case study above).

FOR CONSIDERATION

THE ORIGINS OF THE 'HARDY PERSONALITY'
In the late 1970s, psychologist Suzanne Kobasa conducted a long-term study into stress, on executives at the American telecommunications company AT&T. The organization was being broken up, and many employees were either losing their jobs or being reassigned. Over a period of 8 years she found two patterns emerged in the way these executives responded to stress:
- One group showed deterioration in both physical and mental health. The stress of change was affecting them in adverse ways.
- In contrast, the second group showed no signs of deterioration. Their physical and mental health remained good. If anything, they appeared more healthy and robust. Kobasa referred to this second group as having a 'stress-hardy personality'.

Since Kobasa first coined the term 'stress-hardy personality', psychologists have been attempting to identify its constituent components (Funk 1992). Kobasa (1979, 1986) suggested three characteristics of the hardy personality:
- They are committed individuals who approach tasks with motivation and purpose.
- They perceive situations as challenges rather than threats. By doing this they are often able to use highly effective strategies to minimize stressful effects.
- They frequently attribute a high degree of personal control over their lives. By doing this, they can create a sense of mastery over events. If things aren't going well, they need to adapt their thoughts, feelings and behaviours, rather than having to rely on someone else to change.

HARDINESS TRAINING

Clearly, if the above characteristics have been shown to be associated with the successful management of stress, it would be highly desirable to develop training based upon the development of these traits. This is precisely what Kobasa (1986) and subsequent psychologists have attempted to do. In essence, all hardiness training utilizes three strategies to 'deal' with stress:

- Participants are encouraged to identify symptoms of stress. The argument runs that if you can't recognize that you are stressed, it is unlikely that you will do anything about it. Kobasa calls this technique 'focusing'.
- The second major strategy teaches participants to appraise past stressful events and consider how they dealt with them. Were their perceptions of the event accurate? Were their coping strategies effective? The concept behind this is that people learn from the past. They are encouraged to reinforce the positive aspects of their coping strategies and eliminate the negative. Kobasa refers to this technique as 'restructuring stressful situations'.
- Kobasa also suggested that it is can be useful to take on another challenge in your life. This may sound like bad advice, particularly for someone stressed by work overload. However, the concept behind it is sound. If the participant can master the new challenge it will increase their confidence and feelings of control, which in turn can have positive effects on their perception of the original challenge. Kobasa calls this 'compensating'. For example, imagine that I was stressed because of excessive amounts of paperwork in my job. A trainer might suggest that I take on the responsibility of being chairman for a local model railway society (a role involving administration). If my administration skills were praised at the society, it might encourage me to try out similar administration strategies in my day job.

EVALUATION

Advantages:

- Fischman (1987) used hardiness training with a small number of male executives, and found that there was a significant reduction in reported stress symptoms such as headaches and insomnia.
- Sobel (1993) has shown that providing both information and practical techniques is most effective in developing 'health-enhancing' coping skills.

Disadvantages:

- Because the analysis of the original study was correlational, there has been much debate over the relative importance of each of the characteristics. Does being committed to a task increase hardiness more than attributing personal control to a situation? Because the characteristics are interrelated, it is very difficult to separate them out.
- Hardiness training requires time, money and commitment.
- Schmied and Lawler (1986) studied female secretaries. Having assessed them for a lack of 'hardy characteristics', they found no correlation with increased illness.
- Kobasa's original research was carried out on males. We should perhaps be cautious when generalizing to females.

HOT EXAM HINT

Questions might specifically ask you to describe what hardiness is, or they could ask you to evaluate its effectiveness. Do exactly what the question is asking.

THE ROLE OF CONTROL

INTRODUCTION

As you have seen in previous sections, the way people interpret stress (cognitive appraisal) directly affects its impact upon them. Karen in section 2 was clearly out of control and letting stress get the better of her. Simeon in section 3 did not interpret his lifestyle as stressful. He felt in control of situations. In fact, many psychologists suggest the concept of control is the most important factor when trying to understand stress.

KEY DEFINITIONS

CONTROL
The ability to anticipate circumstances and be prepared for them. A feeling of control can be either real or imagined.

WHAT FORM CAN CONTROL TAKE?

People can impose control over situations in a variety of ways. These could include the following.

Using social support

People can use the support of family, friends and/or work colleagues. This can provide a sense of emotional security – in turn, this can give a sense of control. For example, Jane in section 16 used her friend to spend the evening with to discuss their feelings.

Using information

Seeking knowledge or further information about an issue can provide a rational sense of control for an individual. For example, discovering that a certain illness rarely presents in a person under 50 could put a worried 25-year-old's mind at rest. Statistically, it would be very unlikely that they had it.

Using a belief system

Maintaining a belief that events in life are controlled by a higher power, that has an individual's best interests at heart, can be an effective way of utilizing control. It can also provide a sense of security and stability. Religious beliefs are a good example of this. For example, an effective way of coping with the stress of bereavement is to believe that you will meet that loved one again in an afterlife.

Adapting behaviour

This is where an individual will change their behaviour patterns to increase their actual control, or their perception of control. For example, if a person feels they are struggling on a course because of their limited information technology skills, they may decide to enrol on a computer course to improve their knowledge and their sense of control.

EVIDENCE LINKING STRESS AND CONTROL

Over the years many psychologists have attempted to uncover the links between stress and control. Some studies have found that people who have a strong sense of personal control over their life report stressors having less impact (for example, Elliott et al 1986).

LOCUS OF CONTROL

In 1966, Julian Rotter developed the **I–E** scale of control. He suggested that people attribute control over life events on a continuum, ranging from 'internality' at one end, to 'externality' at the other.

Individuals who believe they have control over their successes and failures in life are described as having an 'internal locus of control'. Those who believe their life is determined by 'outside' influences like luck or fate are said to have an 'external locus of control'. Most of us tend to sit somewhere in the middle.

SELF EFFICACY

Building upon this notion of internality/externality, Albert Bandura (1986) developed the concept of self efficacy. This suggests that people also make an estimation of how successful any coping strategy will be. For example, attempting an exam might be based upon the following features:
- I am intelligent and well prepared (internal locus of control).
- I have passed lots of exams before (an estimation of success).

In fact studies have shown that people with a strong sense of self efficacy, when placed in a variety of stress-provoking situations, show less psychological and physiological distress than those with a weaker sense of self efficacy (Bandura 1985).

It is suggested that our sense of personal control develops throughout our lives, based upon our own personal experiences (Phares 1987). As a child we learn that we are more successful at some things than others. But what happens when someone learns that whatever strategy they employ, it will always lead to a negative outcome?

LEARNED HELPLESSNESS

Martin Seligman (1975) suggests that through a process of 'bad past experiences', people stop striving for goals and instead adopt an apathetic approach to situations, often failing to exert control in situations where control is possible. He called this behaviour **learned helplessness**, and proposed that it was a major characteristic of depression. However, what this theory did not explain was why depressed individuals would blame themselves for things beyond their control. Seligman and his colleagues modified the original idea (Abramson et al 1978) by including the cognitive concept of attribution.

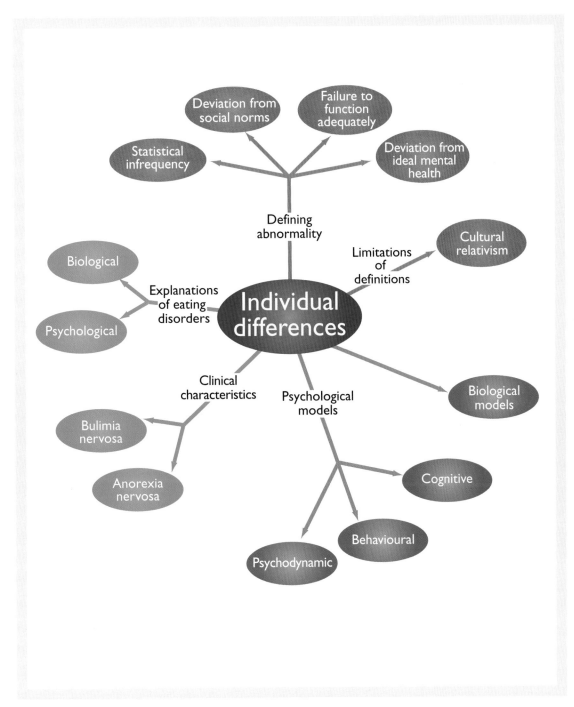

To prepare for the AQA exam you need to know the following things.

Defining psychological abnormality

Attempts to define abnormality
- Statistical infrequency
- Deviation from social norms
- Failure to function adequately
- Deviation from ideal mental health

Limitations of these definitions, including cultural relativism

Biological and psychological models of abnormality

Assumptions made by the biological (medical) model

Assumptions made by the psychological model
- Psychodynamic
- Behavioural
- Cognitive

Treatments of abnormality
- Drugs
- Psychodynamic treatment
- Behavioural treatments
- Cognitive treatments

Critical issue: eating disorders (anorexia nervosa and bulimia nervosa)

Clinical characteristics of:
- Anorexia nervosa
- Bulimia nervosa

Explanations of eating disorders
- Biological explanations
- Psychological explanations

INTRODUCTION

John Slater holds the record for being the only person to have ever walked from Land's End to John O'Groats in his bare feet, wearing only his striped pyjamas and accompanied by a dog (which was wearing suede booties).

Slater has had a number of jobs: Royal Marine bandsman, commando, truck driver, steward on a luxury yacht, social worker, insurance salesman, waiter, painter and decorator and public speaker. He has lived homeless in London so he could learn more about himself.

He has been married three times, and has endless ideas like volunteering to be a human exhibit at London Zoo to raise money for the conservation of pandas. His motto is 'wag your tail at everyone you meet' (Weeks and James 1995).

KEY DEFINITIONS

ECCENTRICITY
Unusual behaviour which does not 'fit' into the medical classification of mental illness.

Fig 5.1 Eccentric or abnormal?

CD-ROM

Individual differences: historical treatments for mental illness.

Would you describe John Slater as 'abnormal'? If you would, what criteria would you use to judge this? Is being abnormal the same as being mentally ill? Often, defining behaviour as abnormal overlaps with issues such as morality (particularly the concept of evil) and the law (Stone 1975). I don't think anyone could say that Slater acted immorally or broke the law; therefore perhaps all we could conclude was that his behaviour was unusual or eccentric.

TWO FACTORS WHICH INFLUENCE THE EXPLANATION OF ABNORMAL BEHAVIOUR

Historical time period

Throughout history, different explanations have been proposed in attempts to understand abnormal behaviour. Arguably one of the earliest of these was the concept of demonic possession. A person's 'strange' or bizarre behaviour was due to the fact they had become possessed by an evil spirit. Treatment involved 'exorcising' the demon, often in very barbaric ways.

During the so-called Dark Ages, particularly in Europe, another explanation for unusual behaviour (as well as unfortunate events) was witchcraft. When a person or an animal fell ill, the first thought was that they had been cursed. Communities believed witches had the power to heal as well as cast spells, making them a major threat to the rulers of the time. If they were found guilty of witchcraft they were drowned or burnt at the stake. The last witch executed by the authorities in England died in 1684; the last in Scotland in 1722. In Ireland the Witchcraft Act was not repealed until 1821!

By the early eighteenth century, people were beginning to realize that mental illness could be cured, or at least managed (controlled). New buildings were opened to house the mentally ill, known as lunatic asylums. In 1808, an Act of Parliament instructed every county in England to provide an asylum for the mentally ill.

Until the late nineteenth century, there were no laws governing the admittance of patients into an asylum. Many people were kept in against their will. In 1959 the law was changed: instead of a magistrate being able to commit a patient to an asylum, two doctors and a member of the family or a social worker were needed to sign.

As you can see, explanations for and attitudes towards abnormal behaviour have varied throughout history.

Culture and society

Not only does the historical time period influence the way in which abnormality is explained, but different cultures and societies have their own ways of explaining it. As you will gather in section 7, Westernized (particularly American) views tend to dominate the world stage. Theories of the causes and treatments of various mental disorders come from a Western scientific perspective. Any view that deviates from this is frequently regarded as primitive or unscientific. This cultural bias even affects what sorts of behaviours are defined as 'abnormal'. Hearing voices or seeing apparitions are seen as signs of illness within the Western model. However, these same behaviours are displayed by tribal witch doctors during rituals, and seen in their culture as vital communication links with the spirit world.

We must be careful not to assume that the modern Western views in explaining abnormality are the only ones. People's behaviour is defined by their culture, and the concept of what is 'normal' varies from society to society.

WESTERN PSYCHIATRY'S EXPLANATIONS

The way Western psychiatry explains abnormal behaviour can be understood by looking at the language it uses. To start with, psychiatry tends to view abnormal behaviour as **pathology**. The term 'mental illness' is used. Also, psychiatry involves recognition and definition of behavioural and emotional signs, symptoms and syndromes.

WESTERN PSYCHOLOGY'S EXPLANATIONS

As well as adopting the psychiatric viewpoint, psychology introduces a wider range of explanations. Sections 11–18 take a closer look at explanations required for your syllabus. In general, perspectives within psychology suggest abnormality is a product of faulty thinking or emotions. This in turn leads to abnormal behaviours.

KEY DEFINITIONS

PATHOLOGY
Related to a physical disease.

MENTAL ILLNESS
A label given to certain abnormal behaviours by psychiatry.

SIGNS
Objective findings observed by the clinician (in abnormal behaviour these might be uncontrolled vocal outbursts or unusual movements).

SYMPTOMS
Subjective experiences described by the patient (e.g. feeling 'down').

SYNDROMES
'Clusters' of signs and symptoms, which tend to present in the same way in most people. According to Western psychiatry, most mental illnesses are in fact syndromes.

PRESENT
When a patient consults a doctor.

FOR CONSIDERATION

DEFINING ABNORMAL BEHAVIOUR
Just as there are numerous explanations for the causes of mental illness, there are equally numerous definitions for it. As you saw at the beginning of this section, what may initially appear to be an easy task very quickly becomes complex. Your syllabus includes the following definitions:
• Statistical infrequency
• Deviation from social norms
• Deviation from ideal mental health
• Failure to function adequately

These will be considered individually in the next four sections.

SECTION 3 | DEVIATION FROM STATISTICAL NORMS

INTRODUCTION

So this was summer camp, thought Mike. Two weeks of activities with a bunch of strangers. His only concern was that apart from one boy, they all looked bigger, stronger and fitter than he did. He decided that out of forty lads he was average, thirty-eight were athletic and one was… well, going to struggle. Mike had noticed that every time this boy got worried he started to suck his thumb. This wouldn't be too bad except this was a camp for 15-year-olds.

If we are honest we have all done this before: made a judgement about someone's behaviour based on how many other people are displaying that behaviour. If the majority of the boys in the case study above had sucked their thumbs, then Mike may have started questioning whether *he* was unusual. Psychologists use this concept of 'rarity' as a basic definition of what is perceived as abnormal behaviour.

KEY DEFINITIONS

NORMAL DISTRIBUTION
A specific pattern in the spread of scores for an attribute in any given population. This pattern, when plotted on a graph, looks like a bell-shaped curve.

THE NORMAL DISTRIBUTION CURVE

Over the decades psychologists have found that in any given population, the degree of intelligence (as measured by an IQ test) tends to be distributed as shown in Fig 5.2. This is referred to as a **normal distribution** curve.

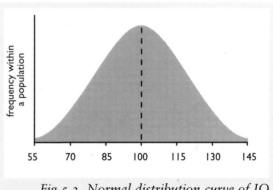

Fig 5.2 *Normal distribution curve of IQ*

KEY DEFINITIONS

STATISTICAL INFREQUENCY
In this model, behaviours that are extremely rare are defined as abnormal.

You can see from the graph that the majority of people score approximately 100. Very few (just over 2%) score below 70. Equally, very few score over 130 (again, just over 2%). The lowest and highest scores are said to be **statistically infrequent**.

Let us now apply this model to happiness. Imagine that we can objectively measure happiness levels and we find that just like IQ, it is also normally distributed, as in Fig 5.3.

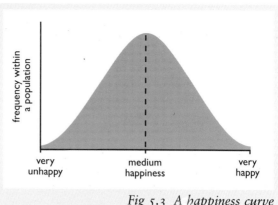

Fig 5.3 *A happiness curve*

On the face of it, it looks very straightforward. As with IQ, just over 2% of this population are extremely unhappy, and the same amount are ecstatic! However there are a number of problems.

- Where do we draw the line? At what point does someone 'move' from happiness to unhappiness?
- The model does not take into account whether the behaviour is socially desirable or not. Do we assume that it is undesirable to be unhappy?
- Using this model assumes that we can objectively measure concepts such as happiness. Converting behaviour into a score is a very touchy area of psychology.
- Because this is a statistical definition, it fails to acknowledge cultural and historical variation.

CRITICISMS OF THE STATISTICAL INFREQUENCY DEFINITION

The biggest issue regarding the 'cut-off' point (for instance between happiness and unhappiness) is that of who should decide where the line is drawn. Should it be psychiatrists, psychologists or the individuals themselves?

Another issue is the assumption that the cut-off point is determined using objective data. In all psychological concepts the collection of objective scores is extremely hard to achieve. In medicine, doctors have a slightly easier task, as all physiological measurements are based on objective biological processes. To say that someone's cholesterol is 'borderline high' indicates that, statistically speaking, he or she runs the risk of being ill. To say that someone is 'borderline unhappy' is an arbitrary term applied to a subjective concept.

The system of measurement used to determine the statistical frequency will not be based upon whether a behaviour is seen as desirable or undesirable. Running 100 metres in less than 10 seconds is statistically rare, but it is unlikely you would call the person who could do it abnormal. It is more likely they would be viewed as an exceptional athlete.

Because this definition also fails to acknowledge cultural and historical variation, another definition is applied, namely deviation from social norms. It is this we will consider next.

KEY DEFINITIONS

SUBJECTIVE
Refers to interpretation of information using personal experience or opinion.

OBJECTIVE
Refers to interpretation of data using measurable outcomes (as opposed to subjective).

HOT EXAM HINT

You may be asked to outline the features of the 'statistical infrequency' definition. Remember this does not require any evaluation of the definition, just a description and an example.

DEVIATION FROM SOCIAL NORMS

Imagine you see a person shouting rhythmically and incomprehensibly in the middle of a shopping centre, their body jerking and contorted. You would probably think their behaviour was abnormal. Now imagine you see a person behaving exactly the same way at the climax of a tribal ritual. For the onlookers this might well appear perfectly normal. The difference is that the first breaks Western social norms of how to behave in a shopping centre. The second is an example of 'socially normal' behaviour for a tribal ritual. The behaviour is the same; the social context has changed.

WHAT ARE SOCIAL NORMS?

Every society has a set of unwritten rules that underlie individual behaviour. These are very different to laws, which are explicit and clearly defined. For example it is unlikely that you ever had lessons in how to behave in a restaurant, yet most of you would know what to do. Even behaviour in class is governed by an unwritten convention. A student who started to do a striptease in class would risk being labelled as weird or abnormal by the rest of the group. Many of these 'rules' are learnt during childhood, through the socialization process. What is deemed acceptable behaviour depends upon the society into which a person was socialized.

Behaviour can be interpreted as normal or abnormal using a number of criteria. Let us now look at the types of norm used to make that judgement.

TYPES OF NORM

Cultural

As we saw in the example at the beginning of this section, the cultural context of the behaviour informs us of its 'normality'. Most of us have not personally experienced a tribal ritual like the one described; however, we have probably seen enough Hollywood films to conclude that as tribal rituals go this behaviour is quite normal. The behaviour of the person in the shopping centre, on the other hand, is not.

Situation and context

Behaviours may be judged using moral criteria or context. Going to the toilet is a normal human behaviour; however, going in the middle of a supermarket is not. This is both a moral and situational issue.

Age

In all cultures, be they Westernized or tribal, behavioural norms depend upon age. A three-year-old can stare at someone, shout out, and even take their clothes off in public, without causing disruption (save embarrassment to the parents!). If a thirty-year-old businessman did the same, onlookers might feel differently.

KEY DEFINITIONS

SOCIAL NORMS
Usually the unwritten rules in a culture or society.

DEVIATION FROM SOCIAL NORMS
Departing from or breaking a society's unwritten rules.

SOCIALIZATION
The way in which people learn the rules of any given society.

PSYCHOSIS
Being out of touch with reality.

SCHIZOPHRENIA
A serious psychotic disorder in which people have episodes of losing touch with reality.

FOR CONSIDERATION

In fact, during the 1950s and 1960s psychiatrists such as Laing and Szasz even proposed that severe mental disorders such as schizophrenia were not physical abnormalities, but conditions in which sufferers were not conforming to the norms and conventions of the society in which they were living. For researchers such as Laing and Szasz, mental illness was not about pathology (physical abnormality), but more to do with the interpretation of behaviour.

Gender

Western cultures have defined specific dress codes and behaviours for males and females. Crossing the boundaries would more than likely be construed as abnormal. However in recent times the norms have shifted. Often high-profile celebrities lead the way with unconventional clothing or opposite sex role behaviours. David Beckham made it cool for men to wear a skirt (in actual fact a sarong). Lily Savage has made a career out of being a transvestite.

Historical

Whether behaviour was classed as normal or abnormal has often depended on the historical time period. In Victorian times, attitudes to sexuality were highly repressed. Women were seen as wicked, deviant or perverse if they engaged in sex outside marriage. Attitudes towards masturbation were harsh, viewing it as an evil sin which led to physical illness including blindness. Today however, overt sexuality is seen as quite a normal way of promoting products, records or films.

Fig 5.4 Lily Savage

Interestingly, changes in social attitudes can influence the medical profession itself. Probably the best example of this is homosexuality. Up until 1973, homosexuality was classified as a mental illness. Owing to pressure from gay rights activists and many within the medical profession, it was removed from the American Psychiatric Association's official classification of mental disorders. Imagine a homosexual 'patient' turning up for his appointment, only to be told that the medical profession no longer views him as ill! This clearly illustrates the problem with labelling behaviours as illnesses.

CRITICISMS OF THE DEVIATION FROM SOCIAL NORMS DEFINITION

The legal position

Often, the laws of our society influence our ideas regarding normality and abnormality. I think most of us would agree that killing someone is an abnormal behaviour. It is also currently illegal. However:
- If it occurred in battle (for instance in the Second World War), the person would be regarded as a war hero.
- If it is deemed acceptable and legal by a peacetime society (as in the death sentence in some states in America), then it is not seen as abnormal.

The ethical/moral position

This is where behaviours are deemed 'right' or 'wrong'. Most of us could define behaviours on a hierarchy of 'rightness' and 'wrongness'. Many people, would put acts such as paedophilia (sexual interest in children) at the top of their 'wrongness' lists; for others it would be murder or rape. Frequently you will hear people say that certain behaviours are 'sick' or 'perverse'. In a way they are making a comment on social acceptability.

HOT EXAM HINT

As with the statistical infrequency definition, you may well be asked to outline this model. Remember to describe it, and give an example.

SECTION 5 | DEVIATION FROM IDEAL MENTAL HEALTH

INTRODUCTION

John was the most successful sales executive they had. Every month he exceeded his targets, and even found time to help other reps who were struggling. His social life was also successful. He was independent, yet needed the company of others. He was confident but not arrogant. He was rarely flustered but wasn't emotionally cold. In fact, all in all he had 'ideal mental health'.

KEY DEFINITIONS

IDEAL MENTAL HEALTH
A set of behaviours which combine to produce a 'healthy state of mind'. It is seen as a state everyone should aspire to.

DEVIATION FROM IDEAL MENTAL HEALTH
Lack of, or movement away from, the qualities that contribute to a healthy state of mind.

SELF ACTUALIZATION
A term coined by Maslow to describe a state in which a person has reached their 'true potential'.

Maslow's hierarchy of needs

Self actualization	To reach one's potential
Self esteem needs	To have self respect, self belief
Social needs	To be accepted by others
Safety needs	Shelter, freedom from danger
Physiological needs	Adequate food, water, temperature

Fig 5.5 People must satisfy each level before they can move up the triangle.

As I am sure you are aware, people like John are very rare. They are usually happy and contented individuals who tend to enjoy a successful life. But what are these 'ideal' characteristics that most of us strive to achieve?

WHAT IS IDEAL MENTAL HEALTH?

Over the years, some psychologists have put together ideas and theories that pick up where philosophers and theologians (people who study religions) have left off. In many ways these areas of psychology are akin to philosophies of life or routes to spiritual enlightenment. Important thinkers include Abraham Maslow, who developed a highly influential theory describing various levels of human motivation – the **hierarchy of needs** (Maslow 1954). He terms the highest level as 'self actualization' – a state in which an individual realizes their own unique potential. According to Maslow, self actualized people are characterized by an acceptance of themselves, profound interpersonal relationships, creativeness and a philosophical sense of humour. These qualities give self actualized individuals an advantage in life as they are more psychologically well adjusted than 'non-self actualizers'.

CHARACTERISTICS OF IDEAL MENTAL HEALTH

The concept of trying to identify characteristics of ideal mental health continued when in 1958 Jahoda published a book entitled *Current concepts of positive mental health*. In it she identified six criteria of mental health. According to Jahoda, any deviation or omissions from these criteria could pre-dispose a person to a mental disorder. Let us briefly look at each in turn and assess their relevance.

Self attitudes

Holding positive attitudes towards yourself is a key feature of psychological health. Accepting who you are, and positively building upon that acceptance, leads to the development of a 'strong' sense of self and high self-esteem.

It is unlikely that any society or culture would disagree with this point. Eating disorders, depression and anxiety have all implicated poor self-esteem as a major symptom.

Autonomy

Jahoda proposed that relying upon yourself (being autonomous) was an important feature of psychological health. Being dependent upon others for your own well-being gives control of your life to other people.

Some commentators have criticized this criterion, suggesting that a sense of independence is culturally relative. In modern Westernized cultures it is a valued commodity; however in many other societies co-operation and reliance on others is valued.

Perception of reality

Jahoda suggested that accurate and realistic judgements of oneself and the world are characteristic of psychological health. Also, being able to adapt judgements, knowing when to be optimistic or pessimistic about events, is an important feature.

There is a philosophical problem with the definition of reality. Many people argue it is not an objective concept. Humans create their own reality within their own minds. On the basis of this it is almost impossible to say whether someone's perceptions of reality are accurate and realistic or not.

Adaptability

Being able to adapt to change quickly and effectively is viewed by Jahoda as an important characteristic of psychological health.

For our ancient ancestors, being able to adapt to a changing environment increased the likelihood of survival. However it must be remembered that not all adaptation has a positive outcome, and to judge mental health on this criteria is quite limiting.

Fig 5.6 *'I'm thinking of saving up for a Mercedes.'*

Self actualization

Jahoda based this criterion on Maslow's theory regarding 'self actualization'. The idea that all humans have the chance to fulfil their true potential has a simplistic appeal. It seems perfectly logical that if a person's 'full potential' is never realized they will remain unhappy and unfulfilled. This emotional state can ultimately manifest itself in a variety of mental illnesses.

The true potential of an individual is always defined by the culture in which they live. A young tribal boy may aspire to be the best hunter in his village; however it is unlikely that this would be a goal for a teenager in London. The idea of 'true potential' is good one, but being able to define and measure it is much more complex.

Integration

'Integration' is the term Jahoda used to describe being able to cope effectively with the stresses of life. Again, she viewed it as an important characteristic of being psychologically healthy. As you saw in chapter 4, stress frequently leads to physiological and psychological illness.

It is important to remember that Jahoda did not suggest that psychologically healthy people don't have stress in their lives; what she said was that they are able to cope with it more effectively.

CONCLUSION

The concept of 'ideal mental health' approaches abnormality from the opposite perspective: measuring the amount of deviation from an 'ideal goal'. However, as with all deviation models it is difficult to know how far we can generalize from one culture to another, and whether there would be universal agreement on the 'ideal qualities'.

SECTION 6 | FAILURE TO FUNCTION ADEQUATELY

INTRODUCTION

Kevin has been out of work for the past five years. His last employer asked him to leave because apart from being continually late for work, he was making so many errors. He has trouble dressing himself in the morning, often putting his trousers over his pyjamas and frequently wears a bow tie with a creased T-shirt. Social services visit once a week to tidy his house and help him with his food shopping. Ironically Kevin is exceptionally bright, possessing an IQ of more than 140.

Having read the case study above it is difficult to know whether Kevin is suffering from a recognizable mental disorder. Clearly Kevin is far from normal, but we are only basing that assumption on the fact that he is not able to function adequately (without help) in a modern Westernized society. So does this mean that 'failure to function adequately' should be seen as a recognizable definition of mental illness?

KEY DEFINITIONS

FAILURE TO FUNCTION ADEQUATELY
Behaviour that interferes with everyday life (for example, inability to dress yourself, or do a job) could be classed as abnormal.

Fig 5.7 Failure to function adequately?

WHAT IS FAILURE TO FUNCTION ADEQUATELY?

An easy way to understand this definition is to think of it in terms of coping. People who cannot cope with the demands of everyday life, and therefore engage in what might be seen as bizarre behaviours, should be defined as abnormal. But how do we know what constitutes bizarre or abnormal behaviour?

THE SEVEN FEATURES OF ABNORMAL BEHAVIOUR

Rosenman and Seligman (1989) proposed that there are seven main features of abnormal behaviour. These are as follows.

Suffering

Frequently mental illness causes anxiety or distress to the individual. They are aware that they are 'different' to many other people and often this compounds the problem.

Some mental disorders do not appear to cause suffering or distress. Patients with anti-social personality disorder (formerly referred to as psychopaths), tend not to suffer themselves, but instead inflict suffering on their victims.

Violation of moral codes

Behaviour is frequently labelled as abnormal if it 'breaks' moral codes. Exposing your genitals in a restaurant or spitting at a teacher are both examples of this.

One of the problems with this is that morality varies from culture to culture and over different time periods. Also, morality varies depending upon context. Exposing your genitals in a strip club could be seen as more socially acceptable (depending upon your view of strip clubs) than exposing them in a restaurant.

Maladaptiveness

Maladaptiveness can refer to behaviours that stop an individual from reaching a particular goal. For example, having a plane phobia may be perfectly acceptable for someone who rarely travels abroad. However, if your job required you to fly frequently, then the phobia would prove to be a major problem. It could be regarded as a 'maladaptive' behaviour.

Using the term 'maladaptiveness' gives no indication of the severity of the maladaptive behaviour, or whether it is specific or more generalized. For example, most of us engage in behaviours that aren't particularly useful or good for us, but it doesn't necessarily make us abnormal.

Vividness and unconventionality

Any behaviour that is unusual will stand out. Having a metal bolt pierced through your nose, your hair dyed green and 'I hate the world' tattooed across your forehead might be viewed by some as a little different. It would be more unconventional if the person who had this done was your GP.

Whether a dress code or behaviour is viewed as unconventional depends upon the views of the person making the observation. The more 'conformist' an individual is, the more 'abnormal' they may view the above example.

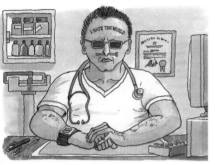

Fig 5.8 'Next!'

Unpredictability and loss of control

A major characteristic of normal behaviour is being predictable and controlled. Being predictable makes relationships run more smoothly, and people feel at ease in your company. Often people are fearful of mental illness because they see sufferers as being unpredictable or 'out of control'. This is particularly true of some of the more extreme disorders such as schizophrenia.

Irrationality

A major criterion for classifying behaviour as abnormal is the view that a person is behaving irrationally. However we must remember that, theoretically, any behaviour can appear irrational if it occurs 'out of context'.

Defining behaviour as irrational depends upon the culture, the historical time period and the context in which it is occurring.

Observer discomfort

Watching someone behave in a way that is out of context frequently causes social discomfort and embarrassment for the observer. This is only true if the observer does not know the motives behind the 'strange behaviour'.

I have witnessed the rather amusing incident of a woman sitting in a shopping centre, a shopping bag in each hand, apparently talking out loud to no one. On closer inspection, I realized that she was speaking into a tiny hands-free mobile phone, which had been totally obscured by her hair. I had judged her talking out loud in public as 'strange', without fully understanding what she was doing.

CONCLUSION

Of the four definitions we have looked at, the definition using failure to function adequately is not based upon the concept of deviation. Its focus is on the fact that an individual is not able to 'function', as they should in any given society. Ultimately this leads to social rejection and stigmatization.

SECTION 7 | CULTURAL RELATIVISM

INTRODUCTION

We have already seen in other sections that cultural differences have a major impact on how mental disorders are defined, even to the point of whether they are classified as abnormal at all. The cultural background a person belongs to shapes their experiences and behaviours. This means all mental illness is **culturally relative**.

KEY DEFINITIONS

CULTURAL RELATIVISM
Refers to the concept that abnormal behaviour must be judged within the context of the culture it occurs in. It is relative to its own culture.

WHY CONSIDER CULTURE?

The psychiatrist Thomas Szasz (1960) argued that physical abnormality could be defined in universally applicable ways. Psychological abnormality involves making moral, philosophical and cultural judgements. This raises the question whether all mental illness can be defined in objective, biological terms. If it can then it wouldn't matter which cultural background you were from. Having tonsillitis is a universal human experience. If you are infected then you will produce symptoms. How those symptoms are interpreted and treated is dependent upon cultural beliefs. However, the jury is still out regarding the biological status of mental illness and until this issue is resolved (if ever), the study of culture has a special importance for psychology and psychiatry. The attitudes and beliefs people have towards an illness can have far-reaching implications. Consider the following example.

John Crook, a British psychologist, was researching the Ladakhi peoples of North West India. When he asked what incidence of mental illness doctors in the region encountered, he was told, rather surprisingly, none (Crook 1997). To a Western scientist this seemed an improbable answer. It transpired that all psychological disturbances were treated and managed by a system outside of Westernized biomedicine. It was viewed as 'possession' ('jug') and treated by village 'oracles' or 'healers'. So why is this example so useful? Well, it demonstrates two important points.

- To have misunderstood or ignored this cultural difference would have meant that Western outsiders might have believed that they had stumbled across the happiest and most psychologically balanced group of people on the planet. In reality of course this was not the case. Cook found evidence of depression and anxiety; it was just that their manifestation and treatment was very different.
- It illustrates that even though the Westernized biomedical model may be the dominant one worldwide, it is not the only one.

Fig 5.9 A tribal witch doctor

KEY DEFINITIONS

CULTURE-BOUND SYNDROMES
Mental illnesses that appear unique to a particular culture.

More recently, Westernized doctors have included cultural relativism in mental illness classification systems. They are referred to as **culture-bound syndromes**.

 **CD-ROM**

Individual differences: Culture-bound syndromes

CULTURE-BOUND SYNDROMES

Some disorders appear to only be found in certain cultures or certain groups. They frequently occur with little warning, they tend to be short lived (acute) and the outcome is usually favourable (they tend to recover).

CULTURAL ISSUES IN DIAGNOSIS

Back in 1851, the American psychiatrist Cartwright introduced two disorders exclusively for black people. These were:

- **Dysaesthesia aethiopis** – which described certain behavioural traits including being idle, clumsy, dirty, drinking too much and stealing, all caused according to Cartwright because they were 'free Negros' and had no master to supervise them.
- **Drapetomania** – which described a condition where black slaves ran away.

It may seem incredible to us today that such contrived and spurious disorders could be invented, just to control and subdue American black slaves. However, there are some commentators who argue that cultural inconsistencies still occur today within diagnosis. Black people in the UK are more likely to be diagnosed schizophrenic or compulsorily admitted to psychiatric hospital (Fernando 1988). It has also been suggested that Asian women frequently 'somatize' (experience physical symptoms) when they are anxious or depressed. So what explains this?

Fernando (1991) argued that because the clinical interview between a patient and a health care professional is a social interaction, it can never be truly objective. Cultural differences between the patient and clinician are an obvious area for subjectivity to creep in. Misunderstandings can occur for a number of reasons – they might include:

- Language difficulties
- Lack of understanding of religious issues
- Different moral codes
- Lack of understanding of the role of family
- Lack of trust (usually from the patient towards the clinician)

Winter (1999) took this explanation a stage further by suggesting that the majority of doctors making diagnoses are white, middle-class men who have been socialized and trained in Western ideals. They 'may be biased against, or insufficiently sensitive to the cultural and social situations of black, working-class or female clients' (Winter 1999).

 KEY DEFINITIONS

CLINICIAN
Someone who works directly with patients.

 HOT EXAM HINT

You may be asked to consider how cultural differences influence the definition of abnormality. Remember this is an analytical/evaluative type question.

CD-ROM

To learn more about analytical/evaluative questions, see the CD-ROM section on exam questions.

CONCLUSIONS

Taking into account the cultural background of the individual demonstrating the abnormal behaviour can help in explaining the origins, the symptoms and the treatment of the condition.

INTRODUCTION

Within any area of human experience, psychologists try to identify gender differences, and mental illness is no exception. Over the years many studies have been published that show the incidence of a particular disorder significantly varies between the sexes. For example, depression seems to be more common in women than in men. As budding psychologists we need to ask ourselves two questions regarding these findings:

- Is this difference due to biological variation between the sexes? If not, then is it due to environmental and social differences?
- Are there other factors that skew these results? For example, incidence of depression can only be recorded when a person presents to their doctor. Men could be just as depressed as women, but on average, they don't present as frequently.

Let us look at some of the classic disorders where differences occur.

GENDER BIAS

KEY DEFINITIONS

GENDER BIAS
In medical statistics, the fact that one gender presents with a particular condition more than the other.

FOR CONSIDERATION

Other examples include **suicide** and **alcohol abuse**.

Suicide is not specifically a mental disorder but many depressed people consider it and some make genuine attempts to end their lives. Men are four or five times more likely to commit suicide (Davison and Neale 1998), though there is evidence that the gap is closing.

Alcohol abuse is a major health problem in Britain and the USA. Kessler et al (1994) found lifetime prevalence rates for alcohol dependence in America of 8% in women and over 20% in men.

An increase in the range of alcoholic products has altered drinking behaviours. In the USA, 50% of men and 40% of women engage in binge drinking (Wechsler 1994).

Eating disorders

Anorexia nervosa (an eating disorder characterized by restricting the amount of food a person consumes) is a disorder on the increase in Westernized cultures.

It is about 10 times more common in women than men, and appears more frequently among groups where body image is of paramount importance, such as models, dancers and so on (Garner and Garfield 1980).

Eating disorders will be looked at in depth in sections 19–22.

Depression

Major depression is arguably the most common mental disorder worldwide. About 17% of sufferers tend to have it throughout their life (Blazer et al 1994).

Depression is almost twice as common in women as in men. On the other hand, bi-polar depression (a form of depression characterized by extreme mood swings) occurs equally often in men and women. However, it has been shown that on average, women tend to experience more episodes of depression (low mood) and men experience more episodes of mania (a 'hyper-mood' state).

Autism

Autism is a disorder in normal development that begins in early childhood. It is very rare, occurring in 0.05% of births.

Approximately four times more boys than girls have autism.

Fig 5.10

Sexuality

Various surveys have suggested approximately 4% of males are homosexual (although Kinsey et al in their ground-breaking report on human sexuality back in 1948 estimated it was nearer 10% – many men wouldn't openly admit to being gay). Lesbianism (female homosexuality) has been estimated at 1%.

Other sexual disorders such as transvestism, voyeurism and exhibitionism are almost exclusively male activities (Moir and Jessel 1989).

EXPLANATIONS

As we pointed out earlier, there could be genuine biological reasons why gender differences occur. However it is unlikely that these alone could explain it. For example, let's suppose that having high levels of oestrogen led people to develop eating disorders. This would mean virtually 100% of women would be sufferers (as women have significantly higher levels of this hormone than men). As this is not the case, researchers look for more individualistic and social explanations (see left).

As we suggested earlier, incidence of mental illness can only become a statistic when it is presented to a doctor. On the whole men tend not to present with psychological disorders as frequently as women. It could be that men tend to use distracting coping strategies such as watching the TV or playing sport more than women do, while women tend to think about issues for longer periods of time and often blame themselves (Nolen-Hoeksma 1990).

FOR CONSIDERATION

One major social explanation (like those based on cultural bias) for the difference could be **differential diagnosis**. Women's symptoms are diagnosed differently to men, based upon sex-role stereotypes. Broverman et al (1981) asked clinicians to identify what they believed to be the characteristics of a healthy adult, a healthy man and a healthy woman. Clinicians tended to use similar adjectives for the adult and male (such as 'decisive' and 'assertive'); however, terms such as 'dependent' and 'emotional' were used to describe the woman. Clinicians were being influence by their own sex-role stereotypes.

HOT EXAM HINT

You could bring in an example from gender when evaluating any aspect of abnormality.

INTRODUCTION

In section 7 we explored the idea that different cultures present with different mental disorders. We suggested that 'abnormality' could only be defined within the context of a specific culture. However, much research has focused upon racial differences in terms of the incidence of specific illnesses, the usage of mental health care and racism within diagnosis. This section will consider each of these in turn.

KEY DEFINITIONS

RACE
The ethnic group to which a person belongs. People in a group tend to inherit the same physical characteristics, such as skin colour or hair type.

RACIAL DIFFERENCES IN VARIOUS MENTAL DISORDERS

It is a fact that the historical mental illness literature (published journal articles) frequently portray black people as being sick. Sometimes this would be in the physical sense, as 'black skin' was often seen as a form of leprosy, or in a psychological sense (black slaves who ran away from their masters were seen as ill – see section 7 for more details).

Even more recent studies suggest that this racial bias continues. Boogra and Mallett (1996; cited in Brewer 2001) conducted a study in Camberwell and Ealing, London, comparing three groups: white, Afro-Caribbean and Asian. They found that the Afro-Caribbeans were nearly twice as likely to be diagnosed as schizophrenic than the other two groups, based on the presentation of the same symptoms.

Sayal (1990) found twice as many black people as white people were given 'compulsory admission' to mental institutions within the UK.

THE USAGE OF MENTAL HEALTH SERVICES

There is very little research looking at how different racial groups require and make use of mental health services. It has been argued that this is partly because as racial minority groups became established in Britain, the need to view them as having specific requirements diminished. They were seen as part of the community as a whole.

Some research has suggested that minority groups tend to use the available mental health services less (Snowden and Cheung 1990). Rack (1982) pointed out that Asian cultures tend to view 'mental disturbance' as a social or spiritual issue, which is best dealt with by a religious leader or family. For this reason conditions such as depression rarely present to a medical doctor and therefore are very 'under-diagnosed' in Asian culture.

WEST INDIAN PSYCHOSIS

This is a term used by many psychiatrists to describe an atypical (not typical) form of psychotic disorder. Frequently the sufferers are black Afro-Caribbean males who do not show the classic symptoms of either schizophrenic or manic depressive psychosis.

Littlewood and Lipsedge (1989) suggest this condition is an acute psychotic stress reaction to racism. It should not therefore be confused with schizophrenia, and does not need the same treatment. They identify other minority groups (for example Arab immigrants in France, Turkish migrant workers in Germany, Eastern European immigrants in Australia) who have also shown paranoid reactions similar to West Indian psychosis. They conclude these reactions can be found in any disadvantaged minority group, and are a response to the experience of discrimination, not a characteristic of race.

RACISM WITHIN DIAGNOSIS

In societies such as Britain, which are predominantly white, the mental health care needs of racial minority groups frequently tend to go unnoticed, or are misunderstood by Westernized health care professionals. Torkington (1991) cites the case of a 51-year-old black man who was admitted to hospital suffering from convulsions and severe leg pains. Rather than treat the man's symptoms as an indication of a physical illness, staff referred him to an acute psychiatric ward where he died about an hour later. Because he was black, they had assumed that his disorder was psychiatric in nature rather than physical.

Fernando (1992), himself a psychiatrist, has for many years argued that western psychiatry is racist. He suggests 'theory and practice are permeated by racist ideology'. Indeed the evidence seems to back this up.

- There is an over-diagnosis of schizophrenia among West Indian and Asian British people. This means that for the same symptoms, disproportionately more individuals from these groups were diagnosed as schizophrenic, rather than any other illness (Fernando 1992).
- Fernando found there was an excessive use of locked wards of West Indian, African and Asian British people, in psychiatric hospitals, when compared with British white people.
- There is evidence that while in psychiatric hospitals, black patients are more likely to be seen by junior doctors, and to receive sedative medication and electroconvulsive therapy (Littlewood and Lipsedge 1989). All these treatments hand control of the management of the disorder to someone else, and away from the patient (as opposed to psychotherapies, which require much more verbal interaction).

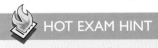

HOT EXAM HINT

Use the information in this section in conjunction with section 7 when answering a question on cultural relativism.

As Brewer (2001) points out, the Royal College of Psychiatrists has set up a working party on ethnic minority Issues to try to address some of the issues we have looked at in this section. However, more cynical commentators suggest that as the great majority of psychiatrists are white men, racial bias will continue.

SOCIAL CLASS AND ABNORMALITY

INTRODUCTION

For over 150 years lower social class has been linked to poorer physical and mental health. But what exactly is social class?

Fig 5.11 Does where people live affect their susceptibility to mental illness?

SOCIAL CLASS

Social class is a method of classifying people, often in terms of their occupation. As you can imagine it is a highly complex and debated area of sociology. The most frequently used system is the Registrar General's classification system, which allocates individuals to one of six occupational groups:

Professional	social class I
Managerial and lower professional	social class II
Skilled non-manual	social class IIIN
Skilled manual	social class IIIM
Partly skilled	social class IV
Unskilled	social class V

RESEARCH LINKING MENTAL ILLNESS AND SOCIAL CLASS

Numerous studies have shown a link between lower social class and mental illness. Below are some examples.

- Merikangas and Weissman (1986) reported that personality disorders tend to affect urban rather than rural populations, and those of lower social class.
- Robins et al (1984) point out that rates of schizophrenia are highest in groups with poor education and lowest socio-economic status.
- Robins et al argued that one reason why women have, on average, the highest rates of depression is that the majority used in research studies are less educated and belong to lower social classes; the poverty element was the key feature. However, no element of society escapes depression. Professionals, the wealthy and the famous suffer from this disorder (see Brewer 2001).

As you are possibly beginning to see, a major contributing factor is poverty. However, some studies have shown that even within the different classes **social adversity** can affect the incidence of mental illness.

RESEARCH EVIDENCE

Dohrenwend et al (1992). Socio-economic status and psychiatric disorders: the causation–selection issue. *Science.*

Aims

A study conducted in Israel by Dohrenwend et al in 1992 attempted to show a causal link between social status and mental illness. Their hypothesis was that within each ethnic group individuals varied in education and occupational attainment (so there was an equal distribution across classes); the only difference was that North African Jews (who have low status in Israel) experienced more 'social adversity'. They would be more prone to mental illness across classes.

Procedure

The researchers used samples of North African Jews (who have low status in Israel and are often vulnerable to prejudice and disadvantage) and compared them with European Jews (who have high status). They were assessed for onset of psychiatric illness.

Findings

The researchers found that disorders such as depression (among women) and anti-social personality disorder (among men) were more frequent in all social classes among the North African Jews than for European Jews. These findings seemed to support the idea that social adversity was responsible. The incidence of schizophrenia was seen equally across both groups of Jews, predominantly in the lower social classes.

Conclusions

Incidence of mental illness does seem to be affected by social adversity. However, disorders such as depression and anti-social personality disorder appear to be 'caused' by social adversity, whereas schizophrenia does not.

Criticisms

- Other factors could have affected the results. Although the method of the study was well constructed, it still does not prove the role of social adversity, even though the results are consistent with it.
- To what extent can we generalize the findings to British populations?

EVALUATION

Having assessed the evidence, why is it that things such as poverty and social adversity correlate so highly with mental illness?

- It is unlikely that the lack of material possessions gives rise to mental disorders. Developing schizophrenia or multiple personality disorder is not dependent on how much money a person has. However, being poor or socially disadvantaged increases stress.
- There is good evidence that when people are stressed they are more vulnerable to illness in general, including mental illness (see chapter 4). Having a poor education, being part of an alienated group in society and having no money (with limited job prospects) increases stress, and makes it very difficult to cope with. This is the most likely link between social class and mental illness.

HOT EXAM HINT

Using evidence about social class is an excellent way of evaluating almost any question on abnormality.

SECTION 11 | THE MEDICAL MODEL OF ABNORMALITY

INTRODUCTION

The professor by now was in full flow, but a casual glance at his watch told Jeremy that he was about to conclude.

'So to summarize. I believe one day all illness, be it physical or mental, will be explainable through biological processes. Let's face it, if we hadn't got a physical brain we wouldn't be capable of thinking at all. Thank you.'

What an interesting lecture, thought Jeremy's mind – or was it his brain?

The dominant assumption made by Western science is that the mind is a by-product of the physical brain. It is logical to conclude that all mental activity has its origins in biology.

KEY DEFINITIONS

THE MEDICAL MODEL
An explanation of abnormal behaviour that suggests it is physiological in nature.

WHAT IS THE MEDICAL MODEL?

The medical model is the name given to a group of explanations that suggest mental illness is caused by underlying biological or physical factors. These factors include structural abnormalities (of the nervous system), bio-chemical imbalances and genetic predispositions. Viewing abnormality as a physical illness means it becomes a medical problem and this in turn influences the types of treatment used.

EVIDENCE FOR THE MEDICAL MODEL

One obvious way of testing the medical model is to assess its predictive abilities (do observed results follow what the model tells us will happen?). Let us imagine that an investigator believes that an imbalance of a particular chemical found in the nervous system is primarily responsible for the symptoms of schizophrenia. It would be easy to test this hypothesis: vary the amounts of this chemical in individuals and observe the resultant effects on behaviour.

THE DOPAMINE HYPOTHESIS

This is exactly what happened (in a more accidental way) when the drug chlorpromazine was first synthesised in 1950. It was developed as an anti-psychotic drug treating the symptoms of schizophrenia. It works because it reduces the effects of a **neurotransmitter** called dopamine (neurotransmitters are chemical messengers within the nervous system). Scientists have long believed that excessive production of dopamine leads to 'psychotic behaviours' (Seidman 1983). Taking chlorpromazine significantly reduces psychotic symptoms. However, if dopamine is too reduced, it leads to a condition known as **tardive dyskinesia**, which produces movement abnormalities very similar to Parkinson's disease.

Fig 5.12 Identical twins

Incidentally, low levels of dopamine are found in Parkinson's disease. Giving the drug L-dopa to sufferers increases dopamine levels, and alleviates the symptoms.

So what was proposed was a 'dopamine seesaw', with psychotic symptoms at one end and Parkinson's symptoms at the other. The prediction would be: decrease dopamine and you will observe Parkinson-like symptoms; increase dopamine and you will see psychotic symptoms.

However, as in most scientific endeavours, inconsistencies have started to emerge within the hypothesis, recently prompting some researchers to question the simplicity of the link (Barlow and Durand 1995).

Another way of testing the medical model of abnormality would be to look for relationships between DNA and behaviours. Identical twins provide an excellent method of assessing the genetic contribution to behaviours, because they share identical DNA. One very contentious area where this has been studied is in homosexuality.

EVALUATION OF THE MEDICAL MODEL

- Even though these scientific explanations are based upon empirical research and objectivity, cures to mental disorders have still remained elusive. Drug treatments have frequently proved effective, but this still does not mean that the disorder was originally caused by biological factors.
- The 'gay gene' example shows that being predisposed towards behaviour is different to causing it. Knowing there are biological differences between people still does not help identify the origins of a disorder.
- A major problem is identifying which came first: the underlying biological abnormality or the psychological disorder. Usually, by the time a person takes part in a study they are already taking medication (it would be unethical not to give them medication). However, this means that the investigators can never be sure whether biological changes are due to the disorder or to side effects of the medication.
- In terms of ethics, labelling a person's 'abnormal' behaviour as 'medically ill' can be problematic. Also, attaching a medical diagnosis to behaviours can excuse the individual from any responsibility. This can lead to all kinds of ethical dilemmas. Imagine a defence lawyer in court saying 'I'm sorry, your honour, my client couldn't stop himself raping those women, it's in his genes'.

SECTION 12 | MEDICAL TREATMENTS

INTRODUCTION

As you saw in the previous section, the medical model of abnormality assumes that abnormal behaviour stems from a physical source. It follows therefore that treatments within this model focus upon changing underlying biological processes. Sometimes medical treatments are referred to as 'somatic' (from the Greek 'soma', meaning body). This distinguishes them from psychological treatments (psychotherapies), which focus on the mind. We will look at three somatic treatments, namely drugs, electroconvulsive therapy (ECT) and psychosurgery.

DRUGS

What do they treat?

Prescription drugs that are specifically intended to change or alter behaviour are collectively referred to as **psychotropic drugs**. It has been estimated that more than one quarter of all prescriptions dispensed by the NHS in Britain are for 'behaviour altering drugs' (DuQuesne and Reeves 1982). Psychotropic drugs are divided into certain categories, depending on the disorders they are intended to treat.

Are they effective?

There is little doubt that psychotropic drugs are effective at changing behaviour. However there are other issues to consider.

Drugs are not a cure: Psychotropic medications cannot cure a disorder as an antibiotic can cure an infection. All they can do is alleviate the symptoms. For this reason patients may become psychologically dependent upon their drugs.

ELECTROCONVULSIVE THERAPY (ECT)

During the 1930s two Italian doctors, Ugo Cerletti and Lucio Bini, proposed that naturally occurring convulsions in epileptic patients could produce positive changes in mood (after the symptoms of the convulsions had subsided). They developed a method of passing a moderate electrical current through a patient's head, by positioning an electrode either side.

Initially it was used with psychotic patients, but later it was found to be highly effective with severely depressed patients.

What is the procedure and is it effective?

In the early days, because patients had not been adequately sedated, often the electrical shock would jerk them off the bed, causing injuries such as broken bones. In some cases the convulsion would cause patients

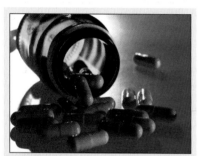

Fig 5.13 Psychotropic drugs

CD-ROM

Individual differences: Psychoactive drugs

FOR CONSIDERATION

DRUGS: IMPORTANCE OF CORRECT DIAGNOSIS

As we have often seen defining abnormal behaviour is difficult. It is assumed that doctors who prescribe these drugs are experts in diagnosing mental illness. However, one American study found that primary care doctors (usually GPs or junior hospital doctors) prescribed 72% of antianxiety drugs during a specified period, compared with 10% for psychiatrists (Beardsley et al 1988). Physicians not specifically trained in psychological disorders were writing the largest percentage of prescriptions. The figures would probably be similar in Britain.

Fig 5.14 *Electroconvulsive therapy*

to bite their tongue off. Nowadays, the procedure is much safer. Patients are totally sedated with muscle relaxants and anaesthesia and the electrical current is kept to a minimum. Electrodes are attached to one side of the head (unilateral) or both sides (bilateral), depending upon various medical decisions. The typical course of treatment involves about six sessions, usually about two or three treatments per week.

Studies have shown that as many as 50–70% of severely depressed patients who do not respond to drug therapy show considerable improvements with ECT. There is also evidence that improvement is far quicker than with drug treatments, which could be very beneficial if there is a chance that a patient is at risk of committing suicide (Janicak et al 1985).

Evaluation

Side effects: One of the most common side effects is temporary memory loss (usually for about 24–36 hours after treatment). MRI scans (brain scans) have shown there is no damage or change to brain structures after ECT (Lader and Herrinton 1990).

How does it work? Despite its widespread use, medical scientists do not still fully understand why or how it works. It is generally assumed to 'kick start' the brain by causing a cascade of chemicals, including noradrenaline and serotonin. This imprecise knowledge of how it works is seen by many as a serious ethical problem.

PSYCHOSURGERY

One of the first and arguably the most notorious of forms of surgery to change behaviour was the **prefrontal lobotomy**. This involved surgically removing the frontal lobes of the brain in an attempt to make schizophrenic and violent patients more compliant. Antonio Moniz was awarded the Nobel Prize for medicine in 1949 for developing this technique.

Is it effective?

A university lecturer of mine once pointed out that you didn't need to be a brain surgeon to understand that removing a great chunk of brain would quieten people down. It was effective but at huge costs. Often patients would be apathetic after surgery and show diminished intellectual functioning. With the development of more sophisticated and targeted psychotropic drugs, the need for 'brutal' surgical techniques diminished. Today drugs have taken the place of psychosurgery, and it is only used in extreme circumstances.

Evaluation

Arguably, out of the three somatic treatments discussed this is the most extreme. Once a patient had surgery they could never return to how they were. The ethics of deciding which patients underwent the treatment and which parts of the brain were to be severed or removed totally were highly controversial.

☕ FOR CONSIDERATION

ETHICS OF DRUGS AND ECT
However effective the treatments, there are always ethical considerations. Changing people's behaviour through drugs or ECT can be viewed as highly invasive, as it takes responsibility for treatment away from the patient. Also, drugs can have unpleasant side effects that have to be weighed against any clinical advantage. What is more, drugs can always have the potential of causing new symptoms, sometimes even worse than the existing ones. In the case of ECT, it is also seen by many as unethical to use a treatment that is not fully understood.

Fig 5.15 *Surgeons performing brain surgery*

🔥 HOT EXAM HINT

It is always a good idea to learn the medical model (section 11) and the medical treatments (this section) together. Questions often ask you to describe or outline both.

THE PSYCHODYNAMIC MODEL OF ABNORMALITY

INTRODUCTION

Juliet had a very unusual style of managing her staff. One moment she would be their best friend, telling them what she did at the weekend, encouraging them to take long lunches and sometimes sharing intimate details about her latest boyfriend. The next minute she would be critical, spiteful and bullying, often subjecting them to verbal humiliation. Certain conversational topics seemed to cause this change in personality – particularly if she felt that she had been made to look foolish or incompetent.

KEY DEFINITIONS

PSYCHODYNAMIC MODEL
Another term for Freud's psycho-analytical theory. It highlights the fact that the psyche is constantly in a state of change or flux (the 'dynamic' part).

UNCONSCIOUS
The part of the mind not directly open to conscious scrutiny.

Fig 5.16 Sigmund Freud

CD-ROM

Individual differences: Freud's psychosexual stages

Nobody likes to feel incompetent, but the way we respond to these emotions tells a lot about our past. Juliet clearly has issues – her response to possibly quite minor comments is nasty and fierce.

Interestingly, it is unlikely she has much of an insight into why she responds the way she does. This lack of insight could arguably make her changes in mood appear abnormal. The psychodynamic model tries to explain abnormality by presenting a theory that attempts to address irrational behaviour.

WHAT IS THE PSYCHODYNAMIC MODEL?

The psychodynamic model of abnormality was based originally on the work of Sigmund Freud (1856–1939). Since his death other psychologists have modified and developed his ideas, but some still adhere to its original form. Thomas (1996) suggested there are a number of principles that underlie the psychodynamic tradition – let us consider each in turn.

The role of the unconscious

Freud proposed that most human behaviour was not what it seemed. The idea that logic or rational thought always preceded an action was often not true. Instead he argued that our motives were driven by 'unconscious forces' to which we do not have direct access. These 'unconscious forces' were based upon early childhood experiences.

The role of childhood

Freud placed great emphasis on the first 5 years of a child's life, during which it undergoes three stages of psychosexual development. If a child experienced 'emotional trauma' during these years, the 'emotional memory' of this trauma would be etched into the unconscious.

In adulthood the 'memory' might manifest itself in a number of ways; perhaps through some behavioural abnormality such as a phobia, or, as in the case of Juliet, by becoming hurtful and aggressive when the person felt 'got at'.

Alternatively, the 'emotional memory' might manifest itself in the form of a physical illness. Freud was particularly insistent that conditions such as eczema and asthma had their origins in early psychological conflict.

The role of the ego

Freud proposed that our understanding of the world is distorted to avoid anxiety. The **ego** (the part of the personality that lives in both the conscious and unconscious mind) uses defence mechanisms to protect us against psychological pain and anxiety.

These mechanisms include:
- **Repression** – this is where painful memories are forced deep into the unconscious mind, thereby forgotten by the conscious.
- **Denial** – this is where the conscious mind convinces itself there is no problem.
- **Projection** – this involves 'projecting' the anxiety onto other people. In many cases it involves criticizing other people. Juliet, in the case study, engaged in this particular mechanism.

Psychoanalysis

The psychodynamic approach uses psychoanalysis as a method for treating abnormality. Analysts are trained to interpret signs and symbols within conscious behaviour, to discover their underlying unconscious motives (psychoanalysis is covered in section 14).

KEY DEFINITIONS

PSYCHOANALYSIS
The name given to the type of treatment developed by Freud during the 1890s.

EVALUATION

The psychodynamic model is arguably one of the few models of abnormality that attempts to explain irrational behaviour. It takes responsibility for abnormal behaviour away from the individual: they can't help doing what they do because their actions stem from their unconscious mind.

Freud believed that early childhood was responsible for all adult abnormalities. Post-Freudians such as Erik Erikson (1963) argue that emotional conflict can influence our behaviour at any stage of life, not just the first five or six years.

This model is almost impossible to test scientifically. Fisher and Greenberg (1977), after an exhaustive review on the evidence on Freud's work, conclude: 'it is a complex structure consisting of many parts, some of which should be accepted, others rejected and the rest at least partially re-shaped'.

SECTION 14 | PSYCHODYNAMIC TREATMENT

INTRODUCTION

As we explained in the previous section, the basic assumption of the psychodynamic model is that traumatic emotional memories from childhood lead to abnormal adult behaviours. It follows therefore that psychodynamic treatment (or **psychoanalysis**, as it is more commonly known) attempts to identify unconscious conflicts. When they are made conscious, the patient is 'relieved' of the trauma and therefore cured.

When I asked you to go back to your childhood, I didn't mean literally...

Fig 5.17

PSYCHOANALYSIS

Traditional psychoanalysis was developed by Sigmund Freud (1856–1939) and became intrinsically linked with his theories. In fact his theoretical ideas were based on his clinical consultations, ironically, exclusively with middle-class Viennese women.

THE METHOD

Free association

The basis of Freud's therapy was listening to then interpreting his patients' **free association** – in which the patient was allowed to talk without interruption or prompting. He was interested in what they omitted in their conversations as well as their choice of words. For example, the word 'home' has more powerful emotional connotations than house. Ignoring your father when describing family events could indicate an unconscious emotional problem with him. Nearly always, the patient is not consciously aware of what they're doing.

Transference and counter-transference

It isn't just dialogue that is important in psychoanalysis. Non-verbal factors are vital also, particularly in the therapeutic process itself. Freud was the first person to suggest that patients use the therapist as a sort of emotional punchbag. This is more technically known as **transference**. The analyst's response to this process is known as **counter-transference**. Freud first noticed transference when a female patient, awaking from hypnosis, put her arms around him and kissed him. Rather than taking it at face value, Freud believed that he was representing someone else in receiving the woman's affections. Perceptive readers may feel that Freud's interpretation of this encounter provides an interesting insight into his own self esteem – think about it!

Fig 5.18 Freud's couch

Dream analysis

Freud also analysed his patients' dreams. He described the interpretation of dreams as 'the royal road to the unconscious' (Freud 1900). He suggested that the content of a dream (what Freud called the 'manifest content') hid the true or underlying meaning of the dream (what he referred to as the 'latent content').

Interpreting the manifest content could reveal the unconscious mind (the latent content).

CD-ROM

Individual differences: Freudian dreams

Cure

Does psychoanalysis cure mental disorders? This is arguably the most important aspect of the treatment, and the most hotly debated. As you can see below this question forms the central theme in any evaluation of psychoanalysis. Freud argued that psychoanalysis did work, but only when a patient was able to 'discharge' a repressed emotion (a process referred to as **abreaction**) by 're-experiencing' it on the analyst's couch.

In the early days of psychoanalysis abreaction was seen to be therapeutic in itself, regardless of whether the patient understood the significance of the repressed experience (Freud 1895). Later, many post-Freudians suggested that patients needed rational insight as well as 'emotional discharge' to cure their psychological disorders.

Duration

Psychoanalysis can continue indefinitely, which can make it a very expensive treatment. Sessions typically last 50 minutes, even though the patient pays for 1 hour. Initially, patients can be recommended to attend four or five sessions per week; however this may be reduced to once or twice after a period of time.

KEY DEFINITIONS

EMPIRICAL
Refers to data obtained using scientific method, as opposed to untested ideas.

EVALUATION

Some empirical studies suggest that psychoanalysis is no more effective as a treatment for mental disorders than doing nothing at all. In one classic study Eysenck (1952) found that while 44% of patients showed 'cure' having undergone psychoanalysis, 66% 'got better' without undergoing any form of therapy at all.

Fonagy (2000) proposes that psychoanalysis is most beneficial to patients with mild neurotic disorders. For more severe symptoms, the benefits appear to be reduced.

Some GPs will not refer patients to psychoanalysts on the NHS – they have to pay privately.

HOT EXAM HINT

If you are asked to evaluate or assess the psychodynamic model of treatment, don't forget to make reference to studies that have looked at its effectiveness.

Garfield (1980) found that psychoanalysis is most effective with patients who are young, attractive, verbally skilled, intelligent and successful (take the first letter of each of these and you get YAVIS). If the patients have these qualities you wonder why they have come for analysis in the first place!

THE BEHAVIOURAL MODEL OF ABNORMALITY

INTRODUCTION

One morning, Lucy was standing in the corner of the playground watching the dustmen empty bins. As the lorry reversed back it accidentally crushed a wheelie-bin against the wall. The sound of cracking plastic was very loud and traumatized the on-looking Lucy. The following day at playtime Lucy refused to go outside and started to cry. Her teachers and parents couldn't understand where this fear had suddenly come from.

ASSUMPTIONS OF THE BEHAVIOURAL MODEL

Unlike the 'deep' irrational, emotional explanations of the psychodynamic model, the behavioural model views abnormal behaviour as inappropriately learnt responses. It is therefore very much a 'surface' explanation. In the above case study, Lucy had learnt an inappropriate response to the playground (being fearful of it) because of a traumatic event. Neither her teachers nor parents could understand the fear, because they had not seen the event occur.

Behavioural psychologists propose that abnormal behaviour can be acquired through the following: classical conditioning, operant conditioning and social learning. Let us look at each in turn.

CLASSICAL CONDITIONING

The principles of classical conditioning are originally based upon the work of Ivan Pavlov (1849–1936). He demonstrated that dogs (the animals he used in his laboratory) could be trained (conditioned) to produce saliva to a variety of stimuli (such as a bell ringing). The natural 'salivary reflex' occurs when animals are exposed to food – the sight, smell or taste is sufficient to produce the response. Pavlov's technique overrode this natural reflex. The typical process is as left.

So how does this apply to abnormal behaviour? Behavioural psychologists argue that if a person experiences a strong emotion when placed in a particular situation or confronted by a particular object, they learn to associate this experience with the event. Lucy may have learnt her abnormal fear of playgrounds through classical conditioning.

Evaluation of classical conditioning

Results from studies such as the one by Watson and Rayner (1920) suggest phobias arise through classical conditioning.

Menzies and Clark (1993) found that only 2% of children who had hydrophobia (fear of water) had experienced any past trauma associated

---

KEY DEFINITIONS

CLASSICAL CONDITIONING
(As applied to abnormality) Learning inappropriate behaviour through association.

Food	→	Salivatory reflex
Food + bell	→	Salivatory reflex
Bell	→	Salivatory reflex

CD-ROM

Individual differences: Classical conditioning: technical terms

FOR CONSIDERATION

A toddler hearing his mother scream when seeing a spider in the bath may be so traumatized by his mother's response that he develops arachnophobia (fear of spiders) himself.

CD-ROM

Individual differences: Watson and Raynor's study

with water. This would suggest that classical conditioning was not responsible. Classical conditioning doesn't explain why some people go on to develop abnormal behaviour while others don't, particularly if they have been exposed to the same event. Also, it doesn't explain why certain associations are made and not others. For example Lucy could have developed a fear of wheelie-bins or walls rather than of the playground.

OPERANT CONDITIONING

The principles of operant conditioning are based on the work of Burrhus Frederick Skinner (1904–1990): behaviour that is **reinforced** (rewarded) will continue, and behaviour that is punished will cease.

Behavioural psychologists argue that these processes can lead to the development of abnormal behaviour. For example, if a person experiences very little social support, or even worse, hostility from others, this becomes a form of punishment. They often become de-motivated and withdraw from social interaction. This can lead to depression (Lewinsohn 1974).

Evaluation of operant conditioning

Suggesting that abnormal behaviour can be shaped through operant conditioning places the responsibility for the disorder in the environment or social setting. This model tends to focus on the present rather than past events. For example, if the 'punishment' is removed from the environment, then arguably the abnormal behaviour will cease.

SOCIAL LEARNING

The third behavioural process assumes individuals learn abnormal behaviours through social interaction. Frequently this involves observation and imitation. If a child observes a maladaptive behaviour they may well 'copy' it without realizing the consequences. For example, observing an adult shake or scream when climbing a ladder may lead a child to do the same in a similar situation. It is likely that at some stage the child will interpret their symptoms as fear, and therefore a phobia of heights may emerge.

Evaluation of social learning

Once again, social learning theory places the blame for abnormal behaviour on those around us. Arguably, spending time with an anxious or a depressed person will encourage the imitation of their symptoms. As we saw with the height phobia, this approach assumes that cognitive interpretation always follows the behaviour. We may become fearful of heights not simply because we have witnessed anyone showing fear symptoms, but because we understand that we might fall.

Social learning is culturally relative. Imitating a behaviour from another culture may well be perceived as abnormal.

KEY DEFINITIONS

OPERANT CONDITIONING
(As applied to abnormality) Learning inappropriate behaviour through reinforcement.

CD-ROM

Individual differences: Operant conditioning: technical terms

FOR CONSIDERATION

Individuals who eat normal amounts of food may be criticized as being 'chubby' or 'fat', which encourages them to reduce their food intake. As time goes on and they lose weight they are praised for how good, attractive or slim they look. This reinforcement encourages the weight loss, creating the potential for the person to develop an eating disorder.

KEY DEFINITIONS

SOCIAL LEARNING
(As applied to abnormality) Learning inappropriate behaviour through observing and imitating others.

MALADAPTIVE BEHAVIOUR
A behaviour that causes you harm (physical or mental).

HOT EXAM HINT

Always be ready to identify the pros and cons of the behavioural model of abnormality.

BEHAVIOURAL TREATMENTS

INTRODUCTION

As we discussed in the previous section, the main assumption of the behavioural model is that abnormal behaviour has been learnt. It should seem quite logical that any behavioural therapy is about 'unlearning' this maladaptive behaviour and replacing it with a more adaptive or appropriate set of behaviours. The other major feature of behavioural treatments is that they do not view the sufferer as 'ill', but as a victim of maladaptive behaviour. While medical and psychoanalytical treatments tend to refer to participants as 'patients', behavioural and cognitive techniques tend to refer to them as 'clients'. Behavioural techniques include aversion therapy, implosion (flooding) therapy, systematic desensitization therapy (SDT) and token economies. Let us briefly consider each in turn.

KEY DEFINITIONS

BEHAVIOURAL TREATMENTS
These are treatments and therapies that focus on 'unlearning' maladaptive and inappropriate behaviour.

CD-ROM

Individual differences: Aversion therapy

AVERSION THERAPY

This technique has been used for many years and is based upon the principals of classical conditioning. An unpleasant association is combined with a behaviour that the individual wishes to stop, or as in some cases, is told to stop by the psychologist. The most widely used application is with addictive behaviours.

Evaluation

Meyer and Cheese (1970) found that 50% of alcoholics who had used this therapy abstained from alcohol for at least 1 year. Using electric shocks and emetics is considered by some as an extreme and unethical form of treatment. However, more commonly today people are asked to imagine unpleasant events or outcomes, and associate them with the addictive behaviour, rather than experience the real thing. The success rate depends upon the participant's motivation and determination.

CD-ROM

Individual differences: Flooding therapy

IMPLOSION (FLOODING) THERAPY

This technique was developed by Wolpe (1960). It is used for the treatment of phobias, and involves a direct and extended exposure to the phobic stimulus. The theory is that after a while the person begins to relax (because they can't escape from it). This feeling of relaxation gets classically conditioned to the original fear.

Evaluation

The biggest problem with this treatment is the ethics. Forcing people to confront their fears head on is seen by many to be extreme. For this reason, people undergoing this form of treatment need to be healthy and give their voluntary consent. Sometimes there are practical limitations on how a client can be exposed to a fear. Forcing someone to go up in an aeroplane or climb a mountain can be costly and time consuming.

SYSTEMATIC DESENSITIZATION THERAPY

Unlike the full-intensity exposure of implosion therapy, systematic desensitization therapy (SDT) involves a step-by-step exposure to the phobic stimulus. These steps are referred to as a 'fear hierarchy', running from the most bearable to the least. Between each step, clients are encouraged to relax often by visualizing a pleasant experience.

Evaluation

This therapy is seen as having fewer ethical problems than aversion or implosion therapy. There is evidence that it is effective as a treatment. For example, Wolpe (1958) was able to treat one of his clients who had developed a fear of dying after the death of her husband. Because a client can monitor their progress as they progress up their fear hierarchy, they get a sense of achievement – this can act as positive reinforcement.

TOKEN ECONOMIES

This is a form of behaviour modification that is based upon operant conditioning (see previous section). In simple terms, clients are given some form of token (usually plastic discs) that can be exchanged for rewards. These might include cigarettes, sweets or access to leisure facilities. This system is most widely used in mental institutions, young offender establishments and prisons.

Evaluation

There is good evidence that token economies are effective in reducing abnormal symptoms. For example, Paul and Lentz (1977) found that long-term hospitalized schizophrenic people, having been exposed to a token economy, showed significant improvements in social and work-based skills, and required less medication. Again there are ethical problems with this approach to treatment. Some commentators argue that token economies are nothing more than a form of social control, where socially accepted behaviours are rewarded: compliance through bribery.

Fig 5.19 'Mr Smith, I think that you've misunderstood the point of token economies...'

If a patient/client has become used to an institution that rewards 'good' behaviour, when they are re-integrated back into the community they may well expect the same treatment. When people they meet in their day-to-day encounters do not respond with positive reinforcement, they may well get despondent and depressed and experience a relapse.

THE COGNITIVE MODEL

INTRODUCTION

On the way to his weekly therapy session, John noticed an old school friend walking on the other side of the road. His old friend appeared to be looking in his direction but showed no sign of recognition; in fact he completely 'blanked' John. John was very hurt by this experience. When discussing it with his therapist, he suggested this as another example of the fact he was 'no good'. Even old friends would rather ignore him than talk to him.

The therapist asked him why he was thinking like this, and John said that his interpretation of events was the only logical explanation. The therapist argued that John was drawn to his interpretation because it made him feel worthless. Over the years he had learnt to select thoughts that made him feel bad. The therapist suggested another explanation that John found difficult to accept, even though it was just as logical as his own: his friend had not been wearing his glasses or contact lenses, and although it looked as though he was looking directly at John, he genuinely couldn't see him.

KEY DEFINITIONS

COGNITIVE
Taken from the Latin word 'cogito' ('think'), it is a term that refers to all human behaviour that requires information processing.

OPTIMISM
A cognitive bias where an individual tends to view things in a positive way.

PESSIMISM
A cognitive bias where an individual tends to view things in a negative way.

Fig 5.20 How do you see the glass?

The above case study is based on a true account given by the eminent cognitive therapist Albert Ellis. He is demonstrating that many of us find it easier to accept one type of explanation for an event than another. Which one we select is often based upon our past learning. A pessimistic or an optimistic outlook on life is something that we are encouraged to develop by those around us.

The optimist and the pessimist

An old Chinese tale depicts a room with a table, and on this table is a glass with water in it. In walks a pessimist, who immediately describes the glass as being 'half empty'. A few minutes later in walks an optimist who describes the glass as being 'half full'.

The amount of water in the glass is the same in both cases; it is the men's perception of the glass that is different. The optimist is thankful for the water, whereas the pessimist feels hard done by, only having half a glass. This tale represents two extreme attitudes to life.

WHAT IS THE COGNITIVE MODEL?

Building upon the behavioural model (which suggests that abnormal behaviour is learnt), the cognitive model proposes that 'unrealistic' cognition (thinking) is responsible for mental illness. As you saw in the above case study, individuals learn to think in a particular way that is nearly always detrimental to their psychological well being.

ASSUMPTIONS OF THE COGNITIVE MODEL

- The cognitive activity (that is, thoughts, perceptions and memories) of an individual directly affects their behaviour. The 'thought frameworks' (more technically known as **schemata**) that a person learns to use in certain situations determine their emotional state. For example, focusing upon the thought of a loved one who has died tends to generate morose and sad thoughts.
- Clients may be seen to demonstrate a variety of maladjusted thinking processes.
- Desired behavioural change may be achieved by changing cognitive processes.
- Cognitive activity can be monitored and altered by a therapist (see section 18).

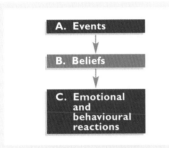

Fig 5.21 The cognitive model focusses on beliefs – the way people interpret events influences their emotional and behavioural reactions.

EVALUATION

The cognitive model has become highly influential in recent years, particularly in conjunction with the behavioural model. Maladaptive thoughts are said to be learnt in the same way as maladaptive behaviours. Linking the two together is not surprisingly known as the cognitive–behavioural approach.

There is good evidence that distorted (or negatively biased) thinking is very common with depression and anxiety disorders (Beck and Clark 1988).

Newmark et al (1973) found that 80% of anxious patients agreed with the statement 'One must be perfectly competent, adequate and achieving to consider oneself worthwhile'. This was compared with 20% of people who did not suffer from anxiety.

This model concentrates on the here and now, rather than revisiting past events that people can do little about. Psychoanalysts would see this as a problem. When evaluating this model, they might object that you may well change the surface thoughts but you won't address the underlying cause.

It is not clear whether biased thinking is the cause of abnormal behaviour, or a by-product of it.

This model depends on the individual being able to reflect upon their own thinking. For severe problems, particularly thought disorders, it is difficult to use it as an explanation.

COGNITIVE TREATMENTS

INTRODUCTION

As you have just seen in the previous section, the cognitive model views abnormality as being caused by 'faulty' or 'maladaptive' thought processes. Not surprisingly, cognitive treatments tend to directly focus on the way in which clients think about the world. The ultimate goal is to change irrational cognitions and replace them with more rational adaptive thinking.

CD-ROM

Individual differences: General issues with treatment

UNDERLYING PRINCIPLES

Beck and Weishaar (1989) identify five underlying principles that typify cognitive treatments. They are as follows:

- Clients are encouraged to monitor their negative, automatic thoughts (cognitions).
- Clients are encouraged to recognize the relationship between cognitions, emotion and behaviour.
- Clients are encouraged to challenge their own automatic irrational thinking.
- Clients are encouraged to provide more rational interpretations of their own experience and behaviour.
- Clients are encouraged to challenge the underlying beliefs that distort their cognitions.

There are a number of different therapies that are regarded as cognitive treatments. We will focus on rational emotive behaviour therapy (REBT).

KEY DEFINITIONS

RATIONAL EMOTIVE BEHAVIOUR THERAPY (REBT)
A cognitive therapy developed by Albert Ellis (1955), which directly challenges the negative assumptions people make through their thinking.

CD-ROM

Individual differences: Albert Ellis – cognitive therapy

RATIONAL EMOTIVE BEHAVIOUR THERAPY

This treatment was established in 1955 by Albert Ellis, a clinical psychologist based in New York. He argued that people with psychological disorders indoctrinate themselves with a series of assumptions, which ultimately lead them to develop irrational thoughts. These include the following.

Irrational beliefs

Clients state these beliefs in absolute terms, for example: 'I'm having a terrible week, it's only Tuesday and hundreds of things have gone wrong already'. Often cognitive therapists will challenge statements such as this, for example by asking clients to write down a few of these 'hundreds' of things. Most clients have trouble reaching ten.

Mustabation and awfulizing

Ellis (1962) proposed that 'mustabation' and 'awfulizing' are two common processes that lead to irrational thinking. Mustabation describes people's belief that they 'must' do something or else they will be viewed as a failure: 'I must go to university'; 'I must get a good job'; 'I must own a big house'; 'I must drive a fast car'.

Awfulizing is the term Ellis gave to the huge over-generalizations that people make when things do not work out for them: 'I didn't go to university, so I must be stupid'.

Self damnation

This is where a person believes that they are 'no good', for example: 'My life is crap and I am a crap person'. Ellis (1962) suggested that REBT should attempt to encourage clients to develop an unconditional acceptance of themselves, recognizing that we are all fallible human beings.

Discomfort disturbance

This is the irrational belief that a person must have comfortable life conditions. This is of course very common in modern Westernized cultures, where a high degree of comfort and affluence is experienced by a large number of people: 'My working life is awful – my boss is very unfair'.

Who ever promised that work should be fun or bosses should be fair in their decisions? These are irrational assumptions we make.

EVALUATION OF REBT

Because practitioners are attempting to change thinking patterns, therapists using REBT tend to be more argumentative and confrontational with their clients than in other forms of therapy.

In their review of the effectiveness of REBT, Haaga and Davidson (1989) concluded the following points:
* REBT is effective in treating excessive anger, depression and anti-social behaviour.
* REBT reduces generalized anxiety and exam anxiety.

Barlow and Durand (1995) conclude that REBT is most effective for clients suffering from anxiety or depressive disorders; however, it is not useful with those suffering from severe thought disorders.

COGNITIVE–BEHAVIOURAL THERAPY

In more recent times, therapists have seen the benefits of combining elements from both behavioural and cognitive treatments to create cognitive–behavioural therapy (CBT). The focus in this type of therapy is on both behavioural and cognitive change. As Kendall and Hammen (1998) point out, thoughts, feelings and behaviours are all interrelated. Techniques involved in CBT actively encourage clients to try out (the behavioural bit) their new-found thinking (the cognitive bit) in real-life scenarios. For example:

A young man pointed out to his therapist that the reason he was single was because he never met women who matched his expectations – highly attractive and intelligent. The therapist pointed out that maybe the man didn't allow himself to socialize enough to test this assumption. The home-work from the therapy session was to socialize with three women during the following week. The client returned having experienced three successful dates – his problem now was he didn't know who to go out with!

> ### KEY DEFINITIONS
>
> **COGNITIVE–BEHAVIOURAL THERAPY (CBT)**
> A therapy that combines both cognitive techniques (getting people to look at their thinking in a different way) and behavioural techniques (putting their newly-found thinking into action).

THE CLINICAL CHARACTERISTICS OF ANOREXIA NERVOSA

INTRODUCTION

Samantha was 17 years old and 5 feet 6 inches tall. She hesitated as she approached the scales. There had been a ceremonial removal of her clothes – the reading must be as accurate as possible. The dial showed 5 stone 8 pounds. What a relief!

KEY DEFINITIONS

EATING DISORDER
The name given to any disorder where there is a serious disruption of the eating habits or appetite of an individual. Usually, this reflects an underlying psychological disturbance.

ANOREXIA NERVOSA
The deliberate loss of weight through restricted food intake.

WHAT IS ANOREXIA NERVOSA?

The term 'anorexia nervosa' literally means 'nervous loss of appetite'. Sufferers of anorexia nervosa deliberately restrict their food intake to remain underweight. Many commentators within this area stress an obvious link between emotional state, food intake and concerns over appearance. In addition, the consumption of food and the rituals associated with it provide an important social function. Beardsworth and Keil (1993) have suggested that not only is eating a nutritional exercise, but it is a highly social activity as well. People who are not participating are emotionally removing themselves from this 'arena'.

WHAT ARE THE SYMPTOMS?

Characteristics of this disorder have been known and recorded since 1694. However, the term 'anorexia nervosa' was first coined in 1874 (Cooper 1995). Some researchers (for example Sue et al 1994) suggest there has been an increase in recent times. However, we should question whether this is a genuine increase or simply due to more awareness of the condition (an increase in diagnosis).

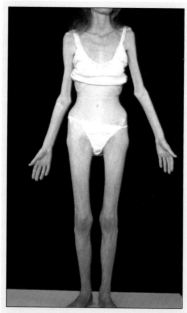
Fig 5.22 A person with anorexia

Classic symptoms of anorexia nervosa include:
- An intense fear of being overweight or becoming fat
- A prolonged refusal to eat adequate amounts of food, which results in deliberate weight loss
- A distorted body image (usually by denying the seriousness of the current low body weight)
- In females, the absence of at least three consecutive menstrual cycles (a condition known as amenorrhoea)

Anorexia nervosa is diagnosed when a person's body weight is 15% below what is expected for their age and height. There are two sub-types of anorexia nervosa: the **bulimic** type in which the sufferer may well engage in periods of binge eating; and the **non-bulimic** type, which is characterized purely by a restriction of diet.

CD-ROM

Individual differences: GP corner: eating disorders

INCIDENCE OF ANOREXIA NERVOSA

It has been estimated that about 70 000 people in Britain suffer from anorexia nervosa (Brooke 1996). It is a potentially fatal disorder, with mortality rates ranging from 5% to 15% (either from suicide or from complications due to starvation). The majority of studies suggest that anorexia nervosa occurs primarily in females. Fombonne (1995) reviewed the literature and found that the ratio of females to males was 20:1 in some studies, but 10:1 in others. Taking an average across studies still demonstrates that women with this disorder significantly outnumber men.

Anorexia nervosa is commonly found in much higher proportions within certain occupations. Models, ballet dancers and high-profile pop and film stars are far more prone to developing this disorder (Garfinkel and Garner 1982).

There is also evidence that eating disorders in general appear to be far more common in industrialized societies such as the United States and Europe compared with non-industrialized societies. In fact, Yates (1989) demonstrated that when women move from a culture with a low prevalence of eating disorders to a culture with a high prevalence, their own susceptibility increases.

Surveys (for example Cooper and Fairburn 1983) also show that eating disorders in general are more common in women from the more wealthy socio-economic classes.

HOT EXAM HINT

Sometimes the examiner will ask you simply 'What is meant by the term anorexia nervosa?'. You could give a brief description of the disorder, the key symptoms and/or the incidence.

THE CLINICAL CHARACTERISTICS OF BULIMIA NERVOSA

INTRODUCTION

Rob was the manager of a trendy clothes shop. Ever since childhood, he had always been interested in looks and fashion. It was the ideal job for him. However, Rob had a secret – he suffered from bulimia. When guests came around for dinner his eating habits appeared normal. 'More potatoes anyone?' Rob reached across and piled more vegetables on his own plate. After consuming a large meal he excused himself from the table for a few minutes. No one noticed his absence.

KEY DEFINITIONS

BULIMIA NERVOSA
A deliberate loss of weight through purging behaviours.

PURGING
The name given to behaviours which expel food from the body. Examples are taking diuretics (drugs to make you urinate more), taking laxatives (drugs to make you excrete more) and self-induced vomiting (usually after a meal).

WHAT IS BULIMIA NERVOSA?

The term 'bulimia' originates from two Greek words, 'bous' meaning ox and 'limos' meaning hunger. This rather unfortunate term 'hungry as an ox' describes two patterns of eating. The first (the **purging** type) involves binge eating then purging (removing the food from the body by vomiting or using laxatives). Sufferers will actually go as far as swallowing a coloured marker (for example food dye) at the start of their binge, then continue to vomit until the marker re-emerges (Colman 1987). This assures them that they have removed all the food they have just eaten. The **non-purging** type involves fasting or excessive exercise.

It is very tempting to think that bulimia nervosa is a relatively new disorder. Psychiatry only officially adopted the term in 1979. However, there are a number of historical references to this sort of behaviour. For example, the Romans had a 'vomitorium', where, after eating a big meal, they could go and make themselves sick. This allowed them to eat and be merry without gaining weight!

WHAT ARE THE SYMPTOMS?

The primary symptoms of bulimia nervosa are:
- An intense fear of being overweight
- Binge eating – feasting on large quantities of food within a short period of time, and feeling a lack of control during these episodes. Usually the food consumed is high in carbohydrates (chocolate, biscuits, and so on)
- Weight loss – engaging in a range of behaviours that prevent weight gain. These could include: **purging** type behaviours (self-induced vomiting and/or the use of laxatives) or **non-purging** type behaviours (fasting or excessive exercise)

Most purging behaviour is usually carried out in secret (as with Rob in the case study above), possibly because of feelings of embarrassment or guilt. Also, bulimia nervosa is possibly more difficult to spot than anorexia nervosa because the sufferer's eating habits may appear quite normal in public (they will sit and eat a meal, then excuse themselves for a few minutes afterwards –just as in the case study).

- To be diagnosed, the individual has to have engaged in a minimum average of two binge episodes a week, for at least 3 months.

As well as primary symptoms, there are sometimes symptoms associated with the excessive purging. These can include:

- A puffy facial appearance (due to swollen glands –particularly those under the jaw) caused by excessive vomiting
- Deterioration in tooth enamel (due to exposure to stomach acid). This pattern occurs on the inside of the teeth and is sometimes noticed first by dentists
- Damage to the digestive tract (particularly ulcers), again due to exposure to stomach acid

INCIDENCE OF BULIMIA NERVOSA

Gelder et al (1999) estimate that the incidence of bulimia nervosa among women (aged 15–40) is approximately 1–2%.

The great majority of sufferers of bulimia nervosa are women, with less than 5% presenting being men (Cooper 1995). However, as we saw in section 8, this statistic might be misleading because men, on average, are more reluctant to visit their GP, therefore are not counted.

Bulimia nervosa typically begins in late adolescence or early adulthood, and as with anorexia nervosa it is more common in the wealthy socio-economic classes.

EVALUATION OF EATING DISORDERS

As you saw in the previous section, some anorexia nervosa sufferers show bulimic symptoms. The fact that some sub-categories of anorexia and bulimia nervosa overlap has prompted a number of researchers to start questioning whether they might in fact be one single disorder.

Bulimia nervosa is not usually regarded as life threatening when compared with anorexia nervosa. However, it takes longer on average to manage, and overall the prognosis is worse (Russell 1979).

Mitchell et al (1982) showed that over 50% of American college students occasionally engaged in binge eating, and some had attempted purging afterwards. Findings such as these could suggest that bulimic behaviours are more common within the general population than suggested. Perhaps classifying it as a disorder is more to do with the severity and frequency of the behaviours than the behaviours themselves.

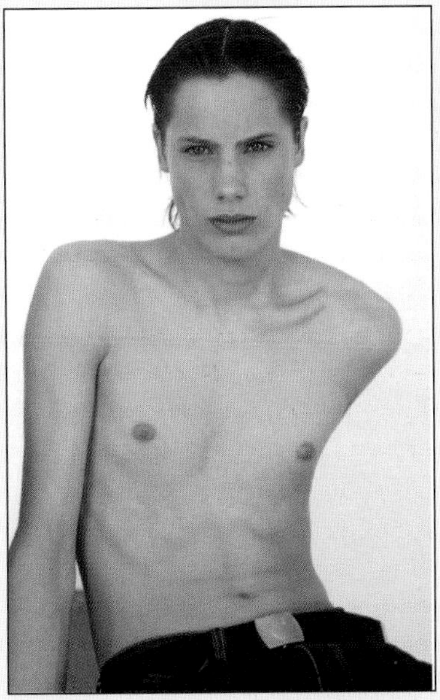

Fig 5.23 *The 'male waif' look – even men are not exempt from social pressures to look slim*

HOT EXAM HINT

It is always useful to learn the characteristics of anorexia nervosa and bulimia nervosa separately, as the examiner could ask you to comment on them as two separate disorders.

BIOLOGICAL EXPLANATIONS OF EATING DISORDERS

INTRODUCTION

Some researchers suggest that the aetiology (root cause) of eating disorders stems from biological abnormalities. These could include genetic, neurochemical or structural abnormalities (see below for more on these). If an individual has a particular 'biological weakness', they would be more prone to developing an eating disorder. Let us consider evidence for each of these in turn.

GENETIC FACTORS

Before we look at studies it is worth spending a few moments briefly outlining how scientists commonly investigate genetic inheritance.

One of the most common methods of determining whether a disorder is influenced by genetic factors is to study twins. There are two types of twin – **identical** (more technically known as monozygotic, MZ) and **non-identical** or **fraternal** (known as dizygotic, DZ). Monozygotic twins share the same DNA (see section 11). In theory, this means that if a monozygotic twin has a particular mental disorder and in every case the other one does as well, that condition could be regarded as 100% genetic. The probability that if one twin has a disorder the other will also is known as the concordance rate.

CD-ROM

Individual differences: Twin and adoption studies

There is evidence that both anorexia and bulimia nervosa run in families (for example, Strober and Katz 1987). Hsu (1990) reviewed the data from several published reports and found a concordance rate for anorexia nervosa of 47% for monozygotic twins and 10% for dizygotic pairs. Similar figures were obtained for bulimia nervosa.

Conclusions

Even though evidence such as this may tempt us to suggest that eating disorders are genetic, we have to remember that other factors must account for the remaining percentage. We may suggest that there is nearly a 50% chance that if one identical twin has an eating disorder, the other will have one; but what explains the other 50%?

Many psychologists feel caution should be used when attempting to link behaviours to genes. Byrne (1994) summarizes: '…genes themselves specify proteins not behavioural or psychological phenomena'.

NEUROCHEMICAL FACTORS

One major area of research within the neurochemical field centres on a group of chemicals located within the nervous system known as

endogenous opioids. These are naturally occurring pain-killing substances – the best known of these are the **endorphins**. During stress, opioids are released into the body, ready to deal with any potential trauma (see chapter 4). A side effect of these substances is a sense of euphoria. Starvation activates the stress response, and in turn the euphoria. This positively reinforces (encourages) the starvation behaviour and perpetuates the condition (Marrazzi and Luby 1986). This is a similar process to 'jogger's high', where a euphoric state is achieved when the body is pushed to its limits.

Conclusions

One major problem with all neurochemical explanations is cause and effect. Did the neurochemical imbalance cause the disorder, or did the disorder cause the neurochemical imbalance?

STRUCTURAL FACTORS

Lask et al (1999), who did research at the Hospital for Sick Children in Great Ormond Street, London, claimed to have found a structural abnormality in the brains of teenage girls, which they believed was related to anorexia nervosa. The region of the brain where this abnormality was identified was the anterior temporal lobe – an area involved in the regulation of appetite, as well as in visual perception. Studies showed that children suffering from anorexia nervosa had a reduced blood flow of at least 10% in this area of the brain, and in some cases the reduction was as much as 30%. The abnormality seemed to affect only one side of the brain.

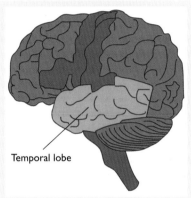

Temporal lobe

Fig 5.24 The anterior temporal lobe

Conclusions

Lask et al (1999) were very keen to emphasize that although this evidence appeared to suggest a 'structural trigger', it was only one of a range of factors that lead to anorexia nervosa. These include much broader issues such as social factors and stress.

GENERAL EVALUATION

As Lask et al pointed out, biological factors are only part of the story.

Most researchers prefer to adopt an 'interactionist' model when attempting to attribute the cause of a particular disorder. This says that eating disorders are caused by both a genetic vulnerability (which could manifest itself in neurochemical or structural abnormalities) and environmental/social triggers. This is referred to as the **diathesis–stress** model.

Biological explanations of eating disorders take responsibility away from the sufferer. Because they assume that there is some underlying illness (or pathology), there is a risk that a sense of control is removed from the patient and placed in the hands of the physician treating them.

CD-ROM

Individual differences: diathesis–stress model: eating disorders

HOT EXAM HINT

The examiner could ask you to evaluate the biological explanations of eating disorders. Try to learn some studies (names of researchers) to provide as evidence.

SECTION 22 | PSYCHOLOGICAL EXPLANATIONS OF EATING DISORDERS

INTRODUCTION

Some researchers suggest the aetiology (root cause) of eating disorders stem from psychological factors. As with many topics within psychology, different psychological explanations tend to align with the various approaches to the subject. We will consider four major psychological approaches, which will provide you with more than enough choice for the exam. These are the psychodynamic, the behavioural, the cognitive and the sociological approaches.

KEY DEFINITIONS

PSYCHOLOGICAL EXPLANATIONS

(As applied to eating disorders) A group of explanations that suggest eating disorders are caused by psychosocial factors.

PSYCHODYNAMIC EXPLANATIONS

The psychodynamic approach has its roots in the work of Sigmund Freud (1856–1939). Some of the early work in this field (for example Walker et al 1940) saw starvation behaviour as a symbolic gesture of sexual conflict. The young female is denying her sexual maturity (at adolescence) by maintaining a 'boy-like' figure.

Later psychodynamic theorists (such as Bruch 1978) take this idea a stage further by suggesting that the young woman has experienced a disturbed relationship with her mother and therefore failed to develop a female body identity. The deliberate restriction in eating can provide a false sense of control, almost a comfort response to feeling out of touch with one's own body.

Evaluation

The psychodynamic explanation focuses upon female sufferers. It does not provide a satisfactory explanation for male sufferers.

The theory is very difficult to evaluate, as empirical research in this area is notoriously difficult to conduct.

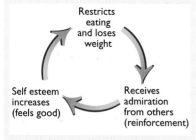

Fig 5.25 Reinforcement

BEHAVIOURAL EXPLANATIONS

Behaviourist explanations suggest that the sufferers of eating disorders have established some sort of reinforcement for avoiding food. In many cases (particularly in modern Westernized societies) this can be admiration they receive for being slim. Unfortunately, once the conditioned response has established, they continue to refuse food and become slimmer and slimmer (see Fig 5.25).

Behavioural explanations tend to focus on the process of eating disorders; they do not really address what caused the disorder in the first place.

Behavioural explanations do not adequately explain why sufferers continue to avoid food when reinforcement (for instance in the form of compliments) stops. When sufferers become obviously too thin admiration tends to cease, yet sufferers tend to continue losing weight.

COGNITIVE EXPLANATIONS

Cognitive explanations focus upon how sufferers think. Many psychologists view this approach as the key to understanding the disorder: it is the sufferer's distorted perceptions of their own body image that motivates them to continue losing weight.

Garfinkel and Garner (1982) found that patients with anorexia tended to overestimate their own body size when compared with a control group. This 'cognitive bias' must be based upon something, and many researchers believe that the media is a major factor. We will look at social explanations next.

Evaluation

It is very difficult to assess whether 'cognitive distortions' of body shape were present before the onset of the eating disorder or appeared as a result of it.

Cognitive explanations tend not to address why some people are more vulnerable to distorted thinking than others.

Fig 5.26 Catwalk model

SOCIOLOGICAL EXPLANATIONS

The underlying belief of this group of explanations is that different societies place undue stress upon individuals (particularly women) to conform to certain standards of beauty. Orbach (1978) suggested that the way in which we perceive body shape is intrinsically linked to wider social issues such as feminism and social identity.

Interestingly, Boskind-White and White (1983) found that bulimic women tended to be overly obsessed with being attractive to men.

Evaluation

This explanation still does not explain why some individuals develop the disorder and some do not. For example, many women admire models in glossy magazines, but do not themselves go on to develop eating disorders.

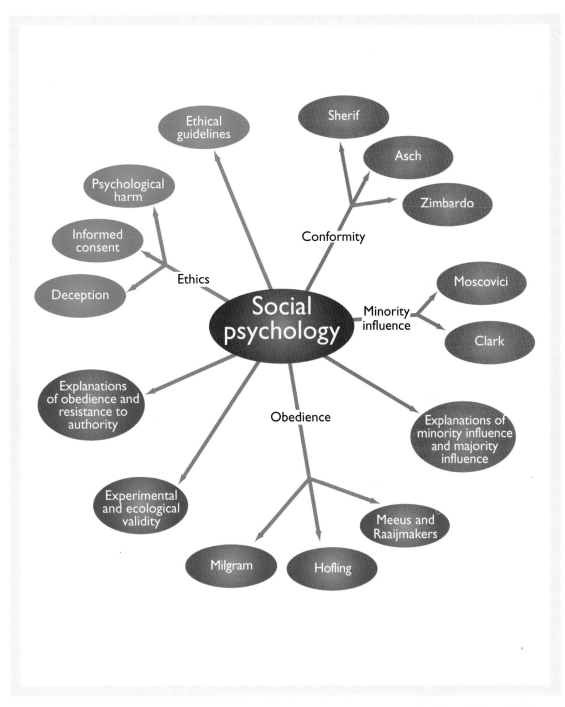

SECTION 1 | WHAT YOU NEED TO KNOW

To prepare for the AQA exam you need to know the following things.

Social influence

Conformity
- Sherif
- Asch
- Zimbardo

Minority influence
- Moscovici
- Clark

Explanations of majority influence (conformity) and minority influence

Obedience to authority
- Milgram
- Hofling
- Meeus
- Raaijmakers

Issues regarding experimental and ecological validity

Explanations of obedience and resistance to obedience

Critical issue: ethical issues in psychological research
- Deception
- Informed consent
- Protection from psychological harm
- The use of ethical guidelines

WHAT IS SOCIAL INFLUENCE?

INTRODUCTION

Marie was at her weekly antenatal class chatting to her friend Bella. They had just being saying how lucky they both were that neither of their children had caught the terrible colds that were going around, when in came the group leader.

'I'm afraid we have a child outside who has German Measles. Does anyone mind if she comes in?'

Marie suddenly felt sick. What about her baby's health?

She looked at the other mothers including Bella. They didn't seem to be bothered.

Despite her anxieties she said nothing and the child came in.

KEY DEFINITIONS

CONFORMITY
Changing behaviour because of group pressure.

OBEDIENCE TO AUTHORITY
Responding to the demands of an authority figure.

CD-ROM

Social Psychology: Conformity in daily life.

HOW DOES SOCIAL INFLUENCE WORK?

Social influence is the effect of other people on a person's behaviour. It is usually manifest in two ways:

- **Conformity** – 'yielding to group pressures' (Crutchfield 1955)
- **Obedience** – responding to the direct demands of an authority figure

These two types of social influence vary in a number of aspects:

- **Nature of influence:** with obedience, the influence is exerted through direct commands ('Tidy your room!'). With conformity, the pressure on a person to change their behaviour is an *indirect* group pressure (nobody might directly tell you that trainers are more fashionable than wooden clogs, but the pressure to conform is there all the same).
- **Power backing up the influence:** with conformity, it is fear of rejection by the group. With obedience, it is more usually official punishment.

Obedience is usually to a leader, while conformity is to a group. Obedience involves an explicit instruction that you are required to obey. Conformity is more voluntary, and involves imitation. An example of conformity is doing something because 'everybody else is doing it'. An example of obedience is not breaking the law.

What is interesting to psychologists is why some people are influenced by these processes, and others are not. Also, what factors affect whether people will conform or obey?

CONFORMITY

Aronson (1976) defines conformity as the 'change in a person's behaviour or opinions as a result of real or imagined pressure from a person or a group of people'. But for Mann (1969) the 'essence of conformity is yielding to group pressures', in whatever way and for whatever motives.

There are a number of factors involved in conformity to the majority, which is usually just known as conformity:

- The group must be important to the individual, either in that particular situation or in the longer term.
- The pressure to conform may be real (for example if the group is physically present) or imagined (for example, creation of group pressure through the media, as with opinion polls giving the majority viewpoint).

Fig 6.1 Some people show their conformity to a group through their clothes and hairstyles.

- The pressure to change is towards that which is accepted or approved by the group.
- It may be conformity to society as a whole or to a specific sub-group (such as your schoolmates or colleagues), which may or may not reflect society's views.
- There is usually no direct request or command to conform.
- There are a choice of responses to conformity pressure: to conform to the majority; independence (where the individual makes their decision not influenced by others); and anti-conformity (deliberately choosing the opposite to the majority view).

Subsequent research has also included conformity to the minority.

TYPES OF CONFORMITY

There are a number of types of conformity, which are discussed below.

Informational conformity

(Mann 1969) The individual is in a new or ambiguous situation, and is unsure how to respond, so they look to others for guidance. This may involve the internalization of the beliefs of the group (that is, private and public acceptance of the group norms). The best example of this type of conformity is shown by Sherif (1935) (see section 3).

Normative conformity

(Mann 1969) Conformity in this case is due to the promise of reward or threat of rejection by the group. It can take two forms. **True conformity** (or **internalization**; Kelman 1958) is where the individual internalizes the group norms (for instance, in a religious conversion experience). **Compliance** (Kelman 1958) means outwardly (publicly) agreeing while inwardly (privately) disagreeing. This latter example is interesting as it is clearly situational conformity, and the individual is aware that they are conforming. Asch (1951) and Crutchfield (1954) are the best known examples of this (see sections 4 and 5).

Identification

(Kelman 1958) This is conformity to a social role. The individual conforms to the social expectations of the particular role they are playing. This is famously demonstrated in the Stanford Prison Simulation (Haney et al 1973) (see sections 10 and 11). The role can become part of the self.

KEY DEFINITIONS

SITUATIONAL CONFORMITY
Conformity depending on your situation.

Type of conformity	Public agreement?	Private agreement?	Why?
Informational	Yes	Yes, usually	Unsure how to behave
Normative: internalization	Yes	Yes	Conversion
Normative: compliance of rejection	Yes	No	Reward of group or fear
Role	Yes	Yes or no	Expectations of role, but can become part of self

HOT EXAM HINT

You may be asked to define 'conformity' or 'obedience to authority'. Memorize short definitions of each.

CONCLUSIONS

Social influence includes conformity and obedience to authority. We shall study forms of conformity in the coming sections.

INFORMATIONAL CONFORMITY: SHERIF

INTRODUCTION

Brian was feeling guilty. Should he have gone to help that man? What if he had? What he knew about first aid wouldn't fill a postage stamp. He would have probably done more harm than good. Anyway why didn't someone else help? There must have been someone there who knew what to do, the crowd had been large enough. No he shouldn't feel guilty.

INFORMATIONAL CONFORMITY

Informational conformity is where individuals conform to the majority because they are unsure of what to do in the situation; they are unsure about what the appropriate social norms are.

SHERIF'S EXPERIMENT

KEY DEFINITIONS

AUTOKINETIC EFFECT
In a completely dark room, a small spot of light appears to move around randomly. This is a visual illusion.

Sherif (1935) made use of the visual illusion known as the autokinetic effect. In a dark room, a stationary dim light appears to move (a different amount for each person). Groups of three male participants had to estimate the distance the light moved from twenty feet away. Estimates were given in this order:
- Individually
- In front of the group (going round the group one at a time)
- Individually again

In the group situations, estimates started to converge and became similar as they went round the group (that is, in the direction of the most confidently stated estimate). But if an individual held to their own view, those who followed would compromise to establish group norms. The experimenter had not instructed the individuals to come to any agreement. Thus conformity is spontaneous because participants are unsure about their estimates.

When the individuals gave their estimates alone for the second time, the estimates remained similar to the group ones. Thus conformity pressure remains even when the group is no longer physically present.

One explanation for the findings is that agreement is important in Western culture.

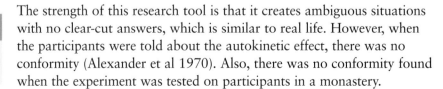

FOR CONSIDERATION

Monks may be a good example of independent behaviour (see section 6).

The strength of this research tool is that it creates ambiguous situations with no clear-cut answers, which is similar to real life. However, when the participants were told about the autokinetic effect, there was no conformity (Alexander et al 1970). Also, there was no conformity found when the experiment was tested on participants in a monastery.

Fig 6.2

Examples of results from this kind of study:

Participant	1	2	3
Estimate of distance light moves (cm)...			
...individually	3	11	7
...in front of the group	6	7	7
...individually again	7	7	8

CRITICISMS OF THE EXPERIMENT

- Similarity of estimates is not a good measure of conformity (as it is not objective).
- It has been argued that the participants are not acting as a group, because there is no interaction between the members of the group. Van Avermaet (1996) believes that merely bringing people with different opinions together is not strictly conformity.

CONCLUSIONS

Individuals will conform to the group because they are unsure about what to do. This is informational conformity, and was demonstrated in Sherif's experiment using the autokinetic effect.

NORMATIVE CONFORMITY: ASCH I

INTRODUCTION

'Go on,' said Theo. 'You do it.'

'What if anyone catches me?' said Paul.

'They won't. You'll be over the fence and out again before anyone sees.'

'I don't know.' The other boys started walking away from Paul.

'We thought you were part of our gang,' said Theo.

'I am,' said Paul.

'Don't think so.'

'Okay. One of you give me a leg up.'

NORMATIVE CONFORMITY

Individuals sometimes conform to the majority when they personally disagree. This is normative conformity. Here individuals are outwardly conforming because they want to be rewarded for doing so, or do not want to be rejected by the group for not conforming. This is 'situational conformity' only.

Fig 6.3 Solomon Asch

ASCH'S EXPERIMENT

Using simple perceptual tasks, Asch (1951) was interested to see whether individuals would publicly conform to the obvious wrong answer to a task when they knew the correct answer.

The tasks involved estimating lengths of lines as shown in Fig 6.4.

A total of 36 participants were initially tested individually, and each participant was given twenty trials. Overall there were three mistakes; thus it was clear that the task was easy and the participants did know the correct answers.

Then the participants were tested on the same types of task in a small group of around six people (see Fig 6.4 for details). In each case, there was only one actual participant; the other members of the group were confederates of the experimenter, told to give the wrong answer at certain times. The participants did not know this. Each participant was given twelve trials where there was pressure to conform to the majority, who were giving the wrong answer.

Overall, 74% of the participants conformed at least once in the twelve trials, and 5% conformed on all trials. There was an average conformity rate of 32%, that is, conformity on one-third of trials.

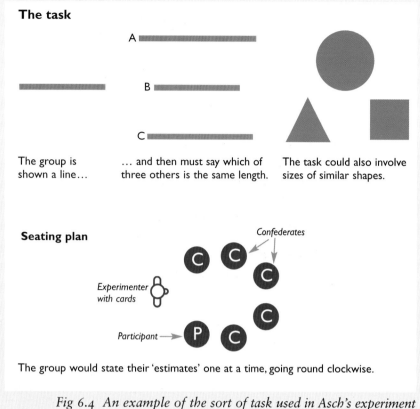

The task

A

B

C

The group is shown a line...

... and then must say which of three others is the same length.

The task could also involve sizes of similar shapes.

Seating plan

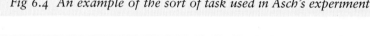

Confederates

Experimenter with cards

Participant →

The group would state their 'estimates' one at a time, going round clockwise.

Fig 6.4 An example of the sort of task used in Asch's experiment

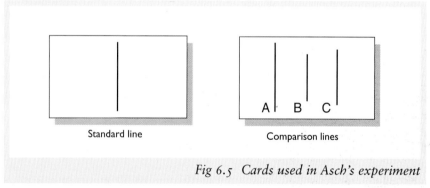

Standard line

A B C

Comparison lines

Fig 6.5 Cards used in Asch's experiment

CONCLUSIONS

Normative conformity is where individuals conform to the majority because they want to be rewarded or do not want to be rejected by the group. Asch's study showed normative conformity in action.

In the next section we shall look at this experiment in more detail, and the factors affecting conformity.

NORMATIVE CONFORMITY: ASCH 2

WHAT INFLUENCES NORMATIVE CONFORMITY IN ASCH'S EXPERIMENT?

Asch spent many years replicating his study (see section 4) with small variations, in order to pin down the factors in this type of conformity to the majority.

Size of group

Increasing the size of the confederate group (surrounding the participant) does not automatically increase the level of conformity; the level peaks at 7:1 (confederates to participant) – see Fig 6.6.

Factor	Most conformity	Least conformity
Size of group	7:1	1:1
Status of members	High	Low
Task difficulty	Lines very similar	Lines not similar

Fig 6.7 Summary of factors influencing normative conformity in Asch's experiment

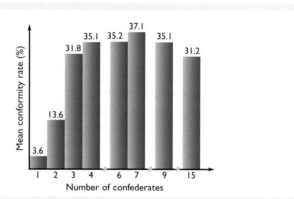

Fig 6.6 Chart showing the mean conformity rate with different numbers of confederates. Remember in each case there was also a single actual participant.

As you can see, conformity was lowest when there was just one confederate besides the participant.

But Wilder (1977) argues that it is not just the size of the group, but the number of apparent independent sources that matters. For example, three 'independent' sources produced greater conformity than five individuals who are seen to be colluding and are thus only one 'independent' source.

Status of group members

Greater status of the confederates leads to greater conformity. (The participants were students, and, in one version of the experiment, Asch gave the confederates name badges showing that they were members of the teaching staff.)

Difficulty of the task

Greater difficulty of the task leads to greater conformity. Where the difference between the lengths of the lines was very small (see section 4), this produced greater conformity.

Deviant in the group

In one version of the experiment, Asch arranged for one of the confederates to give a different answer (to act as a 'deviant'), that is, not to conform to the majority. This reduced the conformity by participants in any group size (mean conformity 18%). It did not matter whether the deviant gave the correct answer or another wrong answer, as long as it was different to the majority.

However, if the 'deviant' gave a different answer, and then changed to conform after hearing the majority, participants were more likely to conform than when the deviant did not change their mind (mean conformity here 28.5%).

Public or private conformity

Where a participant wrote down their answer (private), and then the experimenter read it out, then the next person wrote their answer, and so on, this reduced conformity compared with speaking out the answers in the normal procedure of the experiment (in public, face to face). Insko et al (1983) found that this reduced conformity even further when the situation was ambiguous (that is, there was no clear answer to the task).

Deutsch and Gerrard (1955) tried a variation where participants were hidden from the others and gave their answers by means of lights in front of them. Conformity was halved compared with the face-to-face set-up. However, Crutchfield (1954) using a similar design with business and military men, found similar levels of conformity to Asch.

CD-ROM

Social Psychology: Crutchfield's study

EVALUATION

Often it is assumed that the participants who conformed did so without thinking. Some individuals conformed to the majority knowing the correct answer, but some reported after the experiment that they had been unsure about the instructions and did not want to spoil the experiment. Other participants reported being convinced that the majority were giving the right answer. But were they still conforming or trying to save face by saying this?

Bannister and Fransella (1971) point out that it is easier to say 'Well, I never was much good at measures anyway' as a way of dealing with the situation. Similarly, one participant believed that he was sitting in a position that distorted the visual image. Overall, individuals are seen to be trying to make sense of the social world surrounding them.

CONCLUSION

CD-ROM

Social Psychology: Evaluation of Asch's study

Normative conformity is influenced by various factors including the size of the group, the status of the group members and the difficulty of the task. These have all been demonstrated by replications of Asch's original experiment, with variations.

SECTION 6 | ALTERNATIVES TO CONFORMITY TO MAJORITY: INDEPENDENT AND ANTI-CONFORMITY BEHAVIOUR

INTRODUCTION

The lecture was drawing to a close. The professor had delivered a convincing series of arguments and felt justifiably pleased with herself.

'Any questions?' she said, more out of politeness than a genuine request. Everyone sat there quietly – to question something would almost appear rude.

'I've got one,' said a voice from the side of the room. All heads turned to look at a second-year student with bright green hair and a heavily pierced face.

KEY DEFINITIONS

INDEPENDENT BEHAVIOUR
Where individuals are unaffected by group pressure.

ANTI-CONFORMITY BEHAVIOUR
Where individuals deliberately take the opposite position to the majority of the group.

INDEPENDENT BEHAVIOUR

There has been a small amount of research on **independence** and **anti-conformity behaviour**. The independent individual tends to be unaffected by the group. Either they are resistant to the tension of group pressure, or they can isolate themselves mentally from the group. In Asch's experiments (see sections 4 and 5), the independent individual had high self-confidence about their opinions, could isolate themselves mentally from the rest of the group, and resist the doubt and tension created. Other researchers have found that high self-esteem is an important factor in independence, as is being skilled at judgment tasks.

Asch also noted 'independent behaviour without confidence'. In this case, individuals did not conform to the group's views, but after the experiment reported believing that the group was correct but they themselves were following the instructions of the experimenter. The authority figure's demands were stronger than the majority group pressure (that is, obedience was stronger than conformity).

However, Brown (1985) argues that independence is not just a personality characteristic, but also an interaction with situational variables (that is, factors in the immediate environment or situation).

ANTI-CONFORMITY BEHAVIOUR

Anti-conformity means deliberately taking the opposite position to the majority of the group. Schein (1956) studied American prisoners of war in the Korean War. Some Americans collaborated with their captors. Schein studied the motives of those who did not. There were two types. One type disagreed with the communist philosophy of their captors, and this was their motivation for anti-conformity. The other type had a problem with authority generally.

Fig 6.8 US prisoners of war in Korea

Crutchfield (1954) noted a number of common personality characteristics among anti-conformist individuals:

- More intellectual effectiveness
- More ego strength
- More leadership ability
- More maturity in social relations
- No feelings of inferiority
- No excessive self control (more likely to 'do as they please')
- No authoritarianism (that is, no strict belief in obedience to power and authority)

CONCLUSION

Conformity to the majority in a group situation does not always occur. Alternative types of behaviour are independence and anti-conformity, which we have studied in this section. In the next section we shall go on to consider another alternative to conformity to the majority: conformity to minority influence.

ALTERNATIVES TO CONFORMITY TO MAJORITY: MINORITY INFLUENCE

INTRODUCTION

Xang Fung was standing and clapping along with all the other members of the party. Their leader was acknowledging their respect. The auditorium was drowning in unrestrained applause. On and on it went, no one wanting to be the first to stop. Xang Fung had had enough. His hands were aching, his legs were aching. He stopped and sat down. If it hadn't been for the noise of the clapping you would have been able to hear a gasp from the hundreds of other members. Suddenly, just like a contagion, all the other members stopped clapping and sat down. In less than thirty seconds everyone was seated and sitting in silence ready for the first speaker. After the meeting Xang Fung was arrested for disloyalty and disrespect.

STUDYING MINORITY INFLUENCE

Research has traditionally focused on the power of the majority to change behaviour, but there is evidence also of groups conforming to a minority influence. The original research in this area comes from Moscovici.

In this experiment, groups of six female participants were asked to estimate the colours of 36 slides. Two of the group were confederates of the experimenter, who were told to wait until a group consensus was forming, and then argue together for a different colour. 32% of the groups adopted the confederates' estimate at least once (Moscovici et al 1969).

Fig 6.9 Is this colour 'bluey-green' or 'greeny-blue'?

KEY DEFINITIONS

INVESTMENT
(In conformity experiments) investment means that the participants have something to lose by their decision to conform or not.

However, the minority need to be consistent in order to influence the group. If the minority is inconsistent (for instance if they are seen to change their minds or disagree between them), then their influence is much less. Hogg and Vaughan (1998) note that the minority will be influential if they appear to be making sacrifices for their decision (this is called **investment**), do not appear to be acting for ulterior motives (for example to gain some advantage for themselves), and are flexible when necessary.

MAJORITY INFLUENCE VERSUS MINORITY INFLUENCE

Maass and Clark (1984) attempted to compare the influence of the majority and the minority. Four hundred participants read five articles on 'gay rights', and had to express their views on the articles either publicly or privately. In the 'minority influence' condition, only one article argued against more gay rights, while in the 'majority influence' condition four articles did. The 'minority influence' set of articles was found to influence participants more when they expressed their views privately, whereas the 'majority influence' set of articles was found to influence participants more when they expressed views publicly.

Another important factor is whether the minority is arguing in the direction of prevailing social norms (see Fig 6.10). Whichever side (majority or minority) has the prevailing social norms on their side will tend to be successful.

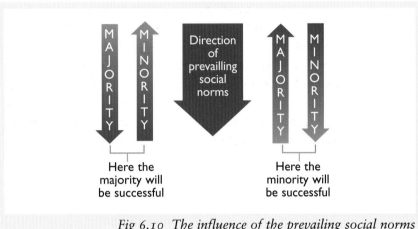

Fig 6.10 *The influence of the prevailing social norms*

Minority	Single	Double
Conforms to group norms	NO	NO
Conforms to social norms	YES	NO

Fig 6.11 *Single and double minorities*

Maass et al (1982) distinguish between **single** and **double** minorities. The former do not conform to the group norms, but do conform to prevailing social norms. Double minorities conform to neither. A member of a jury arguing for leniency towards child sex offenders would probably be in a double minority.

CONCLUSIONS

There are situations where the minority in a group can influence the group's behaviour. This is known as conformity to minority influence. Factors affecting the success of minority influence include:

- Consistency of the minority (but also ability to be flexible when necessary)
- Whether the minority appears to have no ulterior motives, or to be making a sacrifice
- Whether the minority argues with prevailing social norms
- How the views of the group are expressed: publicly or privately

FACTORS AFFECTING CONFORMITY

As there are different reactions to group pressure (as we have seen in the previous sections: conformity, anti-conformity or independence), individuals may conform in certain situations and not in others. There are a number of factors that influence whether someone will conform to the majority or not. These factors can be grouped into **situational factors, characteristics of the source of the influence,** and **personality characteristics**. Briefly, the factors can be listed as follows:

Situational factors:
- Difficulty and uncertainty of group task
- How the individual expresses views in the group: privately or publicly
- Expectation of future interactions with group

Characteristics of the source of the influence:
- How knowledgeable the group appears
- Status of the group
- Group's attractiveness to individual

Personality characteristics of the individual:
- Personality
- Gender

*Fig 6.12 Voting in a group may influence some individuals to conform
to the majority*

In this section we shall study the first of these groups: the situational factors.

SITUATIONAL FACTORS

Difficulty and uncertainty of group task

Sherif, White and Harvey (1955) tested this factor using 60 male students, in small groups or alone. The task set for them was to estimate the sizes of rooms, under three different conditions:

- A brief glimpse of a small room
- A huge theatre, in which the participants were led to their seats in darkness
- The participants taken around a maze in darkness in the room

Greater difficulty and uncertainty in the task led to greater conformity in answers arrived at.

How the individual expresses their view

Research has found that there is more conformity in a discussion group if the participants must state their views publicly, as opposed to writing them down and putting them in a sealed envelope.

Individual and the group

There will be greater conformity to the majority if:

- The individual expects future interactions with the group. (Imagine, for instance, someone in the workplace agreeing with a group decision in order not to cause friction with the colleagues they work with every day.)
- The individual is strongly attached to the group (commitment).
- The individual does not feel completely accepted by the group (that is, they feel insecurity about their position in the group). ('If I behave more like them, perhaps I will be accepted.')

Group size is another important factor, as shown by Asch's work (see section 5).

CONCLUSIONS

Individuals may conform in one group situation but not another. Conformity is influenced by situational factors, characteristics of the source of the influence, and the personal characteristics of the individual. We have looked at the first of these sets of factors in this section. We shall move on to consider the others (characteristics of the source of the influence, and personal characteristics) in the next section.

EXPLAINING CONFORMITY 2

MORE FACTORS AFFECTING CONFORMITY

In the previous section we examined the situational factors that affect conformity. Here we shall look at characteristics of the source of the influence, and also the personality characteristics of the individual.

CHARACTERISTICS OF THE SOURCE OF THE INFLUENCE

Group appears knowledgeable

Mausner (1954) performed an experiment with 28 students who were asked to judge the length of 100 lines on their own, and then paired with confederates of the experimenter to repeat the task (the students were not aware their partners were confederates).

The students were led to believe that the confederates were either very good or very bad at the task. In the former case, there was greater conformity by the students to the confederates' estimates of the length of the lines.

Fig 6.13 Pedestrian crossing

Status of the group

Lefkowitz et al (1955) found greater conformity to misuse of pedestrian signals (that is, crossing the road on a 'wait' signal) with participants surrounded by high-status individuals (based on clothes) compared with low status.

This type of behaviour was also confirmed by Asch's studies (see sections 4 and 5).

Group's attractiveness to the individual

Conformity is likely to be increased if the group appears attractive to the individual.

PERSONALITY CHARACTERISTICS OF THE INDIVIDUAL

Personality

Crutchfield (1954) believes there is a 'conforming personality' type, who will conform in all situations. But other researchers emphasize the importance of the situation in determining behaviour.

Gender

Crutchfield (1954) argues that women are traditionally more conformist. Osman (1980) studied the use of a pedestrian crossing for conformity to group pressure to cross at the wrong time. There was no difference between men and women in this behaviour, but the men were twice as likely to be the initiators of crossing at the wrong time.

CONDITIONS THAT STRENGTHEN CONFORMITY TO THE MAJORITY

FOR CONSIDERATION

Groups that wish to brainwash individuals (e.g. doomsday cults) will use these factors, especially making the individual feel insecure.

The individual is more likely to conform to the majority if:
- The individual is made to feel incompetent or insecure.
- The group is unanimous.
- The group is attractive to the individual, or the individual admires the status of group membership.
- Others in group can observe the individual's behaviour – it seems harder to disagree when you are seen to be disagreeing. It is easier to disagree in private.
- The individual's culture encourages respect for social standards (this might apply, for example, to the practice of queuing at a bus stop).

THEORIES TO EXPLAIN CONFORMITY

FOR CONSIDERATION

Individuals may not be aware of the reasons why they conform. It is the task of psychologists to understand this behaviour.

There are a number of theories of conformity:
- **Social comparison:** this is the idea that individuals look to the group to help compare their own behaviour with social norms.
- **Conflict avoidance:** this explains conformity by assuming that group harmony is desirable and disagreements undesirable.
- **Self-awareness:** individuals do not like to stand out as different to the group – it makes them self-conscious.

These theories have varying success in explaining the ideas of informational conformity (see section 3), normative conformity (see sections 4 and 5) and minority influence (see section 7):
- Both social comparison and self-awareness explain informational and normative conformity, but cannot explain minority influence (where the group bends to the minority).
- On the other hand, conflict avoidance can explain normative conformity and minority influence, but cannot account for informational conformity.

CONCLUSIONS

Individuals will conform more to the group if the group is unanimous and attractive to the individual, and the individual could otherwise be seen to be disagreeing. There are various theories explaining conformity: social comparison, conflict avoidance and self-awareness.

CONFORMITY TO ROLE:
STANFORD PRISON
SIMULATION 1

INTRODUCTION

'Look, we're just going to have to fake it until the real bouncers arrive,' said Phil, looking distinctly worried. 'The mini-bus has got caught up in traffic – they're going to be about half an hour late. We've got to have door staff, otherwise we're going to get in trouble. Mike, Steve, Pete: go and put these jackets and ear pieces on, then come and stand by the door.'
'We're not bouncers!'
'I know you're not – but the punters don't.'
Within five minutes three hard-looking men stood on the door greeting the public on their way in. They were upset when the genuine door staff arrived.
'We were just getting into the role,' said Mike.

WHAT IS CONFORMITY TO ROLE?

In some situations, as we shall see, individuals conform to the social expectations of the particular roles they are playing. This is known as **conformity to role** or **identification**.

This involves a much greater degree of conformity compared with informational and normative conformity, which only involve conformity to one particular aspect of behaviour. In other words, conformity to role means conformity in all aspects of the individual's behaviour.

Conformity to role is best seen in the Stanford prison simulation (Haney et al 1973). This is known under a number of names, including 'the Zimbardo prison experiment' (Philip Zimbardo is remembered as one of the principal researchers).

In this section we shall look at the experimental set-up itself.

Fig 6.14 Philip Zimbardo

THE STANFORD PRISON SIMULATION

Based on responses to newspaper advertisements in the Stanford area of California, 22 male student volunteers were chosen to take part in a prison simulation. They agreed to play the role of 'prisoner' or 'prison guard' (chosen at random) for 14 days in a mock jail built in the basement of the Psychology Department at Stanford University.

The volunteers were given few instructions on how to behave or what was expected. Those volunteers chosen were judged to be the most stable, mature, and least involved in antisocial behaviour. This is important – the volunteers were 'normal' men, and did not have psychological problems. However, it may be important also to ask ourselves what sort of person would volunteer for such research.

The jail contained three small cells (each 6 feet by 9 feet in size). There were three bland meals per day, three supervised toilet visits, and two hours daily of reading and letter-writing privileges. The 'guards' worked three-man 8 hour shifts. To increase the reality of the situation, the 'prisoners' were arrested at their homes by the local police.

Fig 6.15 summarizes some of the advantages that can been seen in this study design.

CD-ROM

Social Psychology: The Stanford prison simulation

KEY DEFINITIONS

REACTIVITY
Participants changing their behaviour because they know they are being observed.

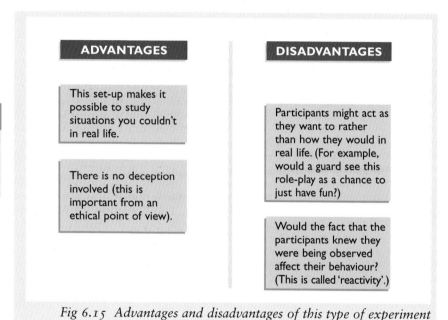

ADVANTAGES	DISADVANTAGES
This set-up makes it possible to study situations you couldn't in real life.	Participants might act as they want to rather than how they would in real life. (For example, would a guard see this role-play as a chance to just have fun?)
There is no deception involved (this is important from an ethical point of view).	Would the fact that the participants knew they were being observed affect their behaviour? (This is called 'reactivity'.)

Fig 6.15 Advantages and disadvantages of this type of experiment

HOT EXAM HINT

You may be asked about the details of the Stanford prison simulation. Remember to describe the method and procedures used.

CONCLUSION

Conformity to role involves individuals conforming in all aspects of their behaviour to the social expectations of the role they are playing.

In this section we have looked at the set-up of a famous experiment intended to investigate this. In the next section we shall look at the findings of this experiment, and evaluate it.

CONFORMITY TO ROLE: STANFORD PRISON SIMULATION 2

FINDINGS OF THE STANFORD PRISON SIMULATION

In the course of the experiment, the 'prisoners' became passive and showed negative emotions. In fact, five had to be released because of extreme emotional depression. The 'guards' were active in the interactions with the 'prisoners', and, though no physical aggression (punching or kicking) was permitted, there was verbal aggression. The 'prisoners' were belittled and humiliated by 'psychological games'. For example, the 'prisoners' were forced to clean the toilets with their bare hands; they were sprayed with fire extinguishers; they were made to do push-ups with 'guards' stepping on them. In fact, the simulation was stopped after 6 days because of the human rights issues (it was supposed to run for 14).

During 25 observation periods over the 6 days, different types of comments of the 'guards' were noted, with the following approximate frequencies:
- Insults: 60
- Deindividuating references, for example calling 'prisoners' by their numbers: 40
- Aggressive: 30
- Threats: 32
- Helping: 0

The 'guards' were the most unhappy when the simulation was terminated unexpectedly. Haney et al (1973) note: 'The extreme pathological reactions which emerged in both groups of subjects testify to the power of the social forces operating'.

This research is important because it shows the powerful influence of the situation and role expectations upon behaviour. 'The environment of arbitrary custody had a great impact upon the affective [emotional] states of both guards and prisoners as well as upon the interpersonal processes taking place between and within those role-groups' (Haney et al 1973).

ARE THE FINDINGS APPLICABLE TO REAL LIFE?

Did the participants believe what was happening, or was it like a game for them? Maybe the participants were playing for the cameras? Philip Zimbardo, one of the three researchers, argues that from the observation of the participants and the post-simulation interviews, it was too real to be just 'role-playing' (Zimbardo 1973).

KEY DEFINITIONS

DEINDIVIDUATION
Denying a person's individual character, and treating them as less than human.

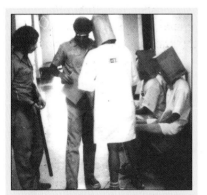

Fig 6.16 The Stanford Prison simulation: prisoners and guards

THE ETHICAL ISSUES

The participants had all agreed to take part (there was informed consent), and the 'prisoners' knew they would be locked up for 14 days (there was no deception involved). All participants knew the simulation was being discreetly filmed by CCTV, though the 'guards' believed the cameras were turned off at night. However, the 'prisoners' had no automatic right to withdraw.

The only deception was the unexpected 'arrest' of the 'prisoners' by the local police at the beginning of the simulation.

Zimbardo defends the simulation's ethics, by saying that it was stopped after 6 days although it was meant to run for 14. There was full debriefing and long-term follow-up of the participants. But could it have been stopped earlier? The evidence of the changes in behaviour of the participants was there from the first day.

Zimbardo admits on the BBC programme 'Five Steps to Tyranny' (2000) that he was caught up in the role of the 'prison supervisor', and the bizarre behaviour seemed normal. Only when an outsider to the research realized the human rights abuses was the simulation stopped.

FOR CONSIDERATION

Because the findings are seen as important, does that justify what happened in the research?

Do you think it is right that Philip Zimbardo should have become famous because of this research?

MOTIVATIONS OF THE RESEARCHERS

Savin (1973) argues that the careers of the researchers were aided by this simulation: 'in pursuit of their own academic interests and professional advancement' they were prepared to 'deceive, humiliate and otherwise mistreat their students'.

Of the three researchers, Zimbardo has become most famous, and much of that fame comes from this research. He replies to the criticism of Savin by emphasizing the importance of the findings: 'a great many prisoners, former inmates, legislators, criminal lawyers and parole officers have gone on record endorsing the findings and implications of our study' (Zimbardo 1973).

CONCLUSIONS

The Stanford prison simulation showed how the behaviour of ordinary students could change drastically when they 'acted' the roles of prisoners and prison officers. McDermott (1993) confirms the importance of this research in the history of psychology. The question has now changed from 'what kind of person will mistreat others?' to 'what are the circumstances under which anyone would behave in this uncharacteristic way?' But would the same ethical debate have arisen if the 'guards' had not mistreated the 'prisoners'?

OBEDIENCE TO AUTHORITY: STANLEY MILGRAM I

INTRODUCTION

Oliver was called to the boardroom. Luke knew that what he was about to do was wrong, but he had no choice. The managing director had given him his orders, and they had to be carried out.

'Oliver, I'll be straight with you. We're going to have to let you go.'

Oliver was visibly shaken.

'Why? I'm performing really well.'

'I know. It's not your performance.'

'What is it then?'

Luke stumbled. How do you sack someone whom you to believe to be really good?

'It's not my decision.'

'Oh that's great, passing the buck. So I suppose if our illustrious managing director told you to shoot me you'd do that as well, would you? Got to obey orders, haven't you – can't think for yourself.'

'Now you're just being stupid,' said Luke.

WHAT IS OBEDIENCE TO AUTHORITY?

Obedience to authority means compliance to the demands of an authority figure (a parent, or an employer, or the President of the United States). There is less opportunity to resist than with requests from ordinary people. It is the abdication of personal responsibility due to social power and status of the authority figure in the social hierarchy.

STANLEY MILGRAM'S EXPERIMENT

Fig 6.17 Stanley Milgram

The topic of obedience to authority is dominated by one set of experiments started in the 1960s, and completed by Milgram (1974). He was interested in why Germans had obeyed their Nazi leaders and committed many atrocities during the Second World War. 'Milgram's decision to frame the obedience project in the shadow of the Holocaust was of paramount significance ... the obedience experiments were seemingly endowed with an undeniably inflammatory, provocative essence' (Miller, Collins and Brief 1995).

Initially Milgram believed that the German people were different to other people, and, because of the type of socialization that existed in German society, had more of a readiness to obey authority figures. So Milgram designed an experiment that would involve obedience to an authority figure to the point of apparently harming (or even killing) a complete stranger. The expectation was that the American participants would not obey the authority figure.

Fig 6.18 The 'learner' was in fact a confederate of the experimenter.

THE STUDY DESIGN

The participants were tested one at a time at the Psychology Lab at Yale University. When the participants arrived, they were introduced to a middle-aged man, who appeared to be another participant, but was a confederate of the experimenter.

The participant was told that they were to investigate memory. Apparently at random, the participant would be chosen to be the 'teacher', and the confederate to be the 'learner'. The participants were not aware that the experiment was a fake; for them everything appeared to be real, and as far as they were concerned it was indeed a memory experiment.

The 'learner' was taken into the next room, where the participant could not see him. The participant was shown a machine with gradings of electrical shocks from 0 to 450 volts. They believed the 'learner' to be wired to this machine (which was of course a fake), and were told that if the 'learner' failed on a series of memory tests, the 'learner' should be given increasing electric shocks as punishment. The participant would be operating the machine.

A shock of 450 volts (the apparent maximum of the machine) can easily kill a person. In case the participant was not sure of the seriousness of electric shocks, each voltage had a label beside it: 300 volts, for example, was labelled 'intense shock'; while 450 volts was labelled 'XXXX'. The participant believed that the machine was real, because they were given a mild electric shock as part of the testing of the machine.

The basic routine went thus: the 'learner' would 'fail' the memory tests, and each time the experimenter would instruct the participant to administer an electric shock, increasing in voltage each time. So Milgram had set up the situation thus: would an ordinary man give increasing punishment to a stranger in the next room because an experimenter in a white coat told them to do so?

Fig 6.19 The machine in Milgram's experiment

SUMMARY

In this famous investigation into obedience to authority, Milgram had set out to show that the atrocities committed by Nazis during the Second World War were only carried out because of the particular socialization of the German people. American people, the study was supposed to show, would not harm another person simply because an authority figure had told them to do so. In the next section we shall look at what actually happened in practice.

OBEDIENCE TO AUTHORITY: STANLEY MILGRAM 2

THE PARTICIPANTS IN THE EXPERIMENT

To find participants for Milgram's experiment, advertisements were placed in newspapers in the state of Connecticut, USA, asking for volunteers for the 'memory' experiment (with a promise of a 5 dollars expenses payment). A total of 40 men aged between 20 and 50 years were chosen for the first experiment (Milgram 1963).

The characteristics of this sample were as follows (Milgram 1974):

Age distribution:
- **20–29:** 8 people
- **30–39:** 16 people
- **40–50:** 16 people

Occupational distribution:
- **Manual workers:** 15
- **Sales/white-collar workers:** 16
- **Professionals:** 9

As you can see, they were a cross-section of ordinary males.

Public Announcement

WE WILL PAY YOU $4.00 FOR ONE HOUR OF YOUR TIME

Persons Needed for a Study of Memory

*We will pay five hundred New Haven men to help us complete a scientific study of memory and learning. The study is being done at Yale University.
*Each person who participates will be paid $4.00 (plus 50c carfare) for approximately 1 hour's time. We need you for only one hour: there are no further obligations. You may choose the time you would like to come (evenings, weekdays, or weekends).

*No special training, education, or experience is needed. We want:

Factory workers	Businessmen	Construction workers
City employees	Clerks	Salespeople
Laborers	Professional people	White-collar workers
Barbers	Telephone workers	Others

All persons must be between the ages of 20 and 50. High school and college students cannot be used.
*If you meet these qualifications, fill out the coupon below and mail it now to Professor Stanley Milgram, Department of Psychology, Yale University, New Haven. You will be notified later of the specific time and place of the study. We reserve the right to decline any application.
*You will be paid $4.00 (plus 50c carfare) as soon as you arrive at the laboratory.

- -

TO:
PROF. STANLEY MILGRAM, DEPARTMENT OF PSYCHOLOGY, YALE UNIVERSITY, NEW HAVEN, CONN. I want to take part in this study of memory and learning. I am between the ages of 20 and 50. I will be paid $4.00 (plus 50c carfare) if I participate.

NAME (Please Print). . . . .
ADDRESS . . . .
TELEPHONE NO. . . . . Best time to call you . . . .
AGE . . . . OCCUPATION . . . . SEX . . . . . .
CAN YOU COME:
WEEKDAYS . . . . EVENINGS . . . . . . WEEKENDS . . . .

Fig 6.20 The original advertisement used by Milgram

DURING THE EXPERIMENT

The experiment was set up as described in section 12, and the participant (in the role of the 'teacher') soon found himself being ordered to administer electric shocks to the 'learner' (a confederate of the experimenter).

The procedure was standardized both in the responses of the 'learner' (which were recorded) and in the words of the experimenter. Some examples of the 'learner's' responses are as follows:

- **75–120 volts:** 'Ugh! Hey this really hurts'
- **135–180 volts:** 'Ugh! Experimenter get me out of here. I told you I had heart trouble. My heart's starting to bother me now. Get me out of here, please. My heart's starting to bother me. I refuse to go on. Let me out'
- **255–300 volts:** '(agonized scream) I absolutely refuse to answer anymore. Get me out of here. You can't hold me here (intensely agonized scream). I told you I refuse to answer. I'm no longer part of this experiment'
- **375 volts onwards:** Silence

If the participant hesitated or stopped, the experimenter would prod him to continue:

- **Prod 1:** 'Please go on'
- **Prod 2:** 'The experiment requires it'
- **Prod 3:** 'It's absolutely essential that you continue'
- **Prod 4:** 'You have no choice'

'Obedience' was defined as obeying the experimenter all the way to 450 volts. If the participants refused to continue, the experiment was stopped at the point of disobedience.

RESULTS

CD-ROM

Social Psychology: Milgram's experiment

Psychiatrists predicted before the experiment that only 0.1% of people would obey until 450 volts (that is, 1 in 1000 people). In fact, in the first experiment, out of the 40 men, 26 obeyed as far as 450 volts.

In addition, nobody stopped before 300 volts, which is still probably enough to kill someone. Thus the level of obedience (to 450 volts) was 65%.

The results in these 40 men are detailed in the table:

FOR CONSIDERATION

Often people reading about this experiment believe they would know it was a fake, and would not have obeyed in the same situation. This kind of attitude is probably due to the hindsight bias, and the actor–observer effect.

Voltage at which participant stopped and refused to continue	Number of participants
300	5
315	4
330	2
345	1
360	1
375	1
450	26

(Milgram 1974)

KEY DEFINITIONS

HINDSIGHT BIAS
Perceiving an event in the past with the knowledge we have now.

ACTOR–OBSERVER EFFECT
Believing that the actor has more control than they actually do.

CONCLUSIONS

Obedience to authority is compliance with the demands of an authority figure. Individuals will sometimes commit atrocities in the name of obedience to authority ('I was only following orders').

Milgram showed in his experiments that ordinary people can do unpleasant things in order to obey an authority figure.

MILGRAM'S OTHER EXPERIMENTS ON OBEDIENCE 1

VARIATIONS ON A THEME

Milgram's original findings were a surprise to him, so he set about trying to discover the exact variables involved in obedience. Over the ten years after the original experiment, he ran another twenty different experiments. Each experiment varied the original in a small way. This is experimental research – isolating variables one by one to see which have the greatest effect on participants' behaviour.

The key components of the original experiment are:

- 'Learner' is in next room and not visible
- 'Learner' feedback
- Male participants
- Experimenter (one, in white coat, sits behind participant)
- Experiment at Yale University
- Participant is alone
- Nature of relationships between individuals in situation

In this section and the next we shall look at some of Milgram's variations on these aspects, and assess their importance.

Remember that the original experiment found that **65%** of the participants obeyed up to 450 volts. Any very different level of obedience in the following experiments would show that variable to be important in the explanation for obedience.

FOR CONSIDERATION

Research can often take a long time and painstaking execution of experiments. Milgram spent over ten years investigating obedience.

'LEARNER' IS IN NEXT ROOM AND NOT VISIBLE

'Learner' in same room (proximity):
- No. of participants obeying to 450 V: **40%**
- **Some importance** in explaining obedience

'Teacher' (participant) must place 'learner's' hand on shock plate to receive electric shock (touch proximity):
- No. obeying to 450 V: **30%**   **some importance**

'LEARNER' FEEDBACK

No voice feedback, but at 300 volts bangs on wall (remote victim):
- No. obeying to 450 V: **65%**   **not very important**

Vocal protests (voice feedback):
- No. obeying to 450 V: **62.5%**   **not very important**

Fig 6.21 'Teacher' holding 'learner's' hand on a shock plate to receive an electric shock.

MALE PARTICIPANTS

Women used:

- No. obeying to 450 V: **65%**   **not very important**

EXPERIMENTER (ONE, IN WHITE COAT, SITTING BEHIND PARTICIPANT)

Softer-spoken experimenter:

- No. obeying to 450 V: **50%**   **not very important**

Experimenter not in room; for example, gives instructions by phone (authority less close):

- No. obeying to 450 V: **22.5%**   **important**

(Clearly having the experimenter in the room is an important factor in obedience.)

Ordinary man gives instructions (not experimenter in white coat):

- No. obeying to 450 V: **20%**   **important**

(It is important to have an experimenter (authority figure) giving the orders.)

Two experimenters giving contradictory instructions:

- No. obeying to 450 V: **0%**   **very important**

(Contradictory messages from authority figures reduce the level of obedience: obedience requires clear messages from authority figures.)

Authority figure is used as victim, and no experimenter giving instructions:

- No. obeying to 450 V: **0%**   **very important**

(Having the authority figure as a victim produces conflict for participants.)

Two experimenters; one of them receives electric shocks:

- No. obeying to 450 V: **65%**   **not very important**

Participants choose level of shocks:

- No. obeying to 450 V: **2.5%**   **very important**

(Having the participant choose the shock level places the responsibility upon them.)

The variations are continued in the next section.

HOT EXAM HINT

The details of Milgram's experiment are important, but it is also important to understand just why people obeyed. The variations on the original experiment help us to do this.

SECTION 15 | # MILGRAM'S OTHER EXPERIMENTS ON OBEDIENCE 2

These variations on Milgram's experiment are continued from the previous section.

EXPERIMENT AT YALE UNIVERSITY

A different part of Yale to the Psychology Lab:
- No. obeying to 450 V: **65%**   **not very important**

Offices outside university in Bridgeport; no connection to University:
- No. obeying to 450 V: **47.5%**   **some importance**

(Clearly the prestige of Yale University plays a part.)

PARTICIPANT IS ALONE

Participant as bystander: confederate takes over giving shocks:
- No. obeying to 450 V: **73%**   **not very important**

Group of 3: 1 participant and 2 confederates who rebel:
- No. obeying to 450 V: **10%**   **some importance**

Group of 2: 1 participant and 1 confederate who gives shocks:
- No. obeying to 450 V: **92.5%**   **very important**

(Group pressure to continue or to stop is important (can combine conformity and obedience).)

NATURE OF RELATIONSHIPS BETWEEN INDIVIDUALS IN SITUATION

'Learner' signs contract releasing legal liability from Yale:
- No. obeying to 450 V: **40%**   **some importance**

(Here the 'learner' releases the University from responsibility.)

'Learner' demands to be shocked:
- No. obeying to 450 V: **0%**   **very important**

(This actually reduces obedience by placing responsibility upon the participant, because it is felt that the 'learner' must just be saying it. The participant would not want to be shocked, and so they are now obliged to use their power and not shock.)

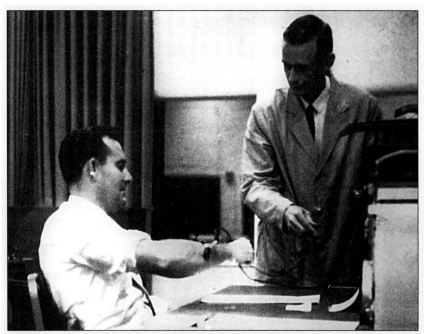

Fig 6.22 The experimenter gives instructions to the 'teacher'.

SUMMARY

Milgram varied aspects of his original experiment in subsequent research, to find out why the participants obeyed. The most important factors in why people obeyed are shown in Fig 6.23.

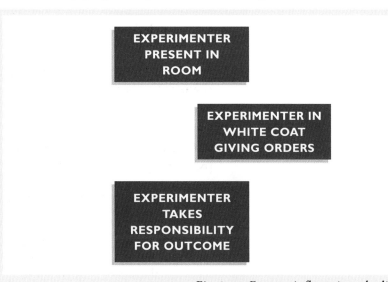

EXPERIMENTER PRESENT IN ROOM

EXPERIMENTER IN WHITE COAT GIVING ORDERS

EXPERIMENTER TAKES RESPONSIBILITY FOR OUTCOME

Fig 6.23 Factors influencing obedience

The proximity of the 'learner', and the presence of the experimenter in a white lab coat proved to be important.

These important factors are discussed further in section 16.

WHY DID PARTICIPANTS OBEY IN MILGRAM'S EXPERIMENTS?

'HOW COULD THEY DO THAT?'

The reason why individuals obey in situations such as the Milgram experiment, and do things that they would not usually do (such as harm a complete stranger without provocation) is due to a number of factors in the situation.

Obedience occurs in small steps, rather than all at once. The study by Gibson and Haritos-Fatouros (1986) of Greek soldiers who were convicted of torture shows that their involvement began slowly. For example, first they would be asked to hold the victim down, later to kick them, and so on. This gradual increase went with dehumanization of the victim, and social support of society and the government for their behaviour.

But it is important to emphasize that the participants in Milgram's experiment were not passive. Most argued with the experimenter, and showed signs of distress, even if they did obey. Milgram notes how arguing with the experimenter protected the individual psychologically as a 'good person' while still continuing to obey the 'callous' experimenter. The participants had no time to reflect, and faced a series of dilemmas: the demands of the experimenter versus those of the victim; and the need for scientific data against the suffering being inflicted.

KEY FACTORS

Overall, Milgram emphasizes certain key factors that led to obedience.

The white-coated experimenter

The experimenter's presence was important. His white coat (uniform) signalled that he was 'legitimate authority'.

Individuals are socialized into obeying 'legitimate authority', whatever is asked of them. Baron and Byrne (1991) emphasize the importance of the authority figure having highly visible symbols of power, such as a uniform. For example, Bickman (1974) set up an experiment where passers-by in the street were told to pick up a paper bag. The command was made by a civilian in a suit or an individual in a guard's uniform. The latter obtained 80% obedience, compared with 40% for the civilian.

Demands of the situation and social roles established by the authority figure

'The entire prospect of turning against the experimental authority, with its attendant disruption of a well-defined social situation, is an embarrassment that many people are unable to face up to' (Milgram

Fig 6.24 Would you pick up this litter if told to? Would it depend on who told you to do it?

1974). Participants were polite to the experimenter despite the unreasonable demands. It may seem absurd to be polite to a 'brutal researcher' (Miller et al 1995). But as well as the explicit orders, there are subtle, implicit aspects to this kind of situation.

Generally, experimental research involves an 'implicit social contract', and this was even stronger here. Refusal to obey was breaking the 'social contract' between authority figure and subordinate, and between experimenter and participant.

The authority figure takes responsibility for the outcome

An American soldier, William Calley, was tried for a massacre at My Lai during the Vietnam war. He based his defence around simply following orders (quoted in Kelman and Hamilton 1989).

However, Lutsky (1995) challenges the importance of this factor in Milgram's work: obedient and disobedient participants did not differ in their attribution of responsibility to the experimenter. Kelman and Hamilton (1989) talk of 'professional authority', where the individual obeys because they respect the expertise of the authority.

Milgram distinguishes between the **autonomous state** (actions based on one's own conscience) and the **agentic state** (acting as an agent for others, with loss of responsibility). When individuals work together, it is easier if control comes from above (a hierarchy forms). The individual comes to accept the commands without measuring them against their own conscience. The individual has become an agent of the hierarchy and obeys unthinkingly. One mechanism here is **tuning**: information from authority figures becomes the only information that matters, as opposed to requests from the victims or those at the bottom of the hierarchy. Furthermore, the situation is redefined by the agents, (for example 'it's not really harming them' or 'they deserve it'). The process of becoming agentic in such situations is socialized into individuals as a good thing.

CONCLUSIONS

The work of Milgram is important because it 'challenges the myth that evil lurks in the minds of evil people – the bad they who are different dispositionally from the good us who would never do such things' (Zimbardo 1992). Milgram showed that obedience was due to situational factors, not individual characteristics. Anybody may find themselves obeying authority figures and performing harmful actions, depending on the situation; it is not reserved to a particular 'sadistic' type of person.

KEY DEFINITIONS

AUTONOMOUS STATE
Actions are based on one's own conscience.

AGENTIC STATE
Acting as an agent for others, with a loss of responsibility.

FOR CONSIDERATION

OTHER FACTORS IN OBEDIENCE
- 'Worthy purpose': participant is swayed by the need for advancement of science.
- Victim appears to be a volunteer, and appears to become the 'learner' by chance.
- Participant is a volunteer and feels obliged to continue the experiment.
- Payment – an unlikely reason because it was a very small amount, and one version of the experiment that did not give expenses found no difference in results.
- The participant believes the experimenter who says the shocks are 'painful but not dangerous'.

ETHICS OF MILGRAM'S RESEARCH 1

THE RIGHTS AND WRONGS OF THE EXPERIMENT

FOR CONSIDERATION

Psychologists follow a set of ethical guidelines for their research, produced by the British Psychological Society (BPS) in the UK, and the American Psychological Association (APA) in the US. (See CD-ROM Introduction: The British Psychological Society's code of conduct.)

This series of experiments stimulated the debate on the ethics of experimentation more than any other. It was the catalyst for the development of codes of conduct for research in psychology.

Psychologists are divided about the rights and wrongs of these experiments. Erikson (1968) calls them a 'momentous and meaningful contribution to our knowledge of human behaviour'. Elms (1972) feels that they are the 'most morally significant research in modern psychology'.

From an alternative viewpoint, Baumrind (1971) argues that 'fundamental moral principles of reciprocity and justice are violated, when the research psychologist, using his position of trust, acts to deceive or degrade'.

Milgram (1964) defends himself thus: 'the problem of destructive obedience, because it is the most disturbing expression of obedience in our time and because it is the most perplexing, merits intensive study'. This is often called the 'end justifies the means' argument.

FOR CONSIDERATION

The debate between Baumrind and Milgram is typical of arguments among psychologists. The existence of different viewpoints is seen as a healthy aspect of psychology.

Diane Baumrind (1964) was the most critical of Milgram. In a series of articles in the 1960s, the two scientists fought out the arguments. The most important arguments centred around the following ethical concerns:

- The participants were not given the opportunity to give informed consent to taking part in the experiment (by the very nature of the experiment they were not fully informed).
- The participants were deceived in a number of ways.
- Psychological distress was caused to the participants during the experiment.
- The participants afterwards had to live with their experiences – that is, there was potential permanent psychological damage.

Now follows a summary of the arguments used by Baumrind and Milgram when contesting these major points. We shall look at the issue of consent in this section, and in the next section we shall move on to the distress and possible permanent psychological damage caused to the participants. Evaluative comments are added – these are based on Brewer (2001).

THE ISSUE OF INFORMED CONSENT

Baumrind's argument

Baumrind argued that there was no informed consent from the participants for what actually happened in the experiment. (Indeed, by the very nature of the experiment, there could be no opportunity for them to be fully informed about it.)

Milgram's argument

Afterwards, participants reported being glad to have taken part in the experiment.
- 84% said they were 'glad' or 'very glad' to have taken part.
- This is compared with 1.3% who said they were 'sorry' or 'very sorry' to have taken part.
- 74% said they felt they had learned something of personal importance.

Evaluation

It is important to ask the question: how do we know that the questionnaire replies were not a product of obedience, in the same way as the obedience in the experiment?

Fig 6.25 Milgram argued that obedience to authority to the point of harming others was 'the most disturbing expression of obedience in our time'. This was why his experiments were justified. Do you agree? Or do you feel his own experiments were too potentially harmful themselves?

ETHICS OF MILGRAM'S RESEARCH 2

In this spread we shall look at other important ethical issues surrounding Milgram's experiments: the distress and potential permanent psychological damage caused to the participants.

THE DISTRESS CAUSED DURING THE EXPERIMENT

Baumrind's argument

In Baumrind's view, an unacceptable level of anguish and distress was caused to the participants during the experiment.

Milgram's argument

Milgram argued that he did not intend the stress to be caused, and before the experiment had no idea of the outcome. (We might consider the fact that he expected the American participants *not* to obey the experimenter – see section 12.)

Evaluation

Milgram may not have been able to predict the outcome initially. However, it must be remembered that after the original experiment, he went on to perform many different variations of the experiment over many years (see sections 14 and 15). It could be argued that he must have known by then the potential for distress.

POTENTIAL FOR PERMANENT PSYCHOLOGICAL DAMAGE

Baumrind's argument

Baumrind argued that there was a potential for permanent psychological damage to be caused to the participants by their experiences.

Milgram's argument

Milgram replied that the participants were debriefed after the experiment. Also they were visited by a psychiatrist one year after, who found no evidence of mental illness caused by the experiment.

Evaluation

The experiment may not have caused major psychological problems, but the individual's self esteem may have been lowered, leaving a general negative feeling about himself or herself.

Elms (1972) defends Milgram with the rather weak point that some people look at themselves in an unreal way anyway.

The debriefing used by Milgram involved:
- Reuniting the 'learner' and the participant (the 'teacher')

- Assuring the participants that no shocks were really given
- Having an extended discussion about the experiment

Elms (1995) argues that Milgram was a pioneer in the development of detailed debriefing.

However, the effectiveness of such a debriefing is questioned by research by Ring, Wallston and Corey (1970). In their study, 57 female undergraduates were involved in an obedience experiment using a loud noise in a victim's ear (52 of them fully obeyed). After the experiment itself, the type of debriefing was varied in three conditions:
- No debriefing
- Traditional debriefing (similar to Milgram's debriefing)
- Traditional debriefing and explanation for their obedience behaviour

When the participants were visited later, those who had been in the first two groups were equally upset, and had negative feelings about the experiment. Participants from the third group (who had had both a traditional debriefing and explanation for their obedience behaviour) were the least upset. This suggests that a form of counselling may be needed as part of the debriefing.

CONCLUSIONS ON THE ETHICS OF THE MILGRAM EXPERIMENT

Aronson (1999) asks the question of whether ethics would be so important in this experiment if none of the participants had obeyed.

ALTERNATIVE ETHICAL RESEARCH METHODS

A role-playing type of study was tried by Geller (1978). A total of 91 adult males aged between 20 and 60 years old were recruited by newspaper advertisements in New York. They all had no prior knowledge of Milgram's experiments.

The participants underwent an experiment similar to Milgram's, with a fundamental difference: all the participants knew the 'learner' was a confederate and that the machine did not give electric shocks. Otherwise, this was a replication of Milgram's experiment. Geller found 51% obedience (compared with 65% for Milgram). However, many participants do not become 'involved' in the scenarios, so there is a tendency to screen participants in order to choose those who are good at role-playing. Are people just guessing how they would behave if they were in a particular situation?

SUMMARY

There are ethical concerns about Milgram's experiments because of the distress experienced by the participants. The issues involved include deception within the experiment, and the fact that there can be no informed consent from the participants for taking part.

Researchers have attempted to find alternative methods with fewer ethical problems.

FOR CONSIDERATION

Because of the ethical concerns surrounding Milgram's experiments, attempts were made to find alternative ways of researching obedience.

HOT EXAM HINT

You may be asked about the ethics of Milgram's experiments. It is therefore important for you to understand what ethical concerns there are, and why.

VALIDITY OF MILGRAM'S EXPERIMENTS I

KEY DEFINITIONS

VALIDITY
In this case, refers to how sure we can be that the experiment really did measure obedience behaviour.

WHAT IS VALIDITY?

Establishing the **validity** of an experiment is very important. This is showing that the experiment really did measure the behaviour of obedience rather than something else.

As Milgram's research was carried out in artificial situations, we must be careful when applying the results to real life. Before we can do so the validity of the results must be established. There are three types of validity: external, internal and ecological. We shall study the first of these in this section, and the next two in the next section.

KEY DEFINITIONS

EXTERNAL VALIDITY
Similar results to the original research will be found in different situations or cultures.

EXTERNAL VALIDITY

This involves the replication of the study in different situations and cultures. Only a few replications were possible before it was decided that it was unethical to continue with this type of study.

Smith and Bond (1993) have summarized the cross-cultural replications as follows.

USA (1962) (original Milgram study):
- Result: 65% obedience
- Comments: male participants used

Italy (1968):
- 85% obedience
- Students; maximum voltage = 330 V

Germany (1971):
- 85% obedience
- 101 males; general population
- There was also 52% obedience where the participant had seen beforehand another scenario where the 'teacher' had refused to shock. There was 0% obedience where participants were reminded of the responsibility for their actions.

Australia (1974):
- 40% obedience for males, 16% obedience for females
- Students
- Foster (1997) believes there were important differences to Milgram. The victim was a 'long-haired' student; there were differences to Milgram in the age, education, social class and status of experimenter; the female participants had a female victim (Milgram always had a male victim). There was 0% obedience when participants were reminded of the responsibility for their actions.

USA (1974):
- 85% obedience
- Students

UK (1977):
- 50% obedience
- Male students

Jordan (1978):
- 62.5% obedience
- 48 students
- There was 12.5% obedience in a control condition in which participants were told beforehand they were free to shock or not.

Spain (1981):
- More than 90% obedience
- Students

Austria (1985):
- 80% obedience
- General population

Holland (1986):
- 92% obedience
- 39 participants from general population (see section 21 for all the studies done in Holland on this area)

Points to note about these replications

- They use different groups of participants to Milgram; for example students were used in Italy and Spain.
- Some studies involved different tasks to obey to the one used in Milgram; for example Meeus and Raaijmakers (1986) (see section 21).
- Different types of victim could be used, for example the 'long-haired student' in Australia.
- There could be differences in authority figures across cultures. For example Moghaddam et al (1993) point out that in Iran, a white-coated scientist would have no authority, but a mullah is an important authority figure.
- Different levels of obedience may show that social context is important. Smith and Bond (1993) argue that: 'These studies suggest that in none of the countries studied is obedience to authority the kind of blind process which some interpreters of Milgram's work have applied. Levels of obedience can and do vary greatly, depending on the social contexts which define the meaning of the orders given. The importance of context may also vary from country to country'.

However, Miller (1995) points out that 'what generalises from the obedience experiments are not the literal findings, but rather the processes underlying them'. This can be seen in real-life cases and the issues of ecological validity (see next section).

VALIDITY OF MILGRAM'S EXPERIMENTS 2

In the last section we looked at the importance of validity in scientific research, and considered the external validity of Milgram's experiment.

Following on from that section, we shall now consider:
- Internal validity
- Ecological validity

INTERNAL VALIDITY

KEY DEFINITIONS

INTERNAL VALIDITY
Participants believe that the situation of the experiment is real.

Did the participants believe the experiment was real, and that they were actually giving electric shocks? Orne and Holland (1968) argue that the participants followed the experimenter's instructions in the same way as when a magician performs a trick to 'chop off your head'. You know it will be all right.

Milgram (1963) is clear that the participants believed the experiment to be real: many of them 'were observed to sweat, tremble, stutter, bite their lips, groan and dig their fingernails into their flesh. These were characteristic rather than exceptional responses to the experiment'. This would not happen if the individuals believe that they were involved in a 'magic trick'.

ECOLOGICAL VALIDITY

KEY DEFINITIONS

ECOLOGICAL VALIDITY
The results of the experiment are applicable to real-life situations.

Are Milgram's findings applicable to real-life situations rather than just artificial experiments?

Coleman (1987) argues that the participants obeyed because it was an experimental situation. However, support for Milgram's findings come from studies in hospitals.

The best known of these studies is Hofling et al (1966). Situations were set up to test whether nurses would obey a doctor in giving a drug to a patient, while knowing that to do so they would have to break various hospital rules:
- Instructions were given over the phone; hospital rules said drug instructions had to be in writing.
- The doctor was unknown to the nurses; the hospital rule was not to take instructions when the doctor was not known.
- The nurses were instructed to give twice the maximum dose; the maximum dose was clearly written on the side of the container.
- Also, the nurses had to go to the pharmacy to collect the drug because it was not on the ward stocklist for the day.

In this study, 21 out of 22 nurses obeyed. However, the drug used was unfamiliar to the nurses.

Rank and Jacobson (1977) replicated the study with a familiar drug (Valium). Of 18 nurses in the study:
- Two obeyed (that is, went to administer the drug).
- Ten prepared the drug but then checked with another doctor before administering it.
- Six checked before preparing the drug.

Foster (1997) argues that these studies are different to Milgram because nurses are contracted to obey doctors. In addition, the situation usually involves female nurses with male doctors, which brings gender and power issues into the equation.

METHODOLOGICAL ISSUES IN MILGRAM

There are a number of methodological criticisms of Milgram's experiment:
- There was no control group, for example of participants told beforehand that they were free to shock or not as they chose.
- There was no version of the experiment where participants were reminded of their responsibility for their actions. In other experiments including this variation there is 0% obedience.
- Apart from 40 participants, all those involved in the experiment were male.
- The victim (the 'learner') was always male.

SUMMARY

Milgram's experiments were artificial situations. In order for the results to be applied to real life, the validity of the experiments must be established.

CD-ROM

Social Psychology: General issues in Milgram

There are three types of validity:
- Internal
- External
- Ecological

These different types of validity have been discussed and explored in relation to Milgram's studies in these two sections.

NEW STUDIES ON OBEDIENCE

Meeus and Raaijmakers (1986, 1995) carried out a series of 19 experiments in the 1980s in Holland, using over 400 participants. They mostly used the following format.

The participant was told that the unemployed person in the next room (actually a confederate) was applying for a job. The participant was asked to 'test their reaction to stress' by using fifteen negative remarks ('stress remarks') from a pre-prepared script.

Each remark became more negative and stressful, and obedience was measured by participants going all the way to the 15th remark. (The participants were under the impression that resistance to stress was not a requirement of the job.)

DIFFERENCES BETWEEN MILGRAM AND THIS STUDY

- **Place:** Milgram took place in the USA, whereas this study took place in Holland.
- **Time:** Milgram took place in the 1960s, whereas this study took place in the 1980s.
- **Task for obedience:** Milgram involved the participant being told to administer electric shocks to a stranger, whereas in this study the participant was required to make stressful comments to an unemployed job applicant (a stranger).
- **Control group:** Milgram used no control group; in contrast this study did use one.
- **Expected behaviour:** in some versions of this study participants were asked to predict beforehand how far they would obey. This did not happen in Milgram's study.
- **Advance information:** in some versions of this study, advance information was given to the participants beforehand, unlike in Milgram.
- **Role-play versions:** some versions of this study were role-play (that is, the participant knew the real aim of the study). This did not happen in Milgram.
- **Original level of obedience:** this was 65% in Milgram, and 91% in this study.
- **'Experimenter absent':** under this condition the level of obedience was 20.5% in Milgram, and 36% in this study.

FOR CONSIDERATION

The replication of an original study in another situation is a good way to show whether the original results were accurate. The replication attempts to copy the original research as closely as possible.

DETAILS OF THE 19 EXPERIMENTS

1 Baseline
Obedience level 91%

2 Control: no instructions to make remarks and participants could choose which remarks to make
Obedience level 0%

3 Baseline replication
Obedience level 83%

4 Participants are personnel officers (experienced in interviewing)
Obedience level 93%

5 Expected behaviour: written description of experiment and participants asked to rate themselves beforehand on how far they will obey
Obedience level 9%

6 Experimenter absent
Obedience level 36%

7 Two peers rebel: two confederates with participant, who refuse to obey
Obedience level 16%

8 Advance information: participants told one week beforehand of experiment and consequences to applicant (expected that obedience would fall in this condition)
Obedience level 100%

9 Legal liability of participants for whatever happens during experiment
Obedience level 30%

10 Advance information and legal liability of participant
Obedience level 20%

11 Advanced information and psychology department legally responsible
Obedience level 67%

12–17
Role-playing variations
Obedience level 14–73%

Milgram replications:

18 Advance information: painful shocks
Obedience level 57%

19 Advance information: deadly shocks
Obedience level 43%

HOT EXAM HINT

Any researchers mentioned by name in the syllabus (such as Meeus and Raaijmakers) are important to know in detail.

SUMMARY

This set of studies on obedience are the most recent and extensive since Milgram. Though they were different to Milgram in certain ways, the studies still found obedience to an authority figure for 'harming' another person.

SECTION 22 | RESISTANCE TO AUTHORITY AND DISOBEDIENCE

INTRODUCTION

A couple of years ago a local newspaper ran an article entitled 'You Ain't Making Me Do Nothing'. It was a story about a local man who appeared to deliberately disobey authority. He had angered the local council when he had refused to clear his back garden, and then deliberately blocked their access to it when they tried to enforce a clearance. He had been to prison on numerous occasions for refusing to pay speeding and parking fines. He had refused to wear a tie to a local club and was promptly arrested for breach of the peace when he tried to force his way in. When asked whether he had any respect for authority, he replied: 'I ain't bowing and scraping to no one.'

KEY DEFINITIONS

RESISTANCE
The refusal to obey an authority figure (for example, if the command is seen as morally wrong).

RESISTANCE IN MILGRAM'S EXPERIMENT

Milgram (1973) was interested in those who did not obey in the experiments he had devised (see sections 12 and 13). Two particular individuals are mentioned. Both of them had experienced the horrors of the Second Word War.

One of them, a Dutch-born man (Jan Rensaleer), continued to believe he was responsible for his actions despite the experimenter claiming to take responsibility, and he also rejected the experimenter's 'prod' that there was no choice but to continue (see section 13).

The other individual, Gretchen Brandt, had grown up in Nazi Germany.

Rochat and Modigliani (1995) note three attitudes among the disobedient participants:
- 'One should not impose one's will on another.'
- 'One is responsible for what one does to another.'
- 'One is always free to choose not to obey harmful demands.'

Also there is evidence of empathy. As one participant said afterwards: 'What if the situation was reversed?'

EARLY RESISTANCE

From a re-analysis of the actual interactions between the experimenter and the 'teacher' (the participant) in Milgram's later experiments, Modigliani and Rochat (1995) point out that 'the earlier in the procedure subjects begin to resist notably, the more likely they will be to end up defiant'.

Using the data from the Bridgeport office version of the experiment, Modigliani and Rochat found that 83% of those who showed defiance

Fig 6.26 Many French people joined the Resistance to fight the German occupation during the Second World War – an extreme form of resistance against an extreme form of authority.

before 150 volts tended to stop at 150 volts. None of those who obeyed to 450 volts had shown any defiance.

In a film that Milgram made of this experiment (and included in a later documentary called 'You Do as You are Told'), there was one participant who stopped at 150 volts. Here are some of his responses to the experimenter's prods (see section 13):

- Prod 3 ('It's absolutely essential that you continue'): 'Essential or not, this programme's not quite that important to me that I should go along doing something that I don't know about, particularly if it's going to injure somebody'
- Prod 4 ('You have no choice'): 'Oh I have a lot of choices. My number one choice is I won't go on if I think it's hurting that man'

Rochat and Modigliani (1995) show evidence for this kind of early resistance in their case study of the French village of Le Chambon during the Nazi occupation in the Second World War. Owing to immediate resistance by the village leaders, the whole village refused to collaborate with the occupiers in persecuting minorities, and in fact would help them to escape. It was estimated that 5000 refugees found safe haven here during the war.

PROVOKING RESISTANCE

Gamson et al (1982) set out to find situations in which individuals would rebel against authority. They posed as a company and told volunteers that they would be taking part in market research.

Discussion groups of nine participants talked about a manager's behaviour while being videotaped. It became apparent that the company was manipulating the discussion for the video, and that the discussion was actually going to be used to fire this manager. When asked whether the company could use the video, 32 of 33 groups refused to continue until the end.

It was important that the group felt it was being manipulated. Group dynamics, however, also influenced the decision. For example, ten groups signed statements allowing the video to be used even though there was dissent within the group.

FOR CONSIDERATION

There have been many examples around the world of obedience leading to others being harmed. Resisting can be an important skill to learn.

CD-ROM

Social Psychology: obedience in real life

CONCLUSION

As much as obedience is important in psychology, there is interest in why some individuals disobey authority figures. An important point is that if individuals obey initially, then they find it harder to refuse or resist later.

CHAPTER **7** ı RESEARCH METHODS

INTRODUCTION

This chapter covers all elements of research methods in the AQA syllabus A. It is meant to be used as a manual. We will look at the main stages of conceiving and designing a scientific experiment in psychology. Even if you have never done any formal research, you should be able to follow the chapter, step by step, and at the end of it have sufficient grounding in the subject area to go on to A2 and begin your research.

I have tried to personalize the experience as much as possible, to involve you in the search for knowledge through other people's research endeavours. Remember that science is a messy business. There are no certainties, just best bets in the constant battle against losing control over unwanted interference. The important thing is to carry out the process as rigorously as possible in accordance with the strict ethical standards required of psychologists, whilst recognizing that perfection is not possible or necessary.

As long as you record your doubts and limits as honestly as possible and take a critical and evaluative approach, then science has proven that it can produce useful results. You are a trainee psychologist and this is the place to start.

EXPERIMENTAL METHOD

Ranjit dyed his hair blond to see what effect this would have on his pulling power with the girl he fancied. Linda, one of his classmates, was well aware that she had a weakness in her exam preparation process: she always seemed to leave it too late. As a result she decided to use a more structured approach to preparing for her AS levels, so that she could improve her performance and gain grades more in line with her ability, compared with her disappointing GCSE results.

As it turned out Ranjit did not achieve his aim, whereas Linda improved her exam performance significantly. The conclusion for Ranjit was that blond hair did not have the powers of attraction he needed for success, whereas Linda is now firmly convinced that the changes she made to her preparation schedule worked, and she will use this strategy again in the future.

Both of the above are examples of experiments and they both have a common pattern:
- You identify a problem.
- You think up a model as a solution to your problem.
- You put the solution into practice.

LOGICAL POSITIVISM

A group of philosophers called the logical positivists tried to formulate a model of how science works so that we could lay down a once-and-for-all code of practice (or 'axiom') that would guarantee us accurate results. However, they failed, in part, because science is not totally logical in that it involves human imagination as well as rational procedures. Experiment is no exception.

CAUSALITY

Kant argued that scientific research is the synthesis of cause-and-effect relationships. Some thinkers, such as Aristotle, believed that the whole universe could be understood in this way. The history of the universe could be seen as a chain of cause-and-effect relationships beginning with the very first cause, or what Aristotle called the 'unmoved mover' (what many people have deemed to be God). Each effect in turn becomes a cause, producing a chain of events in a causal universe. Whether we follow Kant, who gives a formative role to the mind (that is, we tend to interpret things according to the structures of our own minds), or Aristotle, for whom the whole universe is a place of cause and effect, science explores these causal relationships.

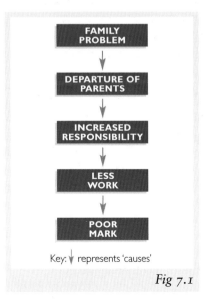

Key: ↓ represents 'causes'

Fig 7.1

- You evaluate the success of your solution. If it works you adopt the solution as useful knowledge for the future – if it doesn't work you try something else.

The above type of informal experiment is something we do all the time as part of living: the German psychologist Heider argued that we are all 'naïve psychologists', in that we subconsciously manipulate psychological variables as parts of our everyday lives. So experimentation is in fact something we understand very well.

However, experimentation also has a formal side. It is seen as one of the most important methods in science. The French sociologist Auguste Comte argued that **positivism** (another word for 'science') was a type of knowledge that required two things:
- A person who develops a theory/model of events as the solution to a problem.
- A method for testing that theory/model to see whether it works in the real world.

Experiments are one of the most important and successful methods of testing scientific models to see whether they work in practice. (For more on Comte's theories see chapter 1.)

CAUSALITY

Let's study causality. Cathy was feeling miserable because she had received a poor mark for her psychology practical. One reason for the poor mark was that she did not have enough time to do the assignment, as she had to look after her family while her parents were away (sorting out a family problem). This meant that Cathy had to shoulder more responsibility than usual, leaving less time for her work.

We can analyse this case study in terms of cause-and-effect relationships:
- Cathy's disappointing mark was the effect of not doing enough work…
- …which in turn was the effect of increased family responsibilities…
- …which in turn was the effect of her parents' departure, caused by the need to sort out the family problem.

This linear description is one way of describing how cause-and-effect chains can be used to analyse events; each effect is in turn a cause, depending on the point at which you decide to analyse the chain (see Fig 7.1). Scientists have spent much time analysing such chains, and have formalized the investigation of cause and effect through what is called **experimental method**.

VALIDITY

Validity is a measure of the accuracy of an investigation. If something is highly valid, it is measuring exactly what we believe it to be measuring: a metre rule measures length; a thermometer measures temperature. Both are valid measures of the variables for which they were designed. However, a thermometer is not a valid measure of length, any more than a rule is a valid measure of temperature.

For cause-and-effect relationships to be properly investigated, valid measures must be used: as experiments focus on very specific relationships between variables they are very useful in this respect.

Another type of validity to consider is ecological validity – how far can we apply the findings of our experiment to real life? The use of laboratories in psychology has been criticized because it has poor ecological validity; that is, measuring variables away from normal environmental conditions is artificial and introduces potential error into the analysis.

RELIABILITY

Reliability is a measure of the ability of our conclusions to stand the test of time. A rule will allow us to measure distance not only today but next year as well. It is therefore very reliable. If it wasn't we wouldn't use it. In psychology there are three methods for testing reliability: test re-test, alternative form and split-half.

Experiments, as a method, offer maximum validity and reliability, where it is possible to use them. Why? Because they offer maximum control over unwanted variables that might interfere with the variables we are trying to measure. Unfortunately, cause-and-effect chains are much more complex than the isolated linear set of events that Cathy believed to be responsible for her problems in section 1. Any single cause-and-effect relationship will be surrounded by a network of other forces that may be having an effect.

This is particularly true of complex problems such as those we find in psychology. We can think of a host of other variables that might have played their part in Cathy's disappointing mark: a row with her best friend, anxiety about the family problem, a problem with the printer on her computer. Any or all of these may have played a part in her difficulties. As experimental scientists we need to control the effects of any variables outside of those we are measuring (called **confounding variables**). Otherwise we may be measuring a distorted relationship between cause and effect.

KEY DEFINITIONS

TEST RE-TEST
Where a measure, such as a test of personality, is applied to many people to see whether it gains the same results for all people with the same personality.

ALTERNATIVE FORM
Using another version of the test to check results. For example, Thompson used a Hebb-Williams T-maze as a test for a rat's problem-solving ability (in this maze the rat always comes to a T junction and can only go left or right, not backwards).

SPLIT-HALF
Checking whether two halves of a test produce the same result. For example, in an IQ test.

CD-ROM

Research Methods: Key researchers

CONTROL TECHNOLOGY AND LABORATORIES

One way of achieving this control is to use technology to shut out external or **extraneous variables** not being measured. If you have ever done chemistry or biology experiments, you will have used test tubes. These offer a highly controlled environment in which to study cause-and-effect relationships. Mix hydrochloric acid and sodium carbonate in a test tube and some very predictable things happen. There is a chemical reaction to form sodium chloride and water, and the gas carbon dioxide is given off.

Tightly controlled environments such as the test tube provide extremely good conditions for the accurate analysis of cause-and-effect relationships involving chemical variables. Such experiments will normally be carried out in a laboratory, to increase even further the level of control over unwanted extraneous variables.

THE RESEARCH PROCESS

However, before we grapple with such control problems we need to recognize that science operates as a *culture* of research. To develop an experiment it is necessary to familiarize ourselves with the work done by other people in our field of interest. In 'state-of-the-art' research we may well address the problems experienced by other scientists in order to offer a solution. Though as psychology trainees we are unlikely to be involved in such problems, we do need to follow a similar procedure as a learning process. We start our experiment, therefore, by reading some general background material related to our area of interest, so that we are familiar with previous findings.

ETHICS

In order to develop our knowledge it is vital that we have an accurate and detailed account of our scientific practice. It is also vital that we control research from an **ethical point of view**.

Therefore within science there are codes of conduct that prescribe certain standards in scientific practice and its reporting, governing professional honesty and respect for the subjects of our research. The idea is that all formal research is published under certain rules, so that scientists can make known their discoveries and have their procedures and findings checked by other scientists. Science is a process of dispute as well as agreement.

CD-ROM

Introduction: The British Psychological Society's code of conduct

FOR CONSIDERATION

Karl Popper argues that science proceeds by a process of falsification. Scientists check theories using factual evidence gathered from techniques such as experiments; the process is supported by mathematical calculation. Elements of the theory that cannot withstand this testing are abandoned. Eventually the theory itself may well be rejected in favour of a more adequate model. Whilst Popper's model has been challenged, most notably by Kuhn, it does signal the importance of dispute in science, and that it is imperative that we standardize our procedures.

AIMS

Once we have established a problem or idea resulting from our review of previous research, we can develop a general statement of intent for our investigation, called the **aim**. Aims can be both theoretical and factual (or **empirical**).

Where the theoretical is concerned, the problems with Wundt's experiments into human perception using introspection were influential in the formation of a new way of doing psychology called **behaviourism** (see chapter 1, section 3). The aim of behaviourism was to focus only on evidence that could be measured, a style of research called **empiricism**. Empiricism is a philosophical idea that suggests that knowledge must be based in the collection of the measurable facts.

CD-ROM

To learn more about Wundt and about behaviourism, see Research Methods: Key terms and Research Methods: Key researchers respectively.

However, the problem with empiricism is that it does not allow the possibility of formulating psychological models, and thus places considerable limits on our psychological knowledge (that is, it does not allow us to suggest new ways of explaining how our minds and personalities work). It was obvious from work done by Köhler that certain types of learning involved problem solving, and that we had to find a model of the brain as an information processor, not just a structure for routing information to different parts of the body, as the behaviourists preferred to think.

CD-ROM

To learn more about Köhler, see Research Methods: Key researchers

Cognitive psychology was developed in relation to problems in behaviourism.
* One aim of Wundt's work had been to understand the psychology of colour.
* One aim of behaviourism was to provide hard objective evidence.
* An aim of cognitive psychology was to develop models of the brain as an information processor to fit the empirical evidence.

However, aims are usually related directly to empirical research, and therefore much less ambitious with respect to the development of experimental research. An aim is a general statement of the experimental or research problem we have decided to consider in a particular psychological area. In the case of Köhler above it might have been as follows:

'To research the relationship between learning and problem solving.'

If we were to take the informal experiments carried out by Ranjit and Linda in section 1, we might describe the aims as follows:
* Ranjit: 'To research the relationship between hair colour and increased attraction.'

- Linda: 'To research the relationship between being more organized and exam performance.'

REMEMBER!

Good hypotheses produce good science.

Aims are an important step towards clarifying our experimental objectives: they are the foundation for the development of a statement which defines exactly what will be tested. This statement is called an **hypothesis**.

HYPOTHESES

Independent and dependent variables

Experimental method offers maximum opportunity for control by isolating the causal relationship of the variables to be tested. The cause and effect are given names: the cause is called the **independent variable**; the effect is called the **dependent variable**. These are often shortened to **IV** and **DV**. Experiments observe and record the relationship between these two: what change in the IV causes what change in the DV? Hypotheses are often statements of prediction about the relationship between an IV and a DV. (For example: 'The more weight I hang from this spring (IV), the longer the spring will get (DV)'.)

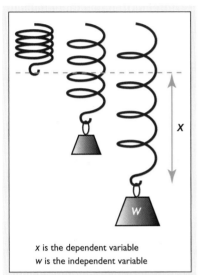

x is the dependent variable
w is the independent variable

Fig 7.2 Independent and dependent variables

Operationalization

One of the essential differences between an aim and an hypothesis is that the hypothesis is **operationalized**. In other words, the variables being tested are stated specifically in the terms in which they are measured. If a hypothesis is to be fully testable then the variables need to be stated in such a form.

Let us look at an example. Jean is interested in the significance of context (surroundings) in memory recall. She intends to give her respondents a list of 20 words to be studied in the laboratory. A short while later, half of the respondents will be asked to write down in the laboratory what they remember of the list; the other half are sent to do this on the sports field.

Her aim is:

'To research the relationship between **remembering** and **context**.'

In order to test this she needs to operationalize her variables ('remembering' and 'context').

From this aim she develops the following hypothesis:

'The level of recall for those carrying out the exercise in the laboratory differs significantly from the level of recall for those carrying out the exercise on the sports field.'

- The variable 'remembering' is operationalized and stated in terms of **level of recall** (this might be, for example, number of words remembered correctly).
- The variable 'context' is operationalized and stated in terms of either **laboratory** or **sports field**.
- Both laboratory/sports field and level of recall are the actual measurements taken of the IV and DV respectively.

CD-ROM

To learn more about contextual memory, see Research Methods: Key terms

REMEMBER!

For successful experimental research it is essential to fully operationalize your hypothesis.

Research methods | 247

TYPES OF HYPOTHESIS (CAUSAL AND NON-CAUSAL)

Causal

This type of hypothesis has a relationship between its variables that is defined in terms of cause and effect: it will therefore have an independent variable (IV) and a dependent variable (DV).

Let's take Jean's experimental hypothesis from section 3. She is predicting that differences in the context will cause differences in the levels of recall. Remember, the variable predicted to be the cause is the IV. The variable thought to be the effect is the dependent variable or DV.

Establish which is which by asking 'What am I actually measuring?' In Jean's case it is level of recall: so this is her DV. Her IV is the predicted cause of changes in level of recall, that is, the context in which recall takes place: either of the two conditions; laboratory or sports field. Her hypothesis predicts a causal relationship between changes in the IV and changes in the DV (the IV has an effect on the DV).

Non-causal

Most psychologists would probably prefer to test causal hypotheses if possible, as they offer high levels of validity and reliability. However, this is often not possible, for practical or ethical reasons. (If I believe long-term isolation to be linked to a psychological disorder, it would be unethical of me to lock people up to find out!)

Fig 7.3 *The different contexts in Jean's experiment*

In non-causal hypotheses we do not test a cause-and-effect relationship; thus there are no IV and DV. The best we can do in these cases is to demonstrate that there is a **relationship** between the variables. A well known example of such a relationship is what we call **correlation**. This is a statistical technique for comparing two variables that we believe may be related.

A significant example of this technique was in the study of disease. Sir Richard Doll, an epidemiologist, suspected there might be a link between many of the serious lung problems in his patients and the long-term effects of smoking tobacco. He and others began collecting data, and found that those who smoked large numbers of cigarettes over an extended period of time were much more likely to contract life-threatening diseases like lung cancer (for this, Doll won a Nobel Prize in 1959). Notice the use of the phrase 'were much more likely to', rather than an absolute like 'will'. Only causal relationships will predict the degree of exactness implied by the word 'will'. With correlation, we can only say that smoking seems to be related to lung cancer – a much less certain prediction.

REMEMBER!

Correlation does not allow us to make statements about cause and effect.

In the research of the cause of fatal diseases the testing of a causal hypothesis would be out of the question for **ethical** reasons – you can't smoke people to death in order to see what they die of. It may also be very difficult to carry out in practice (see section 12).

Alternative – null

The aim of all scientific research is to examine the relationships between variables in as exact a manner as possible. We aim to provide valid and reliable knowledge by measuring the relationship between the variables, avoiding the interference of personal preferences or values in the research process. It is suggested that we need to be **objective** in our thinking and actions. This is impossible to achieve completely, because we are always affected to some degree by our personal values. The best we can do is to control our values (in other words detach ourselves sufficiently from them), so that we can do science.

Hypotheses are statements of intent, and as such include some element of the values of the person developing them. In addition, a danger is that human beings are very good at finding what we are looking for, even when it is not there. There are two examples of psychologists who have been accused of doing just this. Both Burt and Freud have been criticized for their **ethical standards** in relation to carrying out their research and the analysis of their findings.

In order to mitigate this effect, we ask researchers to develop and test hypotheses that state the opposite of what they are predicting. These are what we call **null hypotheses**. Using a null hypothesis enforces greater objectivity, as you are compelled to argue against yourself.

Let's return to Jean's hypothesis from section 3 as an example. Her original hypothesis stated that:

> 'The level of recall for those carrying out the exercise in the laboratory differs significantly from the level of recall for those carrying out the exercise on the sports field.'

Under the **alternative – null** system, this becomes what we call the **alternative hypothesis**. In order to restrict as much as possible the effect that her personal values might have, Jean should test its opposite – the **null hypothesis**. The null hypothesis might be:

> 'The level of recall for those carrying out the exercise in the laboratory **does not differ** significantly from the level of recall for those carrying out the exercise on the sports field.'

By focusing on this hypothesis Jean can detach herself sufficiently from her values to produce valid and reliable findings. The idea is that she has to reject this null hypothesis before she can accept her alternative hypothesis. If she can find evidence to reject the null hypothesis she can, by definition, accept the alternative hypothesis. If she cannot reject the null hypothesis she must not accept her alternative hypothesis.

CD-ROM

To learn more about Burt and Freud, see Research Methods: Key researchers.

FOR CONSIDERATION

There is another feature to this debate. As mentioned in section 2, the philosopher Karl Popper argued that nothing can be proven and that the best we can do is to falsify our findings. In looking for evidence to reject our null hypothesis we are practising falsification.

HYPOTHESIS TAILS AND SIGNIFICANCE

ONE-TAILED OR TWO-TAILED? (DIRECTIONAL OR NON-DIRECTIONAL?)

Hypotheses in psychology generally predict some form of expected change in either a dependent variable (DV) or in two correlated variables. This can be defined in two ways. Returning to Jean's null hypothesis again (see section 4):

'The level of recall for those carrying out the exercise in the laboratory does not differ significantly from the level of recall for those carrying out the exercise on the sports field.'

This is a **two-tailed hypothesis**, because Jean does not predict the direction of the change in the DV in relation to the different contexts (situations) in which recall will take place (this is why this may also be called a **non-directional** hypothesis). In other words, she is open-minded about which condition of the independent variable (IV) will generate the higher level of recall in the DV.

However, this need not have been the case. Jean could have stated her null hypothesis in the following terms:

'The level of recall in the laboratory is not significantly higher than the level of recall on the sports field.'

This hypothesis suggests that Jean is predicting a higher level of recall in the laboratory condition of the IV. This is a one-tailed hypothesis because she is only predicting one outcome.

(These different types of hypothesis can be confusing. In the previous paragraph we have said that in this one-tailed hypothesis Jean is predicting greater recall in the laboratory. Note that Jean actually says 'recall in the laboratory is *not* significantly higher', because she is stating the null hypothesis – see section 4 if you are still unsure about this.)

Many statisticians suggest that you should remain as open-minded as possible and therefore only test two-tailed hypotheses.

SIGNIFICANCE

You will have noticed the word **significance** in the hypotheses mentioned so far. It is not enough to establish that there has been an experimental effect just because a change was observed in the DV as a result of the manipulation of the IV: it is the magnitude of the change which needs to be considered.

There are complex networks of variables that may intrude into psychology experiments even when our controls are well planned and implemented. We must be sure that there is a big enough effect to be confident that our observed change is not due to something extraneous.

One major problem that can affect our measurements is chance. If we throw an evenly balanced coin a number of times, we would forecast that a head would turn up about half or 0.5 of the time. Thus, if we throw the coin 20 times we would expect to get about 10 heads. If we got 12 heads we might still believe the coin to be fair. However, if we got 19 heads we would start to suspect that the result was a lot less likely to be due to chance, and that there was bias in the coin. (In fact, every now and then 19 heads will occur by chance, but very rarely indeed.) The question is: when do you start to suspect the coin?

One standard method of deciding is to set at cut-off point at 5%. In other words when the probability of the result occurring by chance is 5% (.05) or below, we will not believe that the outcome of the coin throwing can be explained by chance; that is, we will presume that some other cause is bringing about the effect.

We carry out a similar exercise when deciding whether or not to reject our null hypothesis in psychology. We will only reject our null hypothesis if the probability of explanation by chance is .05 or less. Other than that we will accept it.

This is the definition of a significant result in standard psychology experiments. Chance is the base-line. It is only when the effect is significantly greater than can be expected by chance that we accept that there has been an experimental effect. For Jean's experiment we will only accept that context causes a change in the level of recall if it is more than 95% certain.

Even though we place such tight limits on our acceptance of experimental findings, there is still a 5% probability that our experimental findings are the result of chance effects. We can tighten the significance level further to .01 (1%). This is done in new research so that there is very little likelihood of the findings being wrong.

Even so, this still means that there is a 1% probability of results being due to chance effects. This may be acceptable where life is not at stake, but in experiments that deal with variables that may be life threatening we will use very tight limits below .01.

Now that we have discussed the development of hypotheses we are in a position to plan the design of our experiment. We will look at this in the next section.

Fig 7.4 At what point do you begin to suspect results are not due to chance?

UNWANTED VARIABLES

Experimental method offers the best possibilities to control unwanted variables. In a perfect world scientists would measure the relationship between the independent variable (IV) and the dependent variable (DV) in isolation in order to find evidence to reject their null hypothesis. In reality it is almost impossible to isolate the IV and DV, even in the natural sciences such as physics and chemistry. A perfectly controlled experiment is certainly not possible in psychology, and we must therefore employ techniques which nullify the presence of interfering or confounding variables.

Such unwanted variables tend to be of three types:
- Subject or respondent variables
- Demand charactersitics
- Extraneous variables

KEY DEFINITIONS

RANDOMIZATION
The standard technique for controlling bias. In a lottery the outcomes are selected by a random number machine to make the game fair. In psychology experiments, we allocate respondents randomly to their positions within the experiment to limit the effects of bias.

REMEMBER!

The British Psychological Society has strict rules to limit distress experienced by respondents in psychological research. Victoria was well aware of the importance of these rules.

CD-ROM

To see the BPS Code of Ethics, see Introduction: The British Psychological Society's code of conduct.

CD-ROM

To learn more about GSR meters, see Research Methods: Key terms.

SUBJECT OR RESPONDENT VARIABLES

Each participant brings to the experiment personal baggage that needs to be accounted for if we are to keep control of the experiment so that we can measure our variables accurately. Subject/respondent variables can be controlled by planning or designing our experiments very carefully. There are three well known design techniques for doing this, which are as follows:
- Randomized or independent subjects
- Matched subjects
- Repeated measures

Randomized subjects

Let's look at an example of randomization. Victoria was interested in different stress reactions in relation to the level of control a respondent experienced. She decided to use an ordinary classroom exercise where respondents read aloud a paragraph from a textbook (**IV**) in front of an audience. However, there were to be two conditions of the IV:
- **Condition 1** gave a degree of control to the respondents: they were told that they could terminate the reading at any time.
- **Condition 2** gave respondents no control because they were asked to read the text from beginning to end.

The **DV** was the level of stress measured in the two conditions. In order to measure stress levels Victoria used a GSR meter.

Victoria decided to carry out an **opportunity sample** of the first 30 people who were available to help her with the experiment. For this experiment an opportunity sample is quite adequate as long as Victoria recognizes the limits this imposes on her findings.

Having found a sample of 30 people Victoria must now allocate them to their test positions within the conditions of the IV. In order to control **subject/respondent variables** this should be done using a random process. The most practical method is probably to give each of the 30 respondents a number and then use a random number table, usually located at the back of a standard statistics book, to assign each respondent to their conditions of the IV: 15 to condition 1, and 15 to condition 2. By doing so Victoria distributes any control problems with subject/respondent variables randomly across both conditions, and therefore minimizes their potential to distort the causal relationship to be measured.

Matched subjects

Edwin is interested in the effect that an audience has on the performance of a simple problem-solving exercise. The exercise is to complete a children's jigsaw puzzle in as short a time as possible. The two conditions of the **IV** are:
- **Condition 1**: solving the puzzle in front of an audience
- **Condition 2**: solving the puzzle alone.

The **DV** is the time taken to solve the puzzle.

However, Edwin is aware that IQ is a subject/respondent variable that will affect performance on the puzzle. If he can distribute the effects of IQ evenly across the two conditions of the IV, so that the average IQ of both conditions is the same, IQ will be controlled.

Of course one method of doing this is to randomize the allocation of respondents to the two groups as per Victoria's experiment above: many purists argue that we should always do this anyway, because in not doing it we may inadvertently introduce unknown control problems into the experiment. Even so, we know that randomization does not guarantee to evenly distribute intelligence across both conditions of the IV, and we may need more certainty: as with all research there is a balance between practicality and accuracy.

We can nullify the effect of IQ by testing all respondents and pairing up people with similar IQ scores. One member of the pair could then be randomly allocated to one condition of the IV, the other member of the pair automatically being placed in the other condition of the IV. By carrying out such a programme of allocation the average IQ of each condition of the IV will be similar enough to limit differences in IQ affecting the DV (puzzle solving time).

Repeated measures

David wants to check out some work originally carried out by Tulving and Pearlstone, who showed that a list of words derived from categories such as types of food was better remembered if the category name (e.g. food) was presented as a retrieval cue. David decided to investigate the level of recall (dependent variable, DV) from two lists of 20 five-letter words (independent variable, IV):

- **Condition 1**: a list of random five-letter words.
- **Condition 2**: a randomized list of five-letter words derived from four categories: food, animals, domestic goods and clothes.

To control **subject/respondent variables** (see section 6) David decided to use a **repeated measures design** (in which all participants do all parts of the experiment). Each of the respondents is given time to study both of the word lists and after an interference exercise (which ensures that the respondent is retrieving from long-term memory, not short-term memory) has time to recall as many words as possible. The respondent experiences the process as follows:

- Study random list (condition 1)
- Count backwards from 20
- Recall as many words as possible
- Rest
- Study categorized list (condition 2)
- Count backwards from 20
- Recall as many words as possible
- **Debriefing**

Because all people tackle both conditions of the IV, subject variables are nullified.

However, there are difficulties with this type of design, known as **order effects**. There is a technique called **counterbalancing** to control these problems.

Repeated measures designs have the advantage of ensuring that the same subject does both conditions of the IV and thus limits the effects of subject variables. However, it does not involve random allocation and thus may bring unknown biases to bear. The less we interfere with the process the better.

CD-ROM

To learn more about Tulving and Pearlstone, see Research Methods: Key researchers.

REMEMBER!

It is always necessary to inform your respondents about the nature of the research in which they took part and to answer any queries they may have. Such practice is polite but also ethical.

FOR CONSIDERATION

ORDER EFFECTS
The respondent has already had **practice** at doing the memory exercise when coming to the second list of words. Such practice may aid recall and therefore increase performance on the second list. Alternatively, the respondent may have a problem with **tiredness** or **boredom**, which may have the opposite effect to that of practice, by lowering the level of recall for the second list.

FOR CONSIDERATION

COUNTERBALANCING
Half of the respondents do list 1 then list 2 and the other half do list 2 then list 1, thus controlling the order effect. Randomly allocate respondents to the different orders: using a coin, define heads as list 1 and tails as list 2. One flip of the coin will decide the order for two respondents at a time: if it comes up heads respondent 1 does list 1 before list 2. Respondent 2 automatically does list 2 before list 1.
- **Respondent 1**: list 1 then list 2
- **Respondent 2**: list 2 then list 1
The coin has decided this order. Repeat the process for respondents 3 and 4, and so on.

DEMAND CHARACTERISTICS

Another major problem for psychology experiments is the effect that the person carrying out the experiment has on the respondent. Orne (1962) called these effects **demand characteristics**. All social situations involve the existence of some kind of personal relationship, and experiments are no exception. The presence of the experimenter will have an effect on the respondent's thinking and behaviour, thereby influencing the outcome of the experiment.

We can control demand characteristics by using standard procedures for the carrying out of experiments. One such technique is to give respondents **standard instructions**.

However, there is some contact between the respondent and the experimenter, which will inevitably have an effect, either enhancing or restricting the performance of different respondents. It is vital therefore that the experimenter and the respondent develop a good **rapport** so that the respondent can perform as naturally as possible.

CONTROL OF EXTRANEOUS VARIABLES

Another major source of variables that can interfere with the measurement of the IV and DV are effects related to the environmental conditions surrounding the respondent. These can involve simple, obvious effects such as light or temperature, or those variables of which we could have no knowledge of in advance.

Laboratories

The standard control method for this type of variable is to site experiments in laboratories. These are spaces where environmental effects are standardized so that all respondents are subject to the same environmental effects. However, as with all control procedures, there is a down side, because our day-to-day experiences are not lived out in laboratories. Placing people under laboratory conditions therefore introduces an element of unreality and potential distortion into the measurement process.

Laboratories, according to Heather (1976), may **dehumanize** people, making them appear more like machines than living beings, thus producing invalid data. However, the control benefits of laboratories may be greater than their drawbacks.

PILOT STUDY/DOING THE EXPERIMENT

Having planned the measurement of the variables with maximum care, the next job is to do a pilot study in order to check that all the procedures work. A thorough pilot study will mean that the experiment will run smoothly and be carried out with maximum precision.

The full experimental procedure can now be carried out. It will give data which needs analysing in order to assess whether the IV has caused a significant change in the DV and there has been an experimental effect.

Having collected our experimental data, we need to summarize it so that we can make judgements about the rejection of our null hypothesis. There are two types of statistics designed for this purpose: **statistics of central tendency** and **statistics of dispersion** (see sections 9 and 10). The two methods of summarizing data allow us to represent a mass of data with a single value.

First of all, however, we need to consider the types of data which can be collected, because they affect which of the types of statistic mentioned above we might legitimately choose.

TYPES OF DATA

There are three types or levels of data:
• **Nominal**
• **Ordinal**
• **Interval/ratio**

In order to explain the nature of these levels of data we will use the outcome of a race as an example.

Nominal data

The outcome of the race could be measured in terms of very broad named categories such as medallists and non-medallists (that is, listing all the people who won medals, in no particular order, and listing all those who did not). All competitors fall into one or the other category. However, this level of measurement provides comparatively little detail of the event: we know nothing about who actually won, the person coming last, the interval between them or their different times. This type of data has least power to describe.

Ordinal data

A more detailed way to describe the outcome of the race is give the finishing positions of each competitor, from first to last. This gives a lot more detail of the relative positions of each competitor and is an ordinal (**rank order**) way of describing the outcome of the race.

Interval/ratio data

Interval: An even more detailed method of describing the outcome is to time each competitor, so that we know not only whether they were a winner or loser, and not only in which position they finished, but also how much faster or slower each was in relation to the others. Time is an **interval variable** in that each second, hour and so on is spaced at equal intervals before or after its neighbour: look at all the divisions on a clock face. The interval level of measurement is the most powerful type of data because it offers most detail and will allow the opportunity for addition and subtraction. We can see that the winner was 3 seconds faster in the race than the runner-up. Variables like weight and distance are also interval in nature.

Ratio: A ratio scale is very similar to an interval scale, but it offers the additional opportunity for multiplication and division. This is because it has a definite zero point. Temperature is a good example.

- If we use the Celsius scale we define the data as interval because we cannot say that 10 °C is twice as warm as 5 °C (the Celsius scale also has minus values).
- However, if we use the Kelvin scale, which begins at absolute zero, we can talk in terms of 100 K being half as hot as 200 K. Celsius is an interval scale, Kelvin is a ratio scale.

In practice we often treat interval and ratio scales as one and the same, which is to some extent the case, because all ratio scales are interval scales as can be seen from the example of temperature above.

CONVERTING LEVELS OF MEASUREMENT

The power of interval data can be seen in how easily it can be translated into the other levels of data. If you have interval data it can be transformed into ordinal or nominal data. Let's take the example of the race. The finishing times were as follows:

| 9.88 | 10.23 | 10.04 | 9.92 | 10.67 | 10.52 | 10.02 | 10.05 |

Converting to ordinal data: from this data we can see that the winner's time was 9.88 and that the person coming last was timed at 10.67. If we finish this process of ranking, each competitor can be given a rank or finishing position as follows:

9.88	10.23	10.04	9.92	10.67	10.52	10.02	10.05	Interval data
1	6	4	2	8	7	3	5	Ordinal data

Similarly, we can transpose interval data into nominal data by defining each athlete as either a medallist (M) or a non-medallist (NM) as follows:

9.88	10.23	10.04	9.92	10.67	10.52	10.02	10.05	Interval data
1	6	4	2	8	7	3	5	Ordinal data
M	NM	NM	M	NM	NM	M	NM	Nominal data

However, you cannot reverse the process, that is, convert nominal data into ordinal, or ordinal into interval. This is an indication of the power of interval data.

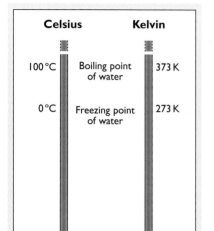

Celsius		Kelvin
100 °C	Boiling point of water	373 K
0 °C	Freezing point of water	273 K
−273 °C	Absolute zero	0 K

Fig 7.5 As you can see, zero on the Kelvin scale is the lowest temperature that can be, whereas there are lower temperatures than zero degrees Celsius.

Measuring central tendency basically means finding the average. It is related to the three types of data available for measuring the dependent variable (DV). These three types (interval, ordinal, nominal) were discussed in section 8. There are three measures of central tendency: the **mode**, the **median** and the **mean**.

MODE

 CD-ROM

To learn more about Eysenck's personality types, see Research Methods: Key researchers.

Richard was interested in measuring the relationship between personality and sporting performance for his project in sports psychology. He interviewed all the competitors who had taken part in the track events in the sixth form sports day in order to decide which runners were extraverts and which introverts.

In order to summarize and compare his findings he organized them in the form of a matrix (or table), as both his variables were nominal:
- **Variable 1:** position in the race (We have to be careful here. We are using this as a *nominal* variable rather than an *ordinal* one.)
- **Variable 2:** extravert or introvert

He then counted the number of competitors in each of the boxes or cells: he did what we call a frequency count. The outcome was as left.

Personality type	Race position		
	1st	2nd	3rd
Extraverts	6	9	7
Introverts	8	5	7

Richard wanted to specify which was the most likely finishing position of each type of personality from his data. The mode is the statistic he could use to do this. The mode is the value that occurs most frequently. From the data, the mode (most frequent value) for Race position and Extraversion is 9 (occurring in the 2nd position); the mode for Race position and Introversion is 8 (occurring in the 1st position). This implies that the most frequent position for introverts is the winner, and for extraverts it is second. We would need to analyse the data more rigorously before we suggested any link between introversion and winning for this sample.

The mode gives an indication of experimental effects based on frequency of occurrence and is a method of summarizing nominal data. However, it does have one major difficulty because there is always the possibility of finding more than one mode. In Richard's results above, we might have found that the extravert group had seven firsts as well as seven thirds. This would make it impossible to define the mode.

MEDIAN

Look again at Jean's experiment on the contextual importance of memory recall (section 3). She recorded the following results from the two conditions of her independent variable (IV) (laboratory and playing field).

Levels of recall (out of 20) for 20 respondents in a randomized design:

Respondent	Lab
1	15
2	9
3	9
4	10
5	13
6	11
7	6
8	14
9	10
10	9

Respondent	Field
11	7
12	6
13	9
14	9
15	7
16	9
17	6
18	0
19	8
20	10

One method of summarizing the data is to find the **median** for each condition of the IV. Arrange the data in each condition in ascending order and find the halfway point. If the median falls between two scores, use the midway point. The lab median is **10**. The field median is **7.5**.

Converting interval/ratio data into ordinal data (the problem of equal scores)

In the above experiment we treat the DV, level of recall, as a ratio variable. By arranging the data in ascending order we find that some of the scores are equal. What do we do with these scores if we want to convert the data to the ordinal level? All equal scores must have equal rank. For Jean's data the ranks are defined as follows:

Lab	6	9	9	9	10	10	11	13	14	15	Ratio
Ranked	1	3	3	3	5.5	5.5	7	8	9	10	Ordinal

These rankings may look a little strange! The reason is that where there are equal values in the array, such as the three 9s in the lab data, they must be given equal rank. As they occupy positions 2, 3 and 4 in the array we give them a mean position of 3: (2 + 3 + 4) divided by 3 = 3.

MEAN

The mean is the arithmetic average. Thus the mean is calculated by adding all the values in the array and dividing this sum by the number of values in the sample.

Using Jean's data above:

Sum of lab sample = 6 + 9 + 9 + 9 + 10 + 10 + 11 + 13 +14 +15 = 106
Mean of lab sample = 106 divided by 10 = 10.6

Repeating the calculation for the field sample: mean = 7.1

Problems with the mean

If we look at the field sample from Jean's data, one person scored zero. This would appear to be an unlikely score, because it is significantly different from the others. The power of the mean is also a weakness. Because it includes all the data in its calculation it may take account of rogue scores at the extreme ends of the array where there was some experimental error. For example, the respondent who scored zero in the field condition may have been affected by some confounding variable such as test anxiety. This will skew the mean downwards.

We may want to ignore such a score and calculate the mean without it. Another alternative is to use the median, which is not sensitive to such extreme results. The median of 7.5 may be more representative of the data than the mean of 7.1.

KEY DEFINITIONS

SYMBOLS
In statistics symbols are used to represent certain concepts:
$\bar{x}$ mean N sample size
Σ 'sigma': means 'add everything up'

We can express a general formula for the mean as follows:

$$\bar{x} = \frac{\Sigma x}{N}$$

As well as techniques for distinguishing the central point in an array of data, we have techniques for describing the way the data is spread around that point.

RANGE

The measure of dispersion related to the median is the range. It is simply the size of the difference between the top and the bottom figure in the data, plus 1. The smaller this number is the better is the median as a summary and representation of the data.

Taking the data from Jean's experiment:

Lab	6	9	9	9	10	10	11	13	14	15
Field	0	6	6	7	7	8	9	9	9	10

REMEMBER!

The rules of algebra state that in calculations involving brackets you work out the part in the brackets first.

Range for lab   = $(15 - 6) + 1 = 10$
Range for field = $(10 - 0) + 1 = 11$

Interquartile range

In order to limit the effect of extreme variables on the range we can find the points a quarter of the way through the array by splitting the data either side of the median into two.

STANDARD DEVIATION

The equivalent measure of spread around the mean is the standard deviation, which is a measure of the average distance of all the items of data from the mean.

There are a number of formulae for calculating the standard deviation and they are all quite complex (this is why GCSE Maths is required to study psychology). The formula I prefer is:

$$\text{Standard deviation} = \sqrt{\frac{\Sigma(x-\bar{x})^2}{N-1}}$$

Whilst this looks difficult, if you follow the rules of algebra it is manageable.

We shall use Jean's lab data for the calculation. The recall score for each respondent is a value of x. As we noted above, we start with the part in brackets. We know that $\bar{x} = 10.6$. Next we develop a spreadsheet for $(x-\bar{x})$ and $(x-\bar{x})^2$:

Respondent	x	$(x - \bar{x})$	$(x - \bar{x})^2$
1	6	$6 - 10.6 = -4.6$	4.6^2
2	9	$9 - 10.6 = -1.6$	1.6^2
3	9	$9 - 10.6 = -1.6$	1.6^2
4	9	$9 - 10.6 = -1.6$	1.6^2
5	10	etc.	etc.
6	10		
7	11		
8	13		
9	14		
10	15		

REMEMBER!

The square of a negative number is the same as if it were a positive number (for example the square of –3 is 9).

Adding up the numbers in the final column will give us $\Sigma(x - \bar{x})^2$.

We have now finished the calculation for the top part of the equation. Next we need to do the division. To do this we need to calculate the part of the formula below the line:

$$N - 1 = 10 - 1 = 9$$

Therefore standard deviation $= \sqrt{\dfrac{\Sigma(x - \bar{x})^2}{9}}$

All we need to do is input our figures into this equation. The larger the result, the greater the degree of spread there is around the mean.

NORMAL DISTRIBUTION

Another feature of interval/ratio data is that it is usually distributed in such a way that it forms an easily recognizable curve in the shape of a bell. Let us look at what this means.

In Edwin's experiment (section 6) we were interested in measuring audience effects on problem solving, and the difficulties caused by variations in the IQ of respondents. IQ is usually defined as an interval variable. If we were to plot a graph with IQ on the horizontal (or x) axis and the numbers of people with each IQ score on the vertical (or y) axis we would get something like Fig 7.6.

There are certain interesting features about this. The mean, median and mode are the same (100), and cut the area under the curve in two. Also, let us assume that the standard deviation is 15 for IQ. If we mark off a distance either side of the mean equal to the standard deviation, along the IQ axis, we find that roughly 68% of all people will have an IQ between these limits. Thus, 68% will have an IQ between 85 and 115. If we mark off a distance of two standard deviations either side of the mean, we find that this covers almost 95% of all the people. Thus, 95% of people will have an IQ between 70 and 130. If we go out to three standard deviations either side of the mean we take care of approximately 99% of the population. Thus, 99% of people will have an IQ between 55 and 145. Only 0.5% will have an IQ above 145, and 0.5% below 55.

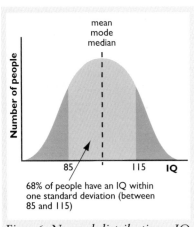

68% of people have an IQ within one standard deviation (between 85 and 115)

Fig 7.6 Normal distribution – IQ

DATA PRESENTATION/FIELD AND NATURAL EXPERIMENTS

Data can be presented in a variety of ways to aid our analysis of the relationship between variables. One of the standard methods is to graph ordinal or interval data as per the normal distribution analysis of the relationship between IQ and frequency in section 10. However, if we want to graphically represent nominal variables, a bar chart or pie chart is preferable.

BAR CHARTS

In her experiment on memory (section 3), Jean wanted a quick visual method of presenting a comparison between her two independent variable (IV) conditions: lab and field. She calculated the mean scores for each condition and presented them in the form of a bar chart as in Fig 7.7.

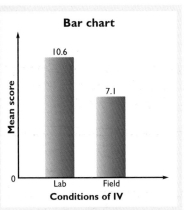

Fig 7.7 Lab and field

PIE CHARTS

Another method of presenting nominal data is in the form of a pie chart. The pie chart takes the form of a circle broken up proportionately in relation to a particular variable. Take Edwin's experiment (section 6) as an example. The normal distribution curve describes the relative proportions of people with various IQs in each sector of standard deviation, both above and below the mean. This could be represented in the form of a pie chart as in Fig 7.8.

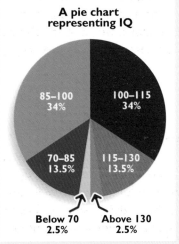

Fig 7.8 Note that to create a pie chart you must work out what proportion of 360° represents each part.

HISTOGRAMS

Another method of representing a relationship is to produce a histogram. To illustrate this we will analyse a coin-tossing exercise. If a coin is fair and we throw the coin once the chances of it coming up heads is one in two or 0.5. If we throw the coin twice in a row there are four possible combinations that might occur: HH; HT; TH; TT. If we throw the coin four times there are 16 possibilities: HHHH; HHHT; HHTT and so on. The relative frequencies of heads can be described in the form of a histogram as in Fig 7.9.

As you can see this looks similar to the shape of a normal distribution curve. The difference between a histogram and bar chart is that in the histogram the size of the rectangle is proportional to its contribution to the total number of occurrences of the variable being measured.

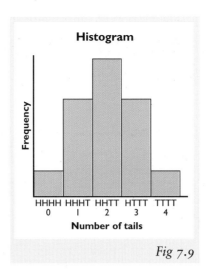

Histogram

Fig 7.9

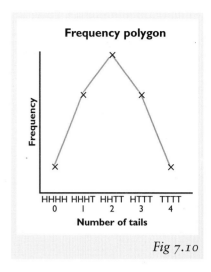

Frequency polygon

Fig 7.10

FREQUENCY POLYGONS

We can draw exactly the same information in another way by joining the central points of each category on the horizontal axis with a series of straight lines. This is called a frequency polygon. See Fig 7.10.

FIELD EXPERIMENTS

CD-ROM

To learn more about Hofling, see Research Methods: Key researchers.

As we have already mentioned, there are problems with the **validity** of laboratory experiments. Thus, psychologists such as Hofling have conducted experiments in the natural environment, in order to avoid the problems of dehumanization described by Heather (1976). Also, in field experiments we circumvent the problem of having to generalize our findings, because, unlike laboratory investigations, we are researching the normal psychological environment. Nevertheless, there is a price to pay in terms of loss of control.

NATURAL EXPERIMENTS

These are experiments where the psychologist is perhaps asked to research the effects of a change in practice. The social services may wish to limit further the risk of children in care becoming detached. They put in place new procedures to provide children with improved foster care. A psychologist is asked to measure the effect by studying, side by side, the new procedure and the old, so as to measure any improvement, using the old procedure as the control.

This type of experiment does not suffer from the problems of the laboratory situation. However, such possibilities are limited and rely on such opportunities arising in the context of the research programme.

NON-EXPERIMENTAL METHODS

CORRELATION

There are often situations where it would be **unethical** for causal experiments to be carried out on people; thus in such investigations there is no independent variable (IV) or dependent variable (DV). A good example was the work carried out in epidemiology, mentioned in section 4, investigating the relationship between smoking and various diseases. We cannot do formal experiments to smoke people to death, so we examine the after-effects of them doing it to themselves. The statistics on smoking are then compared with the statistics on lung cancer, and it is found that the more people smoke the more likely they are to contract lung diseases like cancer. We say there is a significant correlation between smoking and lung cancer.

Correlations are plotted using a **scattergram** relating the two variables together. Fig 7.11 shows a scattergram of the association between smoking and lung cancer.

We see that the trend shows a slope upwards from left to right. This we call a **positive correlation**. As the value of one variable increases, so does the other.

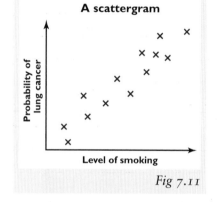

A scattergram

Probability of lung cancer (vertical axis)

Level of smoking (horizontal axis)

Fig 7.11

CD-ROM

To learn more about Thompson, see Research Methods: Key researchers.

A more psychological example: Jonathan was interested in the relationship between inheritance and IQ. He read about some experiments carried out by Thompson, who tested rats' ability to find their way to the end of a Hebb–Williams T-maze and then selectively bred the rats of similar ability to see if they passed on, genetically, their advantage at maze-learning.

This experiment would be difficult to do with people on two grounds:
• It would be **unethical** to selectively breed without consent in this way.
• The practical difficulties of controlling such an experiment, which would take at least two generations, are immense.

Another important feature of **animal experiments** is that the findings may only be of limited value to human psychology. Even though a rat, as a mammal, has a similar physiology to a person, they are sufficiently different to make it extremely difficult to generalize confidently from experiments on rats to people. For instance, rats can consume chemicals which poison people. The nervous system of a rat is far less complex than that of human beings. We have a capacity for self-control far in excess of any rat. There are therefore, limits as to what research into rats can teach us about human psychology.

Thompson did find some evidence to support his hypothesis that the ability to solve maze-learning problems is inherited. But does this mean that those rats who were good at solving mazes were more intelligent than the others? The problem is that we don't have an IQ test for rats. However, will a maze test be an equivalent? This is something Jonathan wanted to investigate.

Of course to test IQ Jonathan would have to use people. He designed a T-maze for an opportunity sample of respondents (see section 6), and gained a score for the number of mistakes they made in learning the maze. He then measured the IQ of the respondents in order to carry out a test of correlation. The raw data was as follows:

Respondent	Maze learning (mistakes)	IQ
1	10	116
2	25	109
3	14	123
4	14	107
5	36	102
6	12	137
7	22	111
8	18	129
9	16	112
10	17	109

Fig 7.12 *We would expect Jonathan's data to show negative correlation.*

REMEMBER!

Even when you get a significant positive or negative correlation, because you are not testing a causal hypothesis you cannot conclude any causal relationship between the variables: a high negative correlation between IQ and maze learning does not offer definitive support for the belief that it is high IQ which is the cause of quick learning of the T-maze. All that is concluded is that IQ is very likely to be a factor.

Jonathan then drew a scattergram of the data, to see whether there was any visual evidence of a trend between the two variables. We would expect to find on this occasion what is called a **negative correlation** between these two variables. Unlike the correlation for smoking and lung cancer, we would expect a trend falling from left to right on the graph. This is because we are predicting that a high IQ will be related to quick learning of the maze (few mistakes) and that a lower IQ will be related to a slower learning of the maze (more mistakes).

Plot the scattergram for yourself and see whether there is a negative trend.

It is often very difficult to see whether there is a significant trend with such data, so we use statistical techniques like Spearman's correlation test to quantify the trend (assign values to it). A perfect trend or correlation can be +1 or −1 depending on whether you are looking for a positive or negative relationship. A value of zero indicates no correlation or trend between the variables: thus, most correlations will be somewhere between the two extremes:

+1 (Perfect positive correlation)
+0.5
 0
−0.5
−1 (Perfect negative correlation)

Naturalistic observation is almost the opposite of the experimental method we have been considering, in that it is what might be called a hands-off approach. Where in an experiment the aim is to control every possible confounding variable, in natural observation the intention is not to manipulate anything but simply record that which occurs naturally in as much detail as possible.

Ethology is a branch of biology that specializes in this approach. *Such an approach is critical of laboratory research*, because laboratory investigations take place out of the natural context and therefore will never be wholly accurate in their conclusions.

Let us look at an example. Paul was interested in researching the possibility that boys are more aggressive than girls. He decided to carry out a series of observations of play-time in a small primary school and record, over a period of ten minutes, the number of aggressive acts displayed by the children.

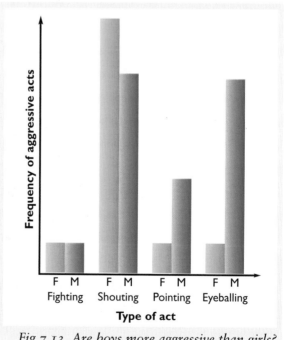

Fig 7.13 Are boys more aggressive than girls?

Initially he had to define exactly what he would record as aggressive behaviour, and he put together a series of categories including both actual and threatened aggression. These were then listed on a table so that he could easily tick any occurrence of aggression he saw, in any of the specified categories for boys or girls. He then produced a bar chart for each sex so that a quick comparison could be made. A sample was as shown in Fig 7.13.

EVALUATION

Whilst naturalistic observation offers maximum realism or **high ecological validity**, it is difficult to control the **value judgements** of the observer and the effect they have on what is being studied. In this example, Paul defines in advance what is to be recorded as aggression, and thus pre-structures the evidence. He then only records what is relevant to this structure and limits his findings accordingly, missing behaviours that do not fit his model, which on reflection could be termed aggressive.

Another disadvantage of naturalistic observation is that Paul cannot consult with those he observes because this would prejudice his findings further. This method is heavily reliant on interpretation: we never simply record anything; our values always intervene no matter how detached we try to be. As a result, what the method gains in realism it loses in control and lack of detachment.

Fig 7.14 *'Ecological validity is all very well – but give me the laboratory every time!'*

Another technique for collecting data is the survey, which is designed to collect both factual and opinion-based knowledge by sampling a population of people on a particular issue. This technique was developed during the nineteenth century in connection with government statistics, and still carries on today with the ten-yearly census.

The census is an attempt to contact every person living in Britain through the household in which they live and asks them to complete a **questionnaire** about their lifestyle. The census is legally enforceable: anyone who fails to complete the questionnaire or who gives false information can be prosecuted. This is indicative of two of the problems with this type of research:

- There is a likelihood that many forms will not be returned.
- There is no guarantee that those who do return them will have answered the questions honestly.

In addition, those who do return their answers may have some social or psychological motive for doing so, which will bias the findings.

However, surveys have certain advantages and can, within certain limits, produce valid and reliable data. The best example is the census, but companies like MORI and Gallup carry out regular surveys in order to estimate our voting intentions, and produce very good forecasts based on only a small sample of the British voting population.

KEY DEFINITIONS

STRATIFIED SAMPLING
A technique whereby a sample is taken in direct proportion to the size of that sample in the whole population. For example, if we were sampling opinions from people on the basis of IQ level, then 50% of that sample should have an IQ less than 100 and 50% should have an IQ greater than 100.

QUOTA SAMPLING
Collecting a limited number of opinions. Each interviewer contacts a specific quota of people of a certain type (e.g. women).

POPULATION AND SAMPLE

In order to cut down the time and cost of surveys we can contact a **representative sample** of the population as a whole and still get an accurate assessment of the findings. The least problematic method of doing this is by doing a **random sample**. (See the earlier analysis of advantages and problems in randomized designs.)

However, there are other non-random techniques such as **stratified** and **quota sampling** which, if applied with rigour, produce relevant findings.

As with experimental design, the design of surveys is a compromise between rigour, cost and practicality. Once decisions on this level have been made the survey comes into its own. It can produce a mass of information, quickly and relatively cheaply.

Many scientists are critical about laboratory experiments not only because they lack realism, but also because they rely on the assumption that it is feasible to generalize from the conclusions of a few experiments to the rest of the humanity. There is no guarantee that results from experiments have application to the wider social network. Surveys have the advantage of measuring these more general networks.

PROBLEMS IN GENERALIZING FROM THE FINDINGS OF EXPERIMENTS

As a prime example of the experimental approach in psychology, behaviourism has the added problem that its primary focus is related to the smallest of psychological entities, the stimulus–response unit. The American psychologist Skinner showed that animals can learn simply by associating the behaviour to be learned with a reinforcement, usually in the form of food, assuming they were hungry. He researched these basic elements of behaviour exhaustively until he felt able to state his findings with confidence. The assumption from here is that such units are the building blocks of many much more complex behaviours and that an understanding of these building blocks will provide useful information about human psychology.

CD-ROM

To learn more about Skinner's work, see Research Methods: Skinner's experiments.

This view was strongly criticized by the Gestalt school of psychologists (see chapter 1), who argued that no psychological knowledge exists in such an elemental form as stimulus–response units. They believed that all psychological material was comprised of 'Gestalts', or compounds of related elements. A Gestalt is a collection of elements that form a unity. This unity cannot be separated without changing so fundamentally that it ceases to exist. We perceive things to exist in relation to other things; not as isolated objects, but as comparison or contrast. Look at the pointillist painting in Fig 7.15. If you were to get too close to it all you would see is the thousands of tiny dots. It is the relationship between the dots that is important.

Or take again the example of the figure/ground relationship (chapter 1 section 3). Look again at the vase/faces picture. We cannot see the figure of the vase; it only becomes understandable in relation to the ground. Then as we focus on the background what was figure becomes background (the vase) and what was background becomes figure (the faces).

Fig 7.15 Young Woman Powdering Herself – *Seurat (1890)*

The Gestalt school would argue that behaviourism is a misguided approach and that a particular stimulus–response unit must be seen in the context of other behaviour before it becomes understandable. Similarly, scientific support for the existence of a specific cause-and-effect sequence does not necessarily mean that we can generalize such a finding to the rest of population. The only place to test this is the wider population, as per the survey.

QUESTIONNAIRES AND INTERVIEWS

Peter wanted to find evidence in support of Erikson's hypothesis (1963) that there may be a relationship between the experience of 'confusion' and difficulty in finding a comfortable career choice. He decided to survey all those students in their final year before leaving for employment or university, by sending them a short **self-administered questionnaire** about their choices and whether or not they had experienced any uncertainty. He decided to use closed questions, which would be quick and easy to answer and quantify. The following is an example:

'Indicate, by ticking, which one of the following best describes your plans for next year:
- Take up employment
- Go to university
- Continue here with another course
- Not really sure'

 **FOR CONSIDERATION**

By carrying out structured interviews, Peter would ensure he contacted every person in the sample (this can be difficult with self-administered questionnaires), and spent half an hour with each of his respondents taking them through a series of pre-prepared questions about their experiences of confusion or otherwise.

Peter planned to contact all those who answered 'not really sure', and a sample of those from the other categories, in order to do a comparison of levels of confusion. For this second part of the survey he decided do a series of structured interviews, because the number of people to be sampled was smaller and the detail Peter required from the respondents was much greater. Such detail is difficult to acquire from closed questions so he decided to use a series of open questions (questions that invite more than a one-word answer) in order to gain a thorough understanding of the feelings of his interviewees.

Peter did consider doing **unstructured interviews**, where there is no specific agenda for the interview apart from a general theme relating to the problem of career choice and how it affects anxiety. However, whilst such a technique might be useful as part of the planning of the survey, in order to learn the sort of question that might be important for the construction of his questionnaire and the structured interview, Peter decided that a whole series of such interviews would take too much time to carry out and analyse. The data collected from unstructured interviews is qualitative and difficult to analyse quickly. Such data is also problematic where generalization is concerned, because it is highly **unreliable**. We can never conduct the same unstructured interview more than once.

The structured interview involved Peter asking respondents a series of **open questions** about opinions on various options such as employment and university and how this affected their self-image. An example was:
- 'Was the process of making a decision about what to do after finishing your present course easy or difficult?'

Depending on the answer given, Peter could ask the respondent to give a fuller account if they so wished. He followed this question with a series of questions aimed at establishing just how anxious the respondent felt in general. The intention was to try to find some association between difficulty in choosing and higher anxiety levels.

Whilst interviews have the virtues of making sure you get replies to the questions set, and that all questions are answered as accurately as possible, they do have a problem. The interview is a social situation and as with all social situations we are affected in our behaviour by the surroundings and most importantly the person who is interviewing us (note the similarity here with demand characteristics in the experimental method – see section 7). Thus, interviewers need to be very carefully trained in ways of facilitating communication by making the respondent feel at ease. Any of the normal tensions that exist in everyday life related to issues of differences in class, gender, ethnicity, age and so on can hinder the retrieval of accurate information from the interview. Interviewers must be careful to develop a good **rapport** with the respondent to ensure the collection of accurate information.

THE ANALYSIS OF SURVEY DATA

When Peter had finished his survey he needed to analyse the data. The great advantage of closed questions is that they are easy to quantify. Let's take Peter's closed question quoted above.

In order to analyse such questions we allocate a number to each answer so as to code it. In the above example the answers can be coded 1 to 4 (1 is 'Take up employment'; 4 is 'Not really sure'). We can then construct a spreadsheet with coded answers for all the questions for each respondent, as left.

Let us suppose that our quoted question is Q1. From the above we can see that respondent C, because they answered Q1 with a 4, is someone to be called for a structured interview as a person who might evidence 'confusion'. We could also calculate the percentage of respondents who were of this category. A whole series of calculations of this type could be carried out.

Respondent	A	B	C
Q1	1	1	4
Q2	4	4	1
Q3	4	2	5
Q4	3	5	1

QUALITATIVE DATA ANALYSIS

Where we collect data from naturalistic observations, or wish to analyse the answers from open questions collected from interviews, we would carry out a **content analysis** of the notes, film, tape recordings and other materials collected during the research.

The first step is to **categorize** information into certain common groupings. Peter studied the answers to his open questions carefully, looking for evidence of 'confusion' and counting the references. He then compared the answers from those respondents who had no difficulty choosing their future options with answers from those who did. He was checking the relative levels of the variable in the two samples.